DELTA URBANISM
NEW ORLEANS

ACKNOWLEDGMENTS

I wish to thank the following institutions for access to the research materials used in this volume: Louisiana Collection, Earl K. Long Library, University of New Orleans; Special Collections, Howard-Tilton Library, Tulane University; New Orleans Public Library; The Historic New Orleans Collection–Williams Research Center; *New Orleans Times-Picayune*; Center for Bioenvironmental Research; New Orleans City Planning Commission; Louisiana Supreme Court Law Library; Louisiana State University CADGIS Lab; Louisiana GIS Digital Map; Louisiana Oil Spill Coordinator's Office; Federal Emergency Management Agency; U.S. Census Bureau; U.S. Army Corps of Engineers; U.S. Geological Survey; and the National Oceanographic and Atmospheric Administration. Gratitude also goes to the all the specific sources cited in the endnotes.

I am indebted to Executive Director Paul Farmer for bringing the resources and membership of the American Planning Association to the problems and promises of delta urbanism, and particularly to Senior Editor Timothy Mennel for stewarding this and other monographs on delta cities from conception to publication.

My deepest gratitude goes to my wife, Marina Campanella, and my parents, Mario and Rose Ann Campanella, for their many years of love, support, and guidance.

Finally, I am grateful to New Orleans, for the way it enriches and inspires the world.

DELTA URBANISM
NEW ORLEANS

RICHARD CAMPANELLA

American Planning Association
Planners Press

Making Great Communities Happen

Chicago | Washington, D.C.

CONTENTS

Deltas, ever-changing land and water interfaces formed by sediment deposits at river mouths, represent some of the most vibrant and diverse ecosystems in the world. Fertile soil, abundant wildlife, and fresh water define the natural landscape. It is no wonder, then, that recent urban development has occurred largely in delta and coastal regions, as people capitalize on the natural advantages the deltas provide. As a result, cities such as New Orleans, Rotterdam, Jakarta, and Alexandria have developed as hot spots of culture, economic activity, and ideas.

But these regions are also some of the most fragile. Plagued by flooding, land subsidence, and strong storms, many delta regions face the constant struggle to manage water and protect life and property. Events such as Hurricane Katrina, the great floods in the Netherlands in 1953, and continual flooding in Jakarta have shown us the vulnerability of delta cities and have highlighted the importance of planning to mitigate these risks and known threats. These examples are not unique. These are the 21st-century problems of 50 urbanized deltas worldwide.

How we build our cities and regions—including our understanding of the interaction between the built and natural environment; the architectural choices we make; our methods of managing water; and the engineering solutions we implement—is more important than ever. Along with known threats, the unknown impacts of climate change and sea-level rise will bring a host of additional challenges.

Thankfully, new solutions and partnerships are beginning to emerge. The past few years have seen an increasing focus on delta regions and knowledge sharing across international borders. Some countries, such as the Netherlands, are farther along in their efforts to understand the ecology of delta regions and have implemented advanced engineering solutions using new paradigms. Dutch practitioners and policy makers are sharing their knowledge with others through conferences, consultations, and workshops such as the Dutch Dialogues, sponsored by the American Planning Association, Waggonner & Ball Architects, and the Royal Netherlands Embassy. Other countries are just beginning to address these issues.

APA believes in the cultural, historical, ecological, and economic value of delta cities and regions, and it is committed to working with partners to seek solutions to these global problems. Through good planning, wise public policy, and an educated and engaged public, delta regions can implement solutions that derive value from water while ensuring high levels of safety. This is the ultimate goal. Although the challenge may seem difficult, even at times insurmountable, we must strive to work across disciplines and across borders to plan and build safe and vibrant deltas.

W. Paul Farmer, FAICP, Chief Executive Officer, American Planning Association

Dale Morris, Senior Advisor, Economic Division, Royal Netherlands Embassy

J. David Waggonner, principal, Waggonner & Ball Architects

vii

For centuries, people have been drawn to the water as a source of life and livelihood. The river deltas and coastal landscapes of the world are the cradles of civilization and the places where trade, industry, commerce, and recreation first emerged. Water provides us with unlimited possibility for advancement, yet its scarcity and at times overabundance has wrought great devastation and posed immense risk to human populations. Learning to live with and manage these risks is a constant and complex struggle.

The history of Louisiana is inextricably linked to the water of our coast and of the mighty Mississippi River that runs through the state. The earliest settlers recognized the vast natural resources and unmatched potential of this special place that sits at the mouth of one of the world's largest and most powerful rivers. Thomas Jefferson recognized the strategic importance of the river and its tributaries and chose its mouth as the starting point of negotiations when he executed the Louisiana Purchase more than 200 years ago.

The future of Louisiana, and in large measure the future of our nation, is directly connected to how we manage these waters, our delta, and the fragile coastal landscape that has been devastated by erosion over the last century.

To secure our future—in Louisiana and throughout the world—we must learn a lesson that seems to be ingrained in the Dutch people: how to live with water, instead of constantly fighting against it. This is one lesson that Americans must learn very quickly if we are to continue to thrive as economic and cultural leaders in the world.

Unfortunately, for more than a century, the federal government has mismanaged critical water-resource projects, placing delicate ecosystems like the Mississippi River Delta at extreme risk of complete and utter collapse. In the decades since our federal government first pursued the channelization of the Mississippi River to promote trade and commerce, the world's seventh-largest delta has been largely deprived of nourishment from sediments carried by the river, which drains roughly two-thirds of the continental United States. Instead of rebuilding the delta, these sediments now are redirected and carried to the Gulf of Mexico, where they disperse.

The effect on the delta is constant and debilitating land loss. This strangulation of natural processes to rebuild the delta is compounded by the ravages of coastal erosion and further aggravated by hurricanes that scrape away barrier islands and coastal plains. Sustainability of life is under dire threat in coastal Louisiana—a rapidly eroding landscape that loses 25 to 35 square miles of wetlands each year. At the current rate of land loss, an area the size of Rhode Island will be underwater by 2050.

And with the loss of this unique area goes our nation's only true working energy coast—an economic engine that contributes 90 percent of America's offshore energy production, 30 percent of the nation's overall oil and gas supply, and 30 percent of the seafood produced in the lower 48 states. It is also home to more than 2.5 million citizens who operate the port and capture the energy so vital to our nation's security.

At the heart of this coast is a massive river system stretching nearly 2,500 miles from the Great Plains to the Gulf of Mexico. The Mississippi River has the third-largest drainage basin in the world, exceeded only by the watersheds of the Amazon River and the Congo River.

Sitting at the mouth of this vast river system is my home of New Orleans—a city that was brought to its knees in 2005 and is still struggling to recover from Hurricane Katrina—one of the most devastating natural and man-made disasters in history. While it bears great strategic importance to the nation, New Orleans is not the only vulnerable area that requires protection. Across the entire Louisiana coast, from east to west, cities such as Lake Charles, Houma, and Lafayette are threatened as well. These cities form the backbone of our nation's fisheries, port system, and offshore oil and gas industry. All of these tremendous assets are at risk of being wiped off the map. With the persistent and rapid loss of land in Louisiana, communities are more

ix

vulnerable to the storm surge of massive storms and the inevitable impacts of sea-level rise.

Louisiana is not alone. The consequences of sea-level rise compound the existing vulnerabilities of populations that have been drawn to rivers, coastal areas, and deltas around the world. Across the globe, millions of people and billions of dollars in assets are at risk. Finding a sustainable balance of water management that keeps communities safe and allows us to prosper is essential to our future.

While this urgent challenge is not unique to Louisiana, it has presented my state with an opportunity to lead the world in discovering new technologies, smarter policies, and successful approaches to integrated water management, flood protection, and ecosystem restoration. I am encouraged that the work being done in Louisiana will be a beacon of hope for cities and peoples across the world.

The river that created this fertile delta I call home is the key to meeting the challenges we face along Louisiana's coast. It is time we learn to live in concert with this water and harness its tremendous power. The very future of Louisiana and coastal communities around the world depends on it.

Senator Mary L. Landrieu

Opposite: Features of the Mississippi Delta, viewed obliquely from the mouth of the Mississippi northwestward. New Orleans appears at center. *Graphic by Richard Campanella; Landsat data courtesy LSU.*

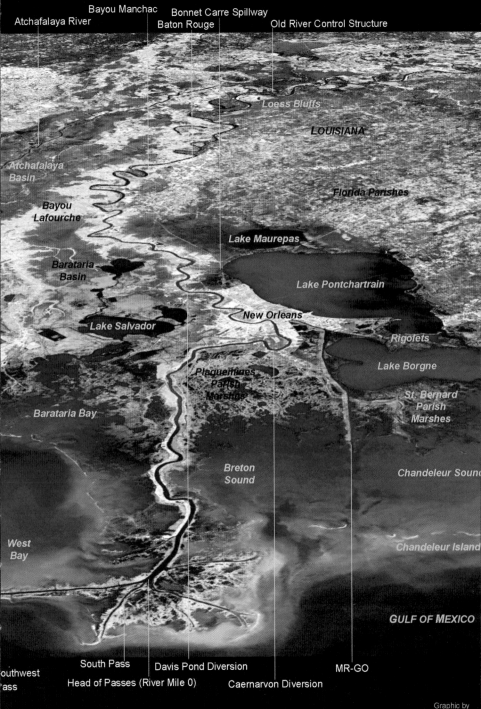

Atchafalaya River
Bayou Manchac
Bonnet Carre Spillway
Baton Rouge
Old River Control Structure

Loess Bluffs

LOUISIANA

Atchafalaya
Basin

Florida Parishes

Bayou
Lafourche

Lake Maurepas

Barataria
Basin

Lake Pontchartrain

Lake Salvador

New Orleans

Rigolets

Lake Borgne

Plaquemines
Parish
Marshes

St. Bernard
Parish
Marshes

Barataria Bay

Breton
Sound

Chandeleur Sound

West
Bay

Chandeleur Island

GULF OF MEXICO

Southwest
Pass

South Pass

Davis Pond Diversion

MR-GO

Head of Passes (River Mile 0)

Caernarvon Diversion

Graphic by

0.5 1 2 3 4
Miles

La...

Lake Pontchartrain Causeway

Kenner

Pontchartrain Shores

Bucktown

Lake S...

Lakevie...

E a s t B a n k

Metairie

Jefferson

Orleans

Armstrong-N.O.
International
Airport

J e f f e r s o n   P a r i s h

Old Town
Kenner

Old Metairie

Jefferson Heights

Hollygrove

Mi...

Ger...

Shrewsbury

Elmwood

Carrollton

Bro...
mo...

Harahan

Bridge
City

Audubon

Park

Frere

...ptown

Waggaman

Westwego

Missis...

W

J e f f...

Population Distribution in 2000
(1 dot = 10 people)

· White population
· Black population
· Asian ancestry
· Hispanic ethnicity

Land Cover

Parks, grassy areas, marsh
Forested areas
Water
Federal levee system, 2006

N
W   E
S

...te...

Laf...

INTRODUCTION

Previous page: Political boundaries, land covers, demographics, and levee system of the delta metropolis. *Map by Richard Campanella.*

Freshwater, arable soil, and waterborne accessibility motivated humans to position their settlements strategically where rivers flow, merge, or disembogue. These site-selection attributes occurred in abundance wherever sediment-laden rivers deposited enough alluvium at their mouths to form rich new earth and productive coastal ecosystems—that is, where rivers formed deltas. Deltaic environments have played an enormously important role in human history, hosting many of our oldest and greatest cities.

The advent of mechanized terrestrial transportation over the past two centuries has radically altered where we build cities. No longer is waterborne accessibility so vital. Yet 37 of the world's 136 largest coastal port cities remain near or upon deltas.[1] Hundreds of millions of people—roughly 7 percent of humanity—reside on or near deltas, while billions more live in similar estuarine, riverine, or coastal environments.

Today, these same geographies find themselves on the front lines of the premier environmental challenge of the 21st century: How do we sustain the world's great coastal cities in light of rising seas?

If risk is viewed as a function of hazard, exposure, and vulnerability, then New Orleans, Louisiana, USA, ranks as exceptionally risky among world cities. The three-century-old port metropolis currently confronts the multiple environmental hazards of coastal erosion, soil subsidence, sea-level rise, and possibly intensifying tropical-storm activity. Its increasingly precarious geography exposes a million metro-area residents, as well as critical national port and petroleum infrastructure, to these mounting hazards. Its high rate of poverty renders many residents particularly vulnerable. Without marked improvements in all three of the variables that drive urban risk, New Orleans's survival into the 22nd century is in question.

This monograph traces the urban development of New Orleans and its affiliated rise in urban risk—or more accurately, its evolution of risk—since its foundation in the early 18th century. We approach the topic geographically, starting with the underlying physical terrain and proceeding with the various transformations humans have occasioned upon it: site selection, settlement, urbanization, population, expansion, drainage, protection, exploitation, devastation, and recovery. Limitations of space require this delta urbanism story to be told episodically; in an effort to capture, albeit briefly, intermediary trends and patterns, the episodes are interspersed with time lines of important moments in the city's historical development.

New Orleans offers a valuable case study for urban planners because its circumstances position it in a prophetic role among world cities. What New Orleans is experiencing today foretells what similar cities will be tackling a generation or century from now. With this in mind, the monograph concludes with some lessons that may be drawn from New Orleans's experience of delta urbanism.

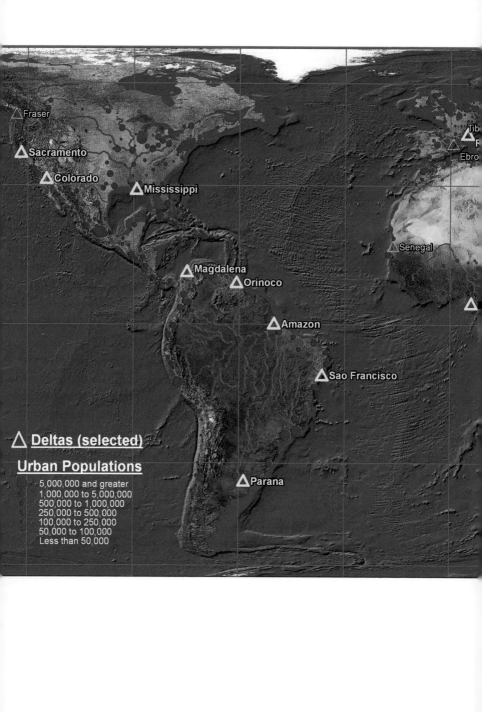

Fraser

Sacramento

Colorado

Mississippi

Tib
F
Ebro

Senegal

Magdalena

Orinoco

Amazon

Sao Francisco

Deltas (selected)

Urban Populations

5,000,000 and greater
1,000,000 to 5,000,000
500,000 to 1,000,000
250,000 to 500,000
100,000 to 250,000
50,000 to 100,000
Less than 50,000

Parana

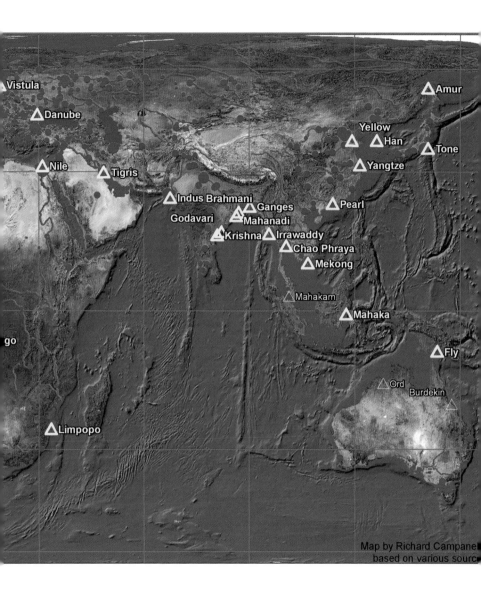

Vistula
Amur
Danube
Yellow
Han
Tone
Nile
Tigris
Yangtze
Indus Brahmani
Pearl
Godavari
Ganges
Mahanadi
Krishna
Irrawaddy
Chao Phraya
Mekong
Mahakam
Mahaka
go
Fly
Ord
Burdekin
Limpopo

Map by Richard Campanell
based on various sourc

By one count, over one-quarter of the world's 136 largest coastal port cities occupy or abut deltaic formations. Hundreds of millions of people—roughly 7 percent of humanity—reside on or near deltas, while billions more live in similar estuarine, riverine, or coastal environments. *Map by Richard Campanella.*

CHAPTER 1   DELTA FORMATION

New Orleans lies not on the ancient, solid North American lithosphere but on a thin, soft alluvial deposit cast out recently upon the continent's margin.[1] The city has occupied this semi-earthen surface for roughly 6 percent of the lifespan of its underlying geology, something few other major cities can claim. Certain oak trees in City Park today have been growing for about one-tenth of the age of their underlying soil; some aged citizens have personally witnessed fully one-fiftieth of the region's geological existence. New Orleans's terrain ranks as the youngest beneath any major American city, while southeastern Louisiana forms, as Mark Twain put it, "the youthfulest batch of country that lies around there anywhere."[2] The entire lower Mississippi Valley, from Cairo, Illinois, to the Gulf of Mexico, constitutes the continent's youngest surface soils.

For millennia, what is now southern Louisiana altered between terrestrial and aquatic states. Cooling global temperatures locked up water in ice sheets, thus lowering sea level and rendering the shallow coastal waters into terrestrial areas. Warming temperatures transferred water from the glaciers back into the world's oceans and returned coastal lowlands to the hydrosphere.

Eighteen thousand years ago, at the peak of the Ice Age, vast quantities of water lay frozen upon earthen surfaces, at the expense of the world's oceans. In North America, those ice sheets stretched as far south as present-day Cairo and radically changed the continent's topography and hydrology, resculpting the Missouri River drainage system to the west and the Ohio River system to the east such that the two rivers joined at Cairo. Rising global temperatures then melted the glaciers and sent increasing amounts of water and sediment toward that confluence. There, at the apex of

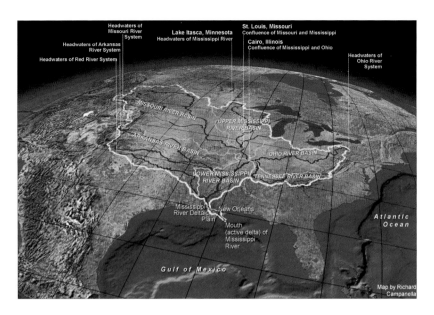

Map by Richard Campanella

an immense down-warping of the Earth's crust known as the Mississippi Embayment (forerunner of the lower Mississippi Valley), a dramatically augmented Mississippi River delivered increasing quantities of sediment-laden water toward the Gulf of Mexico. Minor bluffs and terraces constrained the river to meander within a wide, flat alluvial valley until it passed below a line roughly between modern-day Lafayette and Baton Rouge, Louisiana, beyond which gulf waters lay.

When moving water laden with sediment suddenly hits a slack water body such as the Gulf of Mexico, it loses its kinetic energy and dumps its sediment load. Alluvium began accumulating upon the hard compacted clays—that is, the delta's sub-alluvial surface, formed during Pleistocene Epoch two million years ago—that lay beneath coastal waters. In time, open saltwater transformed into saline marshes and then into freshwater swamps laced with ridges. Because of the Mississippi's immense water volume and sediment load vis-à-vis relatively weak tides and currents in the Gulf of Mexico, the river's dynamics overpowered those of the gulf and extended the coastline farther into the Gulf of Mexico. Southeastern Louisiana began to form, starting approximately seven millennia ago. Longshore currents along the Gulf Coast swept some river alluvium westward, creating the modern-day south-central and southwestern Louisiana coast.

The 1,243,700-square-mile Mississippi River Basin (yellow line) drains 41 percent of the continental United States and 15 percent of the North American continent. Thirty-one states and two Canadian provinces partially or fully drain into the Mississippi. The river discharges entirely along coastal Louisiana—70 percent via the Mississippi River, 30 percent via the Atchafalaya—forming the Mississippi deltaic plain. The Mississippi Delta ranks as one of the best examples of a river-dominated, multi-lobe delta protruding into a sea, and New Orleans represents one of the very few metropolises to occupy such a dynamic young feature. What happened here in the past 300 years represents the continent's purest case study of delta urbanism. *Map by Richard Campanella.*

3

New Orleans ■ Delta Formation

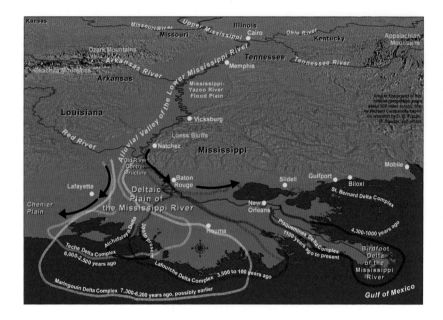

Southeastern Louisiana formed over the past 7,200 years as the Mississippi River emerged from its alluvial valley, shifted channels, and deposited sand, silt, and clay throughout shallow coastal waters. In this map, shades of white-to-red indicate where and when those lobes formed. The New Orleans area is mostly a product of the St. Bernard and Plaquemines deltas, which started to form roughly 5,000 years ago. *Map by Richard Campanella based on Frazier, Russel, Fisk, Kolb, and Van Lopik.*

As that alluvial deposit rose in elevation, the Mississippi sought paths of less resistance around it, and in doing so formed new channels and enlarged the coastline outwardly in new directions. If no longer replenished with soil and freshwater, the original deltaic "lobe" would subside and erode back into the sea, while the new active lobe or lobes grew nearby. Seasonal floods spilled muddy water beyond the banks of the river, depositing more sediment along its inundated flanks and raising still higher the emerging landscape.

Occasionally a crevasse—a breach—would open in the bank, allowing a trickle or a torrent or even the entire water column to divert from the main channel into adjacent wetlands, instigating the same land-building processes in yet another area. The mouth of the Mississippi River in this manner extended farther and wider into the Gulf of Mexico, creating a network of active and abandoned deltaic complexes—a deltaic plain—that would eventually become southeastern Louisiana and home to New Orleans.

One visitor arriving to New Orleans in 1828 observed delta-building processes forming the marshy eastern flanks of the city. "We coasted along, past numerous small, sandy islands," he wrote, "over shallow banks of mud, and through several immense basins, such as Lake Borgne and Lake Pontchartrain, half fresh, half salt, and filled with bars, spits, keys, and . . . shoals [typical of areas] whose Deltas *are silently pushing themselves into the sea[,] raising the bottom to the surface.*"[3] To the French geographer Elisée Réclus, who sailed up the Mississippi in 1853, those processes created a deltaic plain that resembled "a gigantic arm projecting into the sea and spreading its fingers on the surface of the water."[4] American geographer John McPhee described the lowermost river as jumping "here and there within an arc about two hundred miles wide, like a pianist playing with one hand—frequently and radically changing course, surging over the left or the right bank to go off in utterly new directions."[5]

That all of coastal Louisiana, including New Orleans, protrudes so broadly beyond the ancient continental coastline attests to the magnitude of the Mississippi River. Either for lack of water volume or sediment load, most rivers do not form deltas at all but rather admixtures of fresh and saltwater—estuaries—as they discharge into the sea. Two-thirds of the world's 32 most populous cities abut estuaries, including New York City, on the Hudson.[6] Larger sediment-bearing rivers that do form deltas are still usually at the mercy of wave or tidal action in influencing the shape and size of their alluvial deposits. These formations protrude modestly from the coastline, usually in the triangular form of the Greek letter Δ (hence the term *delta*). Others blend in smoothly with adjacent coasts. A number of great cities adjoin or occupy these types of deltas, which are termed *wave-dominated* and *tide-dominated deltas*. Alexandria, for example, sits on Egypt's Nile River Delta, which is dominated by waves. Tides dominate China's Yangtze Delta, home to 80 million people, one-quarter of them living in Shanghai. Dhaka, in Bangladesh, abuts the immense Ganges River Delta, also dominated by tides, with well over 100 million residents.

River-dominated deltas, on the other hand, occur in those rare circumstances when rivers bear enough water and sediment to overpower the dynamics of the receiving lake or sea, enabling the channel to meander, jump, send off distributaries, and build land faster than waves or tides can sweep it away. The resultant formations jut out dramatically into the receiving water body, often with multiple lobes spanning a broad area. River-dominated—or fluvial—deltas are more common in lakes than in seas because few of the world's rivers are large enough to overpower coastal currents. The

5

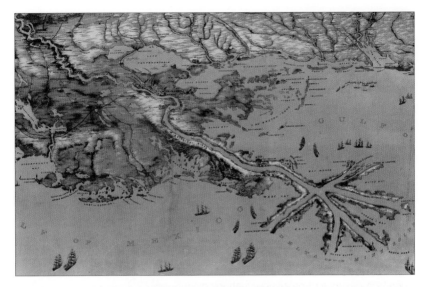

As opposed to those deltas dominated by tides or waves, river-dominated systems such as the Mississippi Delta (shown here in oblique views dating from 1861 and 2002) occur when rivers discharge enough water and sediment to overpower the dynamics of the receiving lake or sea, enabling the channel to meander, jump, send off distributaries, and build land at their mouths faster than waves, currents, or tides can sweep it away. The resultant deltas jut out dramatically into the receiving water body, often with multiple lobes spanning a broad area. *Bird's-eye view of Louisiana, Mississippi, Alabama, and part of Florida, drawn (1861) by John Bachmann, courtesy Library of Congress; Landsat satellite image (2002) courtesy LSU.*

Mississippi Delta ranks as one of the best examples of exactly that: a river-dominated, multi-lobe delta protruding into a sea. New Orleans represents one of the very few metropolises to occupy such a dynamic young feature. What happened here in the past 300 years presents the continent's purest case study of delta urbanism.

Since the 1930s, geologists have generally agreed on where the Mississippi's deltaic complexes have landed over the millennia, although their exact footprints and chronologies have been debated and refined. In the 1940s, geologists R. J. Russel and H. N. Fisk identified six historical delta complexes and subdivided them into a number of sub-deltas. In 1958, C. R. Kolb and J. R. Van Lopik updated these findings to recognize seven deltas, assigned some new names, and mapped them as distinctive lollipop-shaped lobes. In 1967, David E. Frazier advanced the science with radiocarbon dating and other new technologies. Frazier identified five deltaic complexes, subdivided them into 16 lobes, determined that many functioned contemporaneously, and estimated that the entire land-building event transpired over 7,200 years. Other scientists have since added to the body of knowledge on the origins of southeastern Louisiana, but, according to geologist Roger Saucier, "Frazier's work remains the most definitive to date."[7] That research found that the New Orleans region is mostly a product of the St. Bernard and Plaquemines deltaic complexes, which started forming at least 4,300 years ago—a time frame that aligns with earlier investigations.

By 1700, most of the delta's landscape features had reached a developmental stage that would be recognizable today. But these features, at the dawn of the colonial era, were still geologically alive and shifting, driven by gravity and controlled only by the forces of nature. The Mississippi River periodically swelled over its banks and replenished the backswamp with freshwater and new sediment. Enough river water flowed toward the old Lafourche Delta to inspire early French explorers to name it "the fork," and the Bayou Manchac distributary still injected fresh, muddy river water into the Maurepas Swamp.

All this geological dynamism is anathema to European notions of settlement and urbanization. Over the next 300 years, human occupants of the deltaic plain would seize this malleable geography and rework it

7

to improve their safety and circumstances within the time frame in which they lived: the moment and the foreseeable future. New Orleans as an urban system has since become one of the world's great engineering challenges, and southeastern Louisiana and the lowermost Mississippi River rank as one of the most anthropogenically altered regions in the hemisphere. Every blessing seems to be accompanied by a curse; every solution seems to spawn a future problem. The historical geography of New Orleans is, in large part, the story of the benefits, costs, and constant dilemmas associated with this geological tinkering.

8

CHAPTER 2   DELTA TOPOGRAPHY

The highest lands of the deltaic plain lie closest to moving freshwater—precisely the opposite of undulating landscapes, in which water carves downward and flows in the lowest areas.[1] Springtime overflows of the Mississippi River and its distributaries explain this phenomenon, as sediment particles borne by the floodwaters settle on the landscape according to their size and weight. Anything coarser than two millimeters in diameter (gravel, stones, or larger) weighs too much to make it all the way down the vast Mississippi River system. (For this reason, as a visitor in 1750 put it, "in New Orleans there is nothing scarcer than stones.")[2] Finer particles, measuring from 2.0 to 0.05 millimeters (sand), settle in the largest quantities closest to the river, building up those areas highest. Silt (0.05 to 0.002 millimeters) and clay (the finest particles, less than 0.002 millimeters in diameter) settle in lesser quantities farther from the river, where, because of their low elevation, they are joined by larger quantities of standing water and organic matter. By the time of the European arrival, areas closest to the Mississippi River (termed *natural levees*, from the French *lever*, "to raise") had risen about 10 to 15 feet above sea level, while those near Lake Pontchartrain lay only a few feet or inches above the tidally influenced brackish waters of that bay. The rich, coarse particles deposited immediately along the riverbanks (between the river and the natural levee) earned the name *batture*, a corruption of the French *batteur*, as in "beaten down by the river" (*battre*, "to beat").

The relatively well-drained natural levees thus comprise some sand, much silt, some clay, humus (organic matter such as decaying leaves and tree stumps), and water. The backslope of the natural levee contains lesser amounts of sand, mostly silt, more clay, and higher

Mississippi River, moored barges, batture forest, artificial levee (with bike trail along crest), and natural levee in urbanized Jefferson Parish at the Huey P. Long Bridge (1935), upriver from New Orleans. *Photograph by Richard Campanella, 2007.*

New Orleans ■ Delta Topography

quantities of humus and water. The lowest areas farthest from the river contain no sand, some silt, lots of clay, and even more humus and water. As one moves away from the river, then, the soil elevation drops, the soil texture (particle size) becomes finer, the amount of water and organic matter in the soil body increases, and the water table rises closer to the surface (and sometimes *becomes* the surface).

One anomaly lies beneath New Orleans's Mississippi-delivered alluvium: the Pine Island Trend, a sandy deposit of the Pearl River that drifted westward with gulf currents as a barrier island before Mississippi River sediments aggregated around it and froze it into place. The Pine Island Trend, which helped form the tidal lagoon now known as Lake Pontchartrain, today lies below neighborhoods stretching from Lakeview through New Orleans East to the Rigolets.

Rich alluvial soils and a subtropical climate fostered verdant flora and abundant fauna on the deltaic plain. Along the river grew dense bamboo-like reeds, which fronted jungle-like forests of live oaks and other hard-woods atop the natural levee. Farther back, at lower elevations, were palmetto-strewn cypress swamps, which petered out to tidally influenced saline-grass marshes. Unlike today, the entire deltaic plain lay *above* sea level. Any spot that might have subsided below sea level would have quickly filled with water.

The natural levees of the Mississippi River are not the only high ridges on the deltaic plain. Now and then, crevasses would develop in certain weak spots in these features, sending streams of river water flowing into the backswamp. These "distributaries," like the main chan-nel, also deposited sediment along their banks. When the distributaries' natural levees attained sufficient eleva-tion, they divided the flanks of the deltaic plain into hy-drological basins and sub-basins. The major distributary system in the New Orleans area flowed out of the river at a crevasse near present-day River Ridge and wended its way eastward to the sea. Its flooding cycle created a slight ridge—"a certain bulge, called a 'hill' in these parts . . . imperceptible to the naked eye, [perhaps] one me-ter high," according to Réclus.[3] The main channel of the Mississippi River once followed this path (now traversed by Metairie Road, City Park Avenue, Gentilly Boule-vard, and Chef Menteur Highway), creating the Metairie and Gentilly ridge systems. Its offshoot, the Esplanade Ridge, formed a slight upland beneath today's Espla-nade Avenue from City Park to the French Quarter. That ridge would play a key role in the decision to site New Orleans at this locale.

CHAPTER 3 SETTLING THE DELTA

The story of urbanizing the Mississippi Delta begins with the decision to locate a community there.[1] Humans first settled here well before Europeans arrived; indigenous peoples camped on the natural levee now occupied by the French Quarter and altered that environment through hunting, clearing and burning vegetation, and planting crops. Large-scale landscape transformation, however, commenced with the arrival of Europeans. Early Spanish expeditions led by Alonso Álvarez de Pineda (1519), Pánfilo de Narváez (1528), and Hernando de Soto (1539–43) came close to the Mississippi Delta but, seeking riches rather than colonization, left no permanent mark (save for the introduction of European diseases that killed large numbers of indigenous people).

The French in 17th-century North America also sought riches but, invested as they were in New France, pursued a means—trade routes and empire—toward that end. Explorations of the Great Lakes and upper Mississippi region by Marquette and Joliet (1673) helped demystify the interior and refute the notion of a nearby Pacific Ocean, but no French explorer had yet confirmed the connection between the upper Mississippi and the Gulf of Mexico—important, because the French oversaw lucrative colonies in the adjacent Caribbean Sea.

An ambitious young Norman named René-Robert Cavelier, sieur de La Salle, endeavored to do just that. La Salle set out through the Great Lakes in 1682 and, with surprising ease, sailed down the Mississippi and neared the deltaic plain in late March. Father Membré described the historic moment that transpired as the party approached the Mississippi's birdfoot delta and smelled the salty waters of the Gulf of Mexico:

> We arrived, on the sixth of April, at a point where the river divides into three channels [which] are beautiful and deep. The water is brackish; after advancing two leagues it became perfectly salt, and, advancing on, we discovered the open sea, so that on the ninth of April, with all possible solemnity, we performed the ceremony of planting the cross and raising the arms of France, [taking] possession of that river, of all rivers that enter it and of all the country watered by them.[2]

The Mississippi basin, in La Salle's mind, now belonged to France. He named it after King Louis XIV, and *Louisiana* entered the vocabulary.

La Salle promptly returned to France and recommended to the Sun King the establishment of a fortification 60 leagues (150–180 miles) above the mouth of the Mississippi, for its "excellent position," "favourable disposition of the savages," fertile land, mild climate, military advantages, and opportunity to "harass the Spaniards in those regions from whence they derive all their wealth."[3] La Salle set out in 1684 to found his city on the great river. But the expedition missed the foggy, debris-strewn, labyrinthine mouth of the Mississippi and drifted westward until running ashore at Matagorda Bay in what is now Texas. The mistake led to disaster: La Salle was murdered in March 1687 by mutinous crew members, who subsequently died of disease or battle.[4] The vision of a city on the great river died with La Salle, or so it seemed.

La Salle's lieutenant, Henri de Tonti, kept that vision alive. He warned the French government about the English threat to the Mississippi River from the north and the Spanish interests from Mexico and Florida. Not until 1697 did the French Crown, convinced that failing to act on Louisiana would send the region into enemy hands, finally listen. It directed 36-year-old French Canadian warrior Pierre Le Moyne, sieur d'Iberville, to seek "the mouth [of the Mississippi River], select a good site that can be defended with a few men, and block entry to the river by other nations."[5]

Iberville, his younger brother Jean Baptiste Le Moyne, sieur de Bienville, and their men arrived at the modern-day Mississippi Gulf Coast in February 1699 and proceeded westward into the convoluted marshes of the deltaic plain. "All this land is a country of reeds

Bienville situated New Orleans to exploit a convenient portage route that connected the Gulf Coast with the Mississippi River. Traveling from the French colonial coastal outposts of Biloxi and Mobile to the channel of the Mississippi (red lines on top map, which dates from 1732) required sailing across a hundred miles of open sea, then penetrating the debris-strewn mouth of the river. Against the current and often against the wind, this voyage was slow and difficult. The alternative route (green line) passed through the sheltered waters of the Mississippi Sound and Lake Borgne, through the Rigolets channel, into the protected inland bay named Lake Pontchartrain, up a tiny inlet called Bayou St. John (middle map, which dates from 1749). Travelers then disembarked and walked a two-mile portage to the banks of the Mississippi River. Bienville established New Orleans at that spot in 1718; streets laid out in 1722–23 remain in place today as the French Quarter. The ancient portage route also persists in the modern-day street system, as Bayou Road / Gov. Nicholls Street. *Graphic by Richard Campanella; Carte de la côte de la Louisiane (1732) and Carte particulière du cours du fleuve St. Louis depuis le village sauvage (1749) courtesy Library of Congress.*

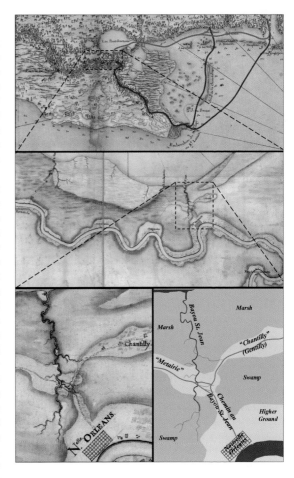

and brambles and very tall grass," Iberville wrote on March 3, 1699—which happened to be Mardi Gras. Six leagues farther was "a bend" the river made to the west, to which they gave the name "Mardy Gras." With those words, Iberville introduced the ancient pagan and Catholic pre-Lenten feast into the colonial society he was about to found. Mardi Gras remains today the single most famous and distinctive cultural trait of Louisiana, and Bayou Mardi Gras ranks as the region's second oldest French toponym (after Louisiana itself).

Iberville at this point spelled out in his journal what was probably quite apparent to him and his men: This entire landscape was a floodplain. "I climbed to the top of a nut tree as big as my body, but saw nothing other than canes and bushes. The land becomes inundated to a depth of 4 feet during high water. I made the decision to go upstream."[6]

As he did, Iberville became convinced that this was indeed the same great river La Salle sailed 17 years earlier. But how to build a city on this soft, wet, dynamic delta? He cast his eyes instead on the solid earth of the Gulf Coast, a hundred miles to the north and east. There, on the edge of Biloxi Bay near present-day Ocean Springs, Mississippi, Iberville established Fort Maurepas in April 1699.

Iberville's Louisiana explorations of 1699 spawned a nascent French colonial society scattered thinly along the Gulf Coast. Following the establishment of Fort Maurepas, a tiny outpost arose on the lower Mississippi River near modern-day Phoenix, Louisiana, in 1700, followed by two larger ones near Mobile Bay in 1702 and 1711 (the latter of which is now modern Mobile, Alabama). A small band of Mobile colonists cleared land at Bayou St. John in 1708, marking the first European development in what is now New Orleans. Scarcity, hunger, disease, natural disaster, official inattention, and a desperate lack of settlers—only around 300 in 1708—made life in early Louisiana a dreaded hardship. Iberville's younger brother Bienville served by this time as the colony's governor; Iberville moved on to other charges and died of yellow fever in Cuba in 1706.

Frustrated and pessimistic about Louisiana, the Crown did what governments often do when they fail to solve their problems: turn them over to the private sector. In 1712, the king ceded a monopoly for the commercial development of Louisiana to a prominent financier named Antoine Crozat. This speculative venture also failed, due to lack of mineral riches, scarcity of settlers for agriculture, and limited commercial interaction with Spain—not to mention mismanagement, feuding, and tensions with American Indians. When Crozat retroceded his monopoly in 1717, Louisiana's prospects seemed dim. But a breakthrough was on the horizon.

King Louis XIV had died in 1715, leaving the throne to his five-year-old great-grandson, Louis XV, for whom Philippe, Duc d'Orléans, would act as Regent of France. Among the Duc d'Orléans's many business associates was a flamboyant maverick named John Law. Born in Edinburgh in 1671, the gifted Law grew rich through high-risk financial affiliations with European aristocracy. He settled with his millions in Paris in the early 1710s,

15

allying himself with French royalty to seek greater opportunities and riches. When Crozat surrendered his Louisiana monopoly, Law pounced. He proposed to the Duc d'Orléans a Louisiana land-development plan than would enrich all investors and the country. The scheming risk-taker found the right patron: the Duc d'Orléans supported the plan.

Less than a month after Crozat formally relinquished Louisiana, John Law's new Company of the West received a 25-year monopoly charter to develop the Louisiana colony for commerce, with a particular emphasis on tobacco cultivation. Law then launched an unprecedented marketing campaign across the continent to drum up investment in Louisiana stock and land, and to entice the lower classes to immigrate there. Although based on grossly exaggerated claims of commercial potential and doomed to fail, Law's efforts thrust Louisiana to the forefront of European attention and, more importantly and more permanently, led to a key resolution:

> Resolved to establish, thirty leagues up the river, a burg which *should be called* New Orleans, where landing would be possible from either the river or Lake Pontchartrain.[7]

Those words, scribed in the company ledger in September 1717, set in motion the foundation of the deltaic city first envisioned by La Salle 35 years earlier.[8] The name honored the Duc d'Orléans, Law's royal sponsor, while the indicated site came from intelligence gathered from American Indians over the previous 18 years regarding a strategic "backdoor" route to the Mississippi River. Rather than sailing up a hundred treacherous miles of the lower Mississippi (the "river route") amid fog and debris, against the current, and sometimes against the wind, voyagers could instead traverse the usually calm waters of the Mississippi Sound, through a channel known as the Rigolets, into the protected waters of Lake Pontchartrain, and up a small rivulet called Bayou St. John. Travelers would then disembark and follow a two-mile-long trail along a slight upland— the Esplanade Ridge—which connected directly with the banks of the Mississippi. The intersection of that portage (called Bayou Road to this day) and the elevated natural levee of the Mississippi formed a particularly compelling place to establish a settlement.

Bienville fulfilled his charge during late March and early

New Orleans ■ Settling the Delta

April 1718, when his men began clearing canebrake precisely at that place, occupied today by the French Quarter. Siting an outpost on that particular riverside perch offered the French a strategic position along a faster, shorter, more reliable, and safer route connecting, on one hand, the Gulf of Mexico–Caribbean–Atlantic world whence they came and, on the other, the vast North American interior they sought to develop. The advantages of slightly upraised land, fine soils, a well-positioned perch for river defense, and deep water for the docking of ships added to the site's appeal.

TIME LINE, 1718–1720s

1718–22	Bienville's siting of New Orleans is contested by rival colonists, who debate relocating settlement to Bayou Manchac site (south of present-day Baton Rouge). Other suggested sites for company headquarters include Natchez, English Turn, Lake Pontchartrain shore, Natchitoches, Biloxi, Mobile, and Pensacola.
1719	Spring floods slow work on New Orleans. Headquarters of Louisiana colony is relocated from Mobile back to Biloxi area; Bienville, an advocate of New Orleans remaining at its present site and becoming headquarters and capital, reluctantly returns to Biloxi to build new fort.
1719	First large group of Africans arrives in chains, commencing 14 decades of slavery in Louisiana. More than 5,000 people, mostly from West African Senegambia region, are imported during 1719–31, first of two major waves directly from Africa. Racial subjugation through slavery, codified in 1724 *Code Noir*, profoundly influences New Orleans's social and urban geography. Compared to Anglo America, racial identities and relationships become more complex and fluid in Caribbean-influenced French Louisiana.
1719–21	Law's company recruits thousands of French citizens, many from society's bottom rung, as well as German and Swiss farmers, representing first major wave of Europeans to settle in Louisiana. New Orleans by 1720 boasts houses for governor and director, company store, church, hospital, more than 100 employees, and 250 concession-holders ready to work their land. But settlement is haphazardly laid out, disease takes its toll, and commercial effort struggles financially.

17

New Orleans ■ Settling the Delta

1720	John Law's highly speculative development scheme for Louisiana fails—one of the great real estate hoaxes of the era. But it lasts long enough to instigate agriculture and urban settlement on the lower Mississippi.
1720s	Germans settle Côte des Allemands, upriver from New Orleans, and help feed struggling city with their agricultural productivity. Teutonic population is later absorbed into French-speaking white Creole society but retains some German ethnic identity for more than a century.
1721	Adrien de Pauger, assistant to Chief Engineer Le Blond de La Tour, arrives in New Orleans and promptly adapts La Tour's designs for new Biloxi capital to New Orleans site, creating today's French Quarter. Pauger's impressive urban plan casts New Orleans in a positive light. But extant haphazard cityscape interferes with deployment of plan.

New Orleans ■ Settling the Delta

CHAPTER 4   URBANIZING THE DELTA

A few years of haphazard development following the 1718 founding of New Orleans inscribed an initial level of urbanization into the deltaic soil.[1] Impressive it was not; nor was it even planned. One observer described the circa-1720 outpost as comprising

> about a hundred forty barracks, disposed with no great regularity, a great wooden warehouse, and . . . a few inconsiderable houses, scattered up and down, without any order or regularity. . . . [They] would be esteemed common and ordinary buildings in a European village. *New Orleans*, in 1720, made a very contemptible figure.[2]

When engineers Le Blond de la Tour and Adrien de Pauger endeavored to rectify that "contemptible figure," the existing hodgepodge impeded their envisioned urban plan. Surely they would have eventually mustered official forces to clear away those first four years of unplanned urbanization, but nature beat them to it. Pauger wrote that at 9 a.m. on September 11, 1722, "a great wind" swept the settlement,[3]

> followed an hour later by the most terrible tempest and hurricane that could ever be seen. . . . It had overthrown at least two thirds of the houses here and those that remain are so badly damaged that it will be necessary to dismantle them. The church, the presbytère, the hospital and a small barracks building . . . are among [those] overthrown, without [there] being, thanks to the Lord, a single person killed. . . . The river rose more than six feet and the waves were so great that it is a miracle that [all the boats] were not dashed to pieces.[4]

New Orleans's first hurricane proved to be a blessing in disguise. Wrote Pauger, who was responsible for surveying the new street system, "all these buildings were old and provisionally built, and not a single one in the alignment of the new city and thus would have had to be demolished. Thus there would not have been any great misfortune in this disaster except that we must act to put all the people in shelter."[5] Pauger prioritized for the unimpeded execution of his street plan and the orderly development of New Orleans. He once ordered the house of a man named Traverse demolished because it violated the grid; when Traverse petitioned the city for indemnification, Pauger personally beat him repeatedly with a stick, then had him bound by the feet in irons and imprisoned.[6]

Establishing a settlement and surveying its urban plat is one thing; ensuring its survival and prosperity is quite another. One way to gain an advantage toward political and economic sustainability is to attain the status of administrative center—in this case, to become the Company of the West's primary "counter office" (financial headquarters), port, and colonial capital. Just as Bienville advocated for New Orleans to attain that status, partisans elsewhere promoted those functions to be located as far east as Mobile and even Pensacola, and as far inland as Natchez and Natchitoches. The worthiest rival to Bienville's site was Bayou Manchac, the Mississippi River distributary south of present-day Baton Rouge. Manchac, like New Orleans, provided a convenient shortcut to the Gulf Coast—via lakes Maurepas and Pontchartrain—but, unlike New Orleans, suffered few of its environmental problems.

Bienville succeeded finally when the company apparently convinced of the strategic superiority of a river site over a coastal position and aware of Pauger's impressive new city plan, designated New Orleans as capital of Louisiana on December 23, 1721. Pauger proceeded, after the 1722 hurricane, to survey a symmetrical 66-block grid around a central plaza, fronted by institutions of church and state and surrounded by fortifications. Contrary to New Orleans's laissez-faire reputation, this first urban environment was "actually military in the insistence of its right angles, like the gridded camps Roman soldiers laid out at the wild edges of their empire." The French Quarter looked like what it was, "the elaboration of a colonial outpost designed by military engineers."[7]

French colonists thus swept away their own messy, unplanned beginnings and imposed upon the newly emptied deltaic space a planned Cartesian sense of urban order. Less than two months after the storm, "the streets of the old quarter had received the names they still bear."[8] The new capital's population of 326 free whites proceeded to alter the deltaic landscape by clearing vegetation, via the enslaved labor of 171 recently kidnapped Africans and 21 American Indians. The 1720s saw the construction of the city's first man-made levees, earthen embankments positioned upon the crest of the natural levee to prevent annual spring-time high water from muddying city streets. Plantations of indigo, tobacco, rice, and foodstuffs replaced old-growth forests; cypress trees were felled for lumber; and species were introduced intentionally as potential agricultural commodities—or unintentionally, such as *Aedes aegypti*, the African mosquito that would later spread yellow fever. Landscape transformation by the early 1720s was under way at every conceivable level, from the geophysical to the biological, hydrological, epidemiological, and cultural. It was in 1722, according to the colonist Dumont, that "New Orleans began to assume the appearance of a city."[9]

21

CHAPTER 5   WHY THERE?

Why did Bienville establish New Orleans where he did?[1] The ultimate motivation was the French imperial need to defend their Louisiana claim by fortifying its Mississippi Valley gateway against competing colonial interests. The proximate motivation was the need for a convenient lower-river port and company office for the commercial development of Louisiana. This particular spot offered the right mix of accessibility, defendability, riverine position, arability, and natural resources toward those ends, in an environment that lacked superior alternatives. What also played roles in the decision were bureaucratic inertia, momentum, pure luck, and personal gain. (Bienville owned vast land holdings in this vicinity and thus stood to benefit if the settlement progressed, although his land grants postdated his 1718 siting decision.) Similarly intertwined commercial, colonial, and military motivations—played out amid hidden agendas, competing egos, miscommunications, and accidents—may be found in the stories of how many great cities ended up at their sites.

Rarely are those site-selection decisions made without controversy. To this day, second-guessing Bienville's judgment has become a favorite topic of local punditry. When the surges of hurricanes Katrina and Rita submerged those lands in 2005, observers worldwide pondered how a major city could have been founded on so precarious a site. Some saw no future for the metropolis, save for its relocation to higher ground. In essence, the circa-1700s debate of the French colonials about where to locate Louisiana's primary city raged again—under very different circumstances, but with similar factors at play.

Indeed, this is a challenging site for a major city. Yet Bienville acted wisely in selecting it in 1718, because he knew that what makes a city great is not its site but its

Physical geographies of New Orleans. *Montage by Richard Campanella based on various sources, 2000–07.*

situation. *Site* refers to the city's actual physical footing; *situation* means its regional context and how it connects with the world.[2] Some human settlements enjoy excellent geographical sites *and* situations; Manhattan is probably the best example in the United States. Many other settlements claim very good sites but lousy situations; we call them small towns, and they're small for a reason. Then we have a few examples of settlements in fantastic situations but on lousy sites—places that seemingly *have* to exist, yet struggle mightily *to* exist. New Orleans and Venice, Italy, are among the best examples in the world. Other deltaic cities are not far behind.

Consider the logic behind Bienville's decision to locate New Orleans. A strategic situation near the mouth of North America's greatest river allowed French colonials to exploit and protect their vast Louisiana claim effectively from a single point. Had Bienville located New Orleans farther upriver, such as at Bayou Manchac or Natchez, the city would have been too inconvenient for coastal traffic and unable to answer enemy incursions. In other words: good sites, but bad situations.

Had he located it farther east, such as at Mobile or Biloxi, he would have relinquished the critical Mississippi River advantage and still suffered flooding problems. Ditto for locations to the west: bad sites, bad situations.

Had he located the city farther downriver, the site would have been that much more vulnerable and precarious. The site he finally selected, today's French Quarter, represented the best *available* site within a *fantastic* geographical situation. French observer Francois Marie Perrin Du Lac captured succinctly in 1807 the horns of Bienville's dilemma:

> There is not for a great distance a finer, more elevated, or healthier position [for New Orleans]. If higher, it would be too distant from the sea; if lower, subject to inundations.[3]

Bienville's wisdom became apparent around the time of Du Lac's visit, as New Orleans emerged as one of the most important cities in America. It was shown again after Hurricane Katrina, when the French Quarter and other historical areas all evaded flooding.

Why, then, is a major American city located on this problematic site? Because it made perfect, rational sense at the time of its founding—a time when people depended heavily on waterborne transportation and when this particular site offered the best waterborne access to what proved to be the richest valley on earth.

German geographer Friedrich Ratzel contemplated New Orleans's site-versus-situation dilemma in his 1870s assessment of urban America. "New Orleans," he judged, "is just as poorly located as a city, or more precisely as a dwelling place, as it is excellently located as a commercial site." He then added: *"This last-mentioned advantage has made up for all disadvantages."*[4]

TIME LINE, 1720s–1760s

1723–27	Capuchin, Jesuit, and Ursuline religious orders arrive at city, playing major role in instilling Catholicism, French culture, education, care for orphans and infirm, and other civilizing aspects into frontier outpost. Ursuline nuns are particularly influential in the education of girls and other activities, remaining active in city's religious culture to this day.
1727	New Orleans's population 938 (729 whites plus 65 enlisted men, 127 black slaves, 17 American Indian slaves).
1727	Man-made riverfront levees, started by La Tour and Pauger earlier in decade, now measure 18 feet wide, three feet high, and one mile long, representing initial attempts to control Mississippi. Anthropogenic river control ultimately succeeds in preventing annual floods but inadvertently starves deltaic plain of critical sediments and freshwater, helping cause catastrophic land loss by late 20th century.
1729	Natchez American Indian uprising at Fort Rosalie kills 250 colonists, sending shockwaves through region. New Orleans responds by constructing primitive rampart and moat around street grid. Fortification remains in altered forms until early American years, affecting urban development of adjacent areas. Angles of old fort line remain visible today in certain parcels and building shapes between Barracks Street and Esplanade Avenue.
1731	Company of the Indies (successor of Company of the West) relinquishes Louisiana to king; era of private development ends after nearly 20 years of consistent under performance. France thence views Louisiana, population around 7,000, as a disappointment at best and burdensome failure at worst, unworthy of great commitment.

1732	New Orleans population 1,294 (1,023 whites, 254 black slaves, nine American Indian slaves, eight free blacks).
1737	New Orleans's population 1,748 (approximately 759 whites, 963 blacks, and 16 American Indians). City becomes majority black in 1730s and remains so until 1830s.
1745	Ursuline Convent designed and built (1749–53) on present-day 1100 block of Chartres Street. Edifice, no longer a convent but still operated by Catholic Archdiocese, stands today as sole surviving complete structure from French colonial era, oldest documented extant building in Mississippi Valley and deltaic plain, and outstanding example of French colonial institutional architecture.
Circa 1750	Claude Joseph Villars Dubreuil excavates canal to power sawmill immediately below city. Waterway eventually establishes trajectory of Elysian Fields Avenue (1805) and Pontchartrain Railroad (1831), which influence layout of numerous street grids and neighborhoods between river and lake over next 200 years.
1754–63	French and Indian War (Seven Years' War in Europe) pits France against England over claims in Ohio Valley; conflict draws in various European states and spreads around world. Defeat of France radically realigns colonial world: French North America, including Louisiana east of Mississippi, is ceded to England. Areas west of river, including New Orleans (thought to be an island, on account of Bayou Manchac distributary and lakes), avoid English possession, having been secretly ceded by King Louis XV in the Treaty of Fontainebleau to his Spanish cousin King Carlos III in 1762. City gains unwelcome new neighbor to north—British West Florida—to which many Anglo settlers immigrate over next 20 years.
1762–69	Dominion of New Orleans passes from France to Spain in stages: secretly in 1762, publicly in 1764, politically in 1766, and militarily in 1769. Population remains largely Francophone in culture.
1763	New Orleans's population 2,524 (1,646 whites, 826 black slaves, 33 American Indian slaves, 19 free blacks).

26

CHAPTER 6   COLONIAL-ERA FLOOD CONTROL

The flooding caused by high waters overtopping the natural levee in spring and by water surging through crevasses quickly convinced French colonials in New Orleans that the natural levee alone provided insufficient protection from the Mississippi.[1] The first organized effort to heighten and reinforce it with an artificial levee began in 1722–23, when city engineers Le Blond de La Tour and Adrien de Pauger planned an earthen embankment about 12 feet wide reinforced with a double palisade of timbers. Original plans had to be scaled back because of an insufficient labor force and the death of La Tour in late 1723. By 1724, the first levee measured six feet wide, three feet high, and 3,000 feet long but was readily breached by the high waters of the Mississippi that spring. Three years later, a solid 18-foot-wide and three-foot-high levee, plus a parallel ditch to collect seepage, lined one mile of the town's riverfront. For manpower, the city at first obligated slave owners to assign their bondsmen 30 days' labor on public works. Later it adopted a tax and hired workers, including slaves, whose wages went to their masters.

Throughout the French colonial era, "extension of the levee line [beyond the city] was almost entirely the work of private land developers supervised at the local level, first by commandants, then by parish and county governments."[2] By 1752, the berms spanned 20 miles below the city to 30 miles upriver and advanced in that direction by about one mile per year.[3]

The tradition of localism continued under the Spanish, as each concession recipient bore the responsibility of levee construction, drainage ditch excavation, and road clearing. Le Page du Pratz, who resided in New Orleans from its founding to the 1730s and published his *History of Louisiana* in 1758, wrote:

> On [both] banks of the river runs a causey,
> or mole [a road following the crest of a levee]
> from the English Reach quite to the town, and
> about ten leagues beyond it; which makes
> about fifteen or sixteen leagues on each side
> [of] the river; and which may be travelled in a
> coach or [on] horseback, on the bottom as
> smooth as a table.[4]

Since a league measures 2.5 to three miles, Le Page's estimates generally concur with those of an English captain who visited New Orleans in the late 1760s:

> The Leveé…extends from the *Detour des Anglois* [English Turn, or Reach], to the upper
> settlement of the Germans, which is a distance of more than fifty miles, [with] a good
> coach-road all the way. The Leveé before
> the town is repaired at the public expense,
> [but] each inhabitant keeps that part in repair
> which is opposite to his own plantation.[5]

An early attempt at centralized levee oversight came with Spanish governor Carondelet's levee ordinance of 1792, which required syndicated residents to raise levees to the recent high-water mark of the river and reinforce their sides by filling in ditches and planting grass. Livestock grazing was strictly forbidden, and in the most vulnerable places the owner had to "have at all times a deposit of pickets, planks, Spanish moss and other articles necessary to stop the crevasses under penalty of a fine of one hundred *piastres*."[6] No integral flood-control infrastructure, of course, can be decentralized and outsourced to individuals as the tradition of localism attempted to do. Failure of any one landowner to install and properly maintain his portion of the levee would compromise the entire system. As a result, colonial levees fell well short of their intended goal of preventing overbank and crevasse flooding. River waters inundated rural areas regularly and afflicted New Orleans proper during 1719, 1735, 1785, 1791, and 1799.[7] Colonial authorities and subjects nevertheless succeeded in commencing the grand effort—which would eventually prove all too successful—to restrain and strangle the very force that naturally built the delta.

TIME LINE, 1750s–1800s

1755–85 British exile French settlers from Acadie region in Nova Scotia. Thousands of displaced Acadians eventually find their way to Louisiana during 1764–85, drawn by French culture and geographical accessibility. Most Acadians settle west of New Orleans, forming agricultural and natural-resource-based rural society separate from, but important to, urban New Orleans. Corrupted local pronunciation of *Acadian* produces term *Cajun*.

1776–81 Six hurricanes strike New Orleans area and cause extensive damage. One, in 1779, was experienced by William Dunbar, who later reported his meteorological observations in *Transactions of the American Philosophical Society*, making him among first to document cyclonic nature of tropical storms.

1777–78 Spanish census enumerates 2,809 residents in New Orleans proper in 1777 and 3,059 in 1778, a sixfold increase since first French census in 1721. The 1,552 whites, 248 free people of mixed race, 105 free blacks, 213 mixed-race slaves, and 941 black slaves live throughout 68 "isles," or blocks making up nearly the entire city proper.

1780 City's first food market, a small pavilion for butchers, opens; later evolves into French Market (1791) and becomes one of New Orleans's most famous features.

1780s Second major wave of African slave importations arrive, the first occurring in 1720s.

1788 Population of New Orleans 5,388 (about 50 percent white, 35 percent enslaved black, and the remainder free people of color). Population of colony is more than 25,000.

1788 Good Friday fire destroys 856 buildings in New Orleans, leveling 80 percent of city's structures and leaving about 70 percent of population homeless. Most original French colonial structures are lost. One of last examples of old French Creole house type, Madame John's Legacy, is built on Dumaine Street immediately after conflagration.

1788 New Orleans's first suburb, Faubourg Ste. Marie (today's Central Business District), is surveyed upon former Gravier plantation above city proper, in response to population pressure and ruins of recent fire. Old plantation boundaries influence layout of emerging street network, as would transpire in many other areas of the city.

New Orleans ■ Colonial-Era Flood Control

1789	St. Louis Cemetery is laid out behind city, reflecting tendency to locate objectionable land uses in back-of-town. New cemetery embodies Spanish tradition of above-ground entombment; replaces old French subterranean burial ground near Burgundy–St. Peter intersection. Still active today, St. Louis No. 1 Cemetery is resting place of many great local historical figures.
1794	Second major blaze in six years destroys 212 structures in New Orleans. New Spanish building codes enacted after disaster phase out traditional first-generation Creole building styles; structures built afterward reflect Spanish colonial traits, often with local embellishments. Village-like appearance of French New Orleans gives way to solid, walled, brick-and-stucco Spanish cityscape.
1794	Governor Carondelet directs excavation of canal from rear of city to Bayou St. John. Carondelet Canal supplants Bayou Road as route to bayou and Lake Pontchartrain; now shipments can be delivered efficiently by water from coast and lake directly to rear of city. Canal, which also serves as early drainage system, provides convenient right-of-way into downtown, used by railroads into 20th century.
1795	Spain and United States sign Treaty of San Lorenzo, granting Americans open navigation of Mississippi River and right of deposit at New Orleans.
1796	First significant yellow fever outbreak strikes New Orleans. Vector, which would remain unidentified until the early 1900s, is *Aedes aegypti* mosquito, probably introduced from Africa through slave trade.
1800	Apprehensive about United States' increasing interest in Louisiana, Spain, an empire in decline, secretly retrocedes Louisiana to militarily powerful France, even as Spanish administrators continue to govern colony. Word of transfer soon reaches United States and alarms President Jefferson, who views New Orleans as critical to western expansion.
1802	Napoleon sends 20,000 troops to control slave insurrection in Saint-Domingue, ongoing since 1791. Yellow fever decimates troops; slave revolt intensifies and eventually leads to expulsion of French regime, creating Latin America's first independent country (Haiti). Loss of extremely valuable sugar colony diminishes Napoleon's interest in France's cumbersome and problematic Louisiana colony.

New Orleans ■ Colonial-Era Flood Control

1802

Spain rescinds American right of deposit at New Orleans, exacerbating tension between United States and colonial powers. President Jefferson launches effort to purchase New Orleans; threat of war emerges, with England casting eyes on Louisiana prize as well. Once perceived as a beleaguered backwater destined for failure, New Orleans is now coveted by three nations.

New Orleans ■ Colonial-Era Flood Control

CHAPTER 7 A RADICAL CHANGE OF DESTINY

Despite its strategic situation, New Orleans was something of a colonial afterthought to its French administrators from the 1720s to 1760s and its Spanish governors for the remainder of the century.[1] The small beleaguered city, with a population of a few thousand, fell further in priority when revolution and insurgency rocked the Atlantic world in the late 1700s. Violence to the north ousted British colonials and launched a new American nation; violence across the ocean overthrew the French monarchy and spawned a shaky new republic; violence in the Caribbean fueled a slave insurrection in France's most valued colony, Saint-Domingue. Agitation for independence bubbled up throughout New Spain, further threatening the imperial status quo.

As political tumult transpired internationally, agricultural breakthroughs began to affect the lower Louisiana landscape. Eli Whitney's 1793 patent for the cotton "gin" (engine), which efficiently separated lint from seed, made cotton cultivation lucrative and fostered its dramatic spread into newly cleared lands in the lower Mississippi Valley. Two years later, Jean Etienne de Boré of New Orleans succeeded in granulating Louisiana sugarcane—a process practiced for centuries in the tropical West Indies but elusive in a subtropical clime—and replicated the process commercially. Sugarcane cultivation swiftly replaced fading colonial-era crops throughout the delta. There was only one economical way for sugar and cotton to reach sources of demand: down the Mississippi for deposit at *Nueva Orleans* and transshipment to world markets, where new steam-engine technology had revolutionized the processing of cotton lint into fabric and clothing.

Dramatic political news punctuated these advancements. Spain, declining in might and apprehensive about the United States' mounting interest in *Nueva Orleans*, in 1800 secretly retroceded its Louisiana colony to Napoleon's militarily powerful France and in 1802 rescinded Americans' right to deposit cargo at New Orleans. Upon learning of these developments, an alarmed President Thomas Jefferson aspired to gain control of the once neglected, now treasured port city, one way or another, as France shockingly returned to the North American stage. But where Jefferson saw strategic advantage, Napoleon saw subservience: The future emperor viewed his regained *Nouvelle Orleans* and the Louisiana colony as little more than a bread-basket to feed the astonishingly lucrative sugar colony of Saint-Domingue—once, of course, its insurgent slaves were crushed.

Instead, Napoleon's 20,000 troops, sent to Saint-Domingue in 1802 to restore order, were vanquished through bloody battles and lethal yellow fever out-breaks. Loss of the key colony undermined whatever passive interest Napoleon had in Louisiana. Wary of overextending his colonial empire, in need of money, and in light of impending war, Napoleon decided to sell the entire colony to the United States, which had bargained previously only for *Nouvelle Orleans*. "A vast and unlimited territory [became American] without the loss of a drop of blood," marveled one sanguine West-erner of the era. The 85-year-old port once envisioned to command that territory for France instead became the new American city of New Orleans.[2]

Colonials lowered the French tricolor for the last time in the Place d'Armes during the Louisiana Pur-chase ceremony on December 20, 1803. In only a few years, New Orleans's fortunes had dramatically reversed. For decades the colonial orphan of two distracted Old World monarchies, the city now found itself strategically positioned under the dominion of an ascendant, expanding, unabashedly capitalistic New World democracy. Westward-bound American settlers received the news "with elated heart and joy-ful countenance," enthused that they could now do business with the "friendly hand of a fellow citizen" rather than what they perceived to be foreign "ty-rants whose every glance was dire jealousy and suspicion . . . bombastic pride and ostentation . . . bribery, fraud, and chicanery."[3] Prominent observers routinely predicted that this new American city would, as one put it, "doubtless one day become the greatest [on the] continent, perhaps even in the world."[4] Another went further, foreseeing New Orleans as "one of the greatest commercial cities in the universe."[5]

TIME LINE, 1800s–1820

1803

Napoleon sells entire Louisiana territory to United States, ending colonial era; Louisiana Purchase is signed April 30 and ceremonially finalized on December 20. New Orleans's population at the time is 8,056 (3,948 whites, 2,773 slaves, and 1,335 free people of color) residing in roughly 1,000 dwellings. Another 2,000 people live nearby.

Early 1800s

Shifting river channel deposits sediment and forms batture along Faubourg Ste. Marie riverfront; instigates legal controversy regarding public versus private ownership of valuable new riverside land, reflecting differing Creole and American legal philosophies. Complex legal case involves President Jefferson and lasts for decades; court decisions between 1836 and the 1850s resolve that batture is public. Area is eventually incorporated into urban grid, spanning between river and Tchoupitoulas and South and North Peters streets corridor, from Toulouse to Felicity streets (including entire Warehouse District). Laws regarding batture ownership remain complex and convoluted to this day.

1800s

Outbreaks of cholera, malaria, and especially yellow fever give New Orleans highest death rate of any major American city: 4.3 percent annually in the 1800s, representing an improvement from the 7 percent death rate of the late 1700s. Yellow fever strikes mostly during August through October, disproportionately affecting poor "strangers"—usually working-class immigrants without childhood resistance, particularly those who live near stagnant mosquito-breeding water. Virus kills more than 100,000 Louisianians and nearly 40,000 New Orleanians between 1796 and 1905, deeply influencing human geography, economics, seasonal migration patterns, public image, and daily life of city.

1804–25   Three attempts to improve public health through sanitation and nuisance-abatement regulatory boards arise and fail due to minimal government support and commercial opposition to quarantines. New Orleans becomes nation's filthiest, least healthy, and most death-prone major city for much of 19th century, a fact often denied or covered up by city's commercial interests and newspapers.

1805   New Orleans is incorporated as a municipal entity, legally establishing city government, mission, duties, privileges, and boundaries. Charter ends colonial-era notions of city management and makes New Orleans official American city. Process of Americanization is under way.

1807   Act of Congress clarifies ownership of disputed lands in New Orleans; influences development of commons between the old city and Faubourg Ste. Marie. Act also reserves right-of-way for waterway to connect Carondelet Canal with river, paralleled by 60-foot-wide public highways. Although canal is never built, 171-foot-wide corridor gains name Canal Street. Act also confirms most land titles of settlers from colonial times, preserving old French arpent land-surveying method in cadastral (land parceling) system.

1809   More than 9,000 Saint-Domingue (Haitian) refugees arrive at New Orleans via Cuba. Composed of roughly even numbers of whites, free people of color, and enslaved blacks, refugees double city's population and revive city's Francophone culture. They integrate into Creole neighborhoods and society, adding new layers of ethnic complexity.

1810   New Orleans's population reaches 17,224 (approximately 6,316 whites, 5,961 black slaves, and 4,950 free people of color), seventh largest among American cities.

1810   Plantation of Claude Tremé is subdivided for urban development. Faubourg Tremé spreads New Orleans toward back-swamp, exploiting trunk of Esplanade Ridge–Bayou Road upland. Neighborhood, known for its black Creole and immigrant population, is described today as America's oldest black neighborhood but was actually quite mixed.

1812   Louisiana admitted to Union as 18th state.

New Orleans ▪ A Radical Change of Destiny

1812	First Mississippi River steamboat docks at New Orleans. Successful demonstration of emerging steam technology promises efficient upriver-bound transportation, replacing slow-moving keelboats for contra-current travel. Steamboat era begins in earnest by early 1820s, after technological, logistical, and legal barriers (namely, monopoly granted to inventors Robert Fulton and Robert Livingston) are surmounted. With city in American hands and hinterland under intensive cotton and sugar cultivation, new steamboat transportation puts New Orleans in strategic position to become principal Southern city.
1815	On January 8, local militia under command of Maj. Gen. Andrew Jackson defeats advancing British troops at Chalmette. Battle of New Orleans ends War of 1812, terminates English threat to young American nation, brings city's society to national attention, and helps integrate isolated, once foreign outpost into national fold. Anglo-American immigration increases, followed by foreign immigration.
1816	Crevasse at Macarty's Plantation floods backswamp to rear streets of city. Water damages infrastructure and crops but coats land with layer of sediment, building up elevation and helping enable early development of Carrollton. Flood may have actually saved lives, by cleaning city and reducing death rate by more than half.
1820	New Orleans's population reaches 27,176 by some accounts, 41,351 by others (approximately 19,244 whites, 14,946 black slaves, and 7,188 free people of color). Inclusion of adjacent areas may account for difference.

36

New Orleans ■ A Radical Change of Destiny

CHAPTER 8 UNWRITTEN RULES OF URBAN EXPANSION

New Orleans under American administration saw its population double roughly every 10 to 20 years and its urban footprint expand upriver and downriver along the natural levee of the Mississippi River.[1] By a two-to-one ratio, urbanization spread mostly in an upriver direction, starting from Pauger's original urban grid and into the former plantations of the upper *banlieue* (outskirts). These areas attracted English-speaking Anglo-American Protestants who arrived from the North and upper South after the Louisiana Purchase. This incoming ethnic group often found itself at odds with the older Creole population living in the Old City (French Quarter) and the lower *banlieue*, who were more likely to be French in tongue, Catholic in faith, Latin in culture, and native to the city and region for generations. Immigrants, refugees from Haiti, free people of color, enslaved African Americans, and seasonal transients further diversified the city's complex and often contentious social landscape. The Anglo–Creole tension, which manifested itself in everything from law to land use to race relations to architecture, underlies much of the history of New Orleans during the antebellum era.

From 1788 to the early 1900s, New Orleans expanded in a manner that was planned at the intra-subdivision scale (usually by professional surveyors and engineers) but unplanned at the citywide scale. What guided the spread of the city was a set of conditions and unwritten rules.

The first condition was *immediate adjacency to an already urbanized area*. The appeal to pedestrians of minimal walking distances encouraged new developments to occur quite literally across the street from existing ones. Faubourg Ste. Marie, New Orleans's first suburb, was laid out in 1788 immediately upriver from the original city, while Faubourg Marigny was founded

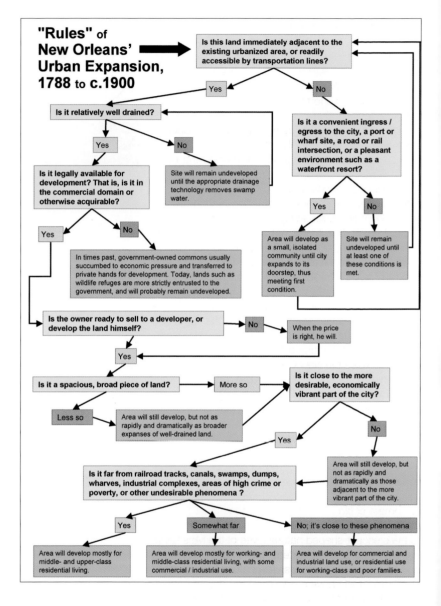

"Rules" of New Orleans' Urban Expansion, 1788 to c.1900

Is this land immediately adjacent to the existing urbanized area, or readily accessible by transportation lines?

Yes → Is it relatively well drained?

No → Is it a convenient ingress / egress to the city, a port or wharf site, a road or rail intersection, or a pleasant environment such as a waterfront resort?

Is it relatively well drained?
- **Yes** → Is it legally available for development? That is, is it in the commercial domain or otherwise acquirable?
- **No** → Site will remain undeveloped until the appropriate drainage technology removes swamp water.

Is it a convenient ingress / egress to the city, a port or wharf site, a road or rail intersection, or a pleasant environment such as a waterfront resort?
- **Yes** → Area will develop as a small, isolated community until city expands to its doorstep, thus meeting first condition.
- **No** → Site will remain undeveloped until at least one of these conditions is met.

Is it legally available for development? That is, is it in the commercial domain or otherwise acquirable?
- **Yes** →
- **No** → In times past, government-owned commons usually succumbed to economic pressure and transferred to private hands for development. Today, lands such as wildlife refuges are more strictly entrusted to the government, and will probably remain undeveloped.

Is the owner ready to sell to a developer, or develop the land himself?
- **No** → When the price is right, he will.
- **Yes** →

Is it a spacious, broad piece of land?
- **More so** → Is it close to the more desirable, economically vibrant part of the city?
- **Less so** → Area will still develop, but not as rapidly and dramatically as broader expanses of well-drained land.

Is it close to the more desirable, economically vibrant part of the city?
- **Yes** → Is it far from railroad tracks, canals, swamps, dumps, wharves, industrial complexes, areas of high crime or poverty, or other undesirable phenomena ?
- **No** → Area will still develop, but not as rapidly and dramatically as those adjacent to the more vibrant part of the city.

Is it far from railroad tracks, canals, swamps, dumps, wharves, industrial complexes, areas of high crime or poverty, or other undesirable phenomena ?
- **Yes** → Area will develop mostly for middle- and upper-class residential living.
- **Somewhat far** → Area will develop mostly for working- and middle-class residential living, with some commercial / industrial use.
- **No; it's close to these phenomena** → Area will develop for commercial and industrial land use, or residential use for working-class and poor families.

A series of unwritten rules guided urban expansion in New Orleans, from its initial 1788 spread beyond the original plat to the early 1900s. In the 20th century, the "rules" began to change on account of municipal drainage, flood protection, and modern city planning. The urban-growth sequence on the opposite page was made by digitally coregistering historical and aerial imagery, delineating developed areas, then overlaying the results on an elevation model. From its initial 0.3-square-mile footprint at the French Quarter in the early 1700s, the deltaic conurbation now spans about 200 square miles across four parishes. *GIS processing, analyses, and graphics by Richard Campanella.*

in 1805–06 directly below it. Faubourgs Duplantier, So-let, La Course, and Annunciation (1806–10) immedi-ately abutted Faubourg Ste. Marie once its blocks were urbanized with parcels and structures. Faubourg Tremé (1810) also closely adjoined an established urbanized area, across the old fort line from the original city. Exist-ing development, then, was a strong predictor of the location of future development—until new transporta-tion systems altered spatial relationships.

Roads, canals, and railroads diminished the need for immediate adjacency, broadening the expansion "rule" to include accessibility. Bayou Road had allowed a tiny agricultural community to thrive at Bayou St. John, about two miles away from the city, since early colonial times, but it was not subdivided into a fau-bourg until 1810, when the Carondelet Canal made it accessible to the old city. Navigation canals also made distant Spanish Fort and West End into lakefront mini-ports and resorts in the early to mid-1800s. Ridge-following roads enabled development along present-day Metairie Road and Gentilly Boulevard years before the metropolis enveloped these areas. The Pontchar-train Railroad (1831) turned Milneburg into a busy lake-front port, while the New Orleans & Carrollton Railroad (1835) fueled the establishment of Lafayette, Jefferson, Carrollton, and other communities now constituting Uptown, which were at the time otherwise unattached to the city proper. With these new conveyances, New Orleanians could now live farther from the city center yet still partake of its attributes; real estate developers were more than eager to accommodate them.

In addition to adjacency or accessibility, land in New Orleans needed to be high and dry before urban de-velopment could occur. For most of the city's first two centuries, this important topographic rule restricted it to the crescent-shaped natural levee of the Mississippi River and, to a lesser extent, the smaller Esplanade and Metairie–Gentilly ridges. The natural levee crested at 10 to 15 feet above sea level near the riverfront (the "front-of-town") and sloped downward to uninhabited swamp and marshland, which lay inches above sea level. The backswamp edge roughly aligned with what is now Claiborne Avenue—a few blocks closer to the river in the early 1800s, and a few blocks closer to the lake by the late 1800s, as early drainage efforts took ef-fect. Neighborhoods near the backswamp edge were dubbed "the back-of-town," a term still heard today.

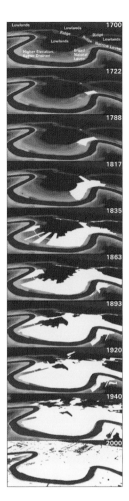

Yellow indicates general extent of urbanized area. Interpretation and map by Richard Campanella.

New Orleans ■ Unwritten Rules of Urban Expansion

Land also had to be legally acquirable for subdivision. Sugarcane plantations surrounded New Orleans; as the city spread, planters had to decide whether they could make more money by continuing to cultivate their holdings or by surveying them into blocks and selling them off for development. Nearly all eventually chose the latter—though at different times and through various surveyors, who each independently designed street grids into the elongated parcels.

A few government-owned commons also succumbed to private-sector development. The Canal Street corridor is one such example: For 22 years, it comprised a dusty commons between the Old City (roughly what is now Iberville Street) and Faubourg Ste. Marie (along the aptly named Common Street). It was finally subdivided in 1810, at an angle that unified the extant street grids of its neighbors.

Terrains' expansiveness and adjacency to the more prosperous, amenity-rich, desirable section of town also drove development patterns. Because of the broad meander of the Mississippi in uptown, its natural levee sprawled wider than those abutting the straight section of river flowing below the French Quarter. Developers thus had more fine land to subdivide uptown than in the lower city. Fortuitously, those same uptown areas were also physically adjacent to the economically vibrant and socially fashionable part of New Orleans. This was the American section, where English predominated, business and industry reigned, and American culture prevailed. Horse-drawn streetcars and hackney cabs transported uptown residents to their downtown offices in St. Mary (anglicized from Faubourg Ste. Marie), fast replacing the Old City as New Orleans's economic and professional heart.

Uptown also benefited from a fundamental hydrological advantage over downtown areas: Refuse flows downriver. In a city where the Mississippi River served as the premier source of all water needs (as it does today), areas upriver from the urban core evaded most of the local sewage, debris, carcasses, and other pollutants dumped in the Mississippi. For this and aforementioned reasons, New Orleans grew on a faster, bigger, and grander scale in an upriver direction, compared to downriver or away from the river.

Downtown communities, by contrast, looked more toward a European past than an American future. This predominantly Creole and immigrant section mostly spoke French, practiced a religion that differed from the American norm, and culturally referenced the fading colonial worlds of France and Spain and their Afro-Caribbean sphere of influence. Granted, the Old City boasted its share of professional districts, fancy hotels, theaters, and other amenities, but it increasingly fell behind what Faubourg St. Mary had to offer. The faubourgs carved from lower-city plantations were usually poorer and humbler—for example, the Poor Third, meaning the Third Municipality below Esplanade Avenue—than those uptown. Wealth and urban amenities tended to gravitate upriver; indigence and urban nuisances often ended up downriver (or away from the river, at the back-of-town). Planters who subdivided their lower-city parcels for urbanization saw little of the quick economic success enjoyed by their uptown counterparts; neighborhoods a mile below the French Quarter took 60 to 80 additional years to reach the urban-density levels realized by areas a mile above the Quarter as early as the 1810s. It is no coincidence that the neighborhood now called Bywater (located one to two miles below the French Quarter) is home to the last riverfront plantation home on the city's east bank: the Lombard House, which presided over one of the area's last agrarian riverfront parcels. It is also no coincidence that the Lower Ninth Ward ended up as one of the city's poorest and most isolated neighborhoods, and among the slowest to urbanize.

Thus, 19th-century New Orleans steadily expanded upriver more so than downriver, as sugarcane plantations were subdivided into grids, transformed into low-density villages, municipally annexed by New Orleans, and finally developed into streetcar-suburb environments. Uptown's developmental success is reflected in the various adjustments of Orleans Parish's official borders. The upper limits of New Orleans expanded upriver six times between 1797 and 1874, from its original location along modern-day Iberville Street to its final position on Monticello Street, over eight river miles upriver. The lower parish line, on the other hand, has contracted over the past 200 years, from the eastern marshes of what is now St. Bernard Parish to within a few hundred feet of Jackson Barracks, three miles below the French Quarter.[2]

The ad hoc "rules" driving 19th-century urban expansion encountered revolutionary new circumstances in the 20th century. Electrified streetcar lines and, later, automobiles undercut the historical need to develop adjacently to extant subdivisions. Municipal drainage negated the ancient requisite to build on higher ground. Modern water treatment, sewerage, electrification, telephony, steel-frame high rises, and other technological breakthroughs fostered the outward movement of residential land use and the transformation of the inner city to commercial use. The new nature and geography of urbanization inspired a nationwide rethinking of the decentralized, individual-driven processes that had prevailed previously. "In every large city of our country," lamented one New York planner in 1915, "a land owner could put up a building to any height, in any place, of any size and use it to any purpose, regardless of how much it hurt his neighbor."[3] Authorities responded to the emerging crisis by creating city planning commissions and zoning ordinances, intervening in bottom-up piecemeal development with top-down expert planning and regulation. New York City adopted its zoning ordinance in 1916; by 1933, well over a thousand American cities, home to 70 percent of the nation's urban population, had followed suit. New Orleans was no exception, creating its City Planning and Zoning Commission in 1923 and adopting its first Comprehensive Zoning Ordinance in 1929. "Complete individualism is anarchy," admonished the commission in writings entitled *What Is Zoning?* and "Something similar to anarchy has prevailed in the development of American cities. . . . Orderly living[,] public peace and convenience cannot exist without government power to control and direct the acts of individuals."[4]

They were right, of course. But one cannot help observing that the New Orleans cityscapes created by the bottom-up forces of the 18th and 19th centuries are far more distinctive and appealing than those overseen by the top-down forces of the 20th century.

42

TIME LINE, 1820s–1830s

Early 1800s   Travelers from Europe and eastern seaboard marvel at New Orleans's social and physical distinctiveness, particularly its ethnic diversity. National perceptions about New Orleans as a unique and exotic city, or alternately as a wicked "Sodom and Gomorrah," begin to form.

1822

According to John Adems Paxton's *New-Orleans Directory and Register*, city and suburbs count "1,436 brick, and 4,401 wooden dwellings; 1,258 brick and 1,567 wooden warehouses, workshops, &c.; 28 brick and 15 wooden public buildings, making in the whole 8,705 buildings of every description. New buildings are daily rising particularly in the upper part of New Orleans."

1823–36

First effective municipal water system, designed by Benjamin H. B. Latrobe, replaces various makeshift efforts. Located at foot of Ursulines Street, system uses steam pump to draw river water into three-story pumphouse, where it is stored in raised reservoirs and distributed to residential households through network of cypress pipes.

1824–28

First Jewish congregations founded in New Orleans, notably Congregation Shangari Chassed (Gates of Mercy) in 1828, predecessor of Touro Synagogue. Later-arriving German Jews form small enclave at foot of Jackson Avenue, which would migrate to uptown–University area by turn of 20th century. This older, established Reform Jewish population lived separately from Eastern European Orthodox Jews who settled near Dryades Street in late 19th century.

1825

Erie Canal in upstate New York connects Great Lakes with Hudson River. Waterway gives New York City access to western frontier, suddenly challenging New Orleans's monopoly on Mississippi Valley trade. Conservative New Orleans business community fails to diversify economy during ensuing decades, focusing instead on booming river trade. Seed for New Orleans's decline is planted but is buried amid antebellum prosperity. Erie Canal inspires rampant waterway excavation elsewhere—more bad news for New Orleans.

1830

New Orleans's population reaches 49,826 (21,281 whites, 16,639 black slaves, and 11,906 free people of color), fifth largest among American cities.

1830s

Esplanade Avenue is extended from river to Bayou St. John. Avenue is designed in French manner and developed as garden suburb for wealthy Francophones departing old city. Corridor exploits upraised Esplanade Ridge and forms axis of orthogonal street network of Sixth and Seventh wards but does not replace its prehistoric predecessor, Bayou Road, which wanders across Esplanade at an angle all its own.

1830s	Black population in New Orleans, majority since 1730s, falls into numerical minority as Irish and German immigration augments city's white population. Urban slaves are often replaced by immigrant servants and laborers, contributing to steady decline in absolute number of black New Orleanians from 1840 to emancipation. City remains majority white until late 1970s.
1831	Pontchartrain Railroad built to connect river and lake. Early railroad establishes Elysian Fields Avenue trajectory through backswamp a century prior to area's urban development. Railroad serves as ingress/egress for passenger traffic between New Orleans and Gulf Coast cities.
1832–38	At cost of thousands of mostly Irish lives, New Basin Canal is excavated between rear of Faubourg St. Mary and Lake Pontchartrain, giving city (particularly uptown Anglo business community) improved access to lake trade. Waterway competes with circa-1790s Carondelet Canal and new Pontchartrain Railroad, both of which draw lake trade to Creole lower city. Canal and turning basin (downtown docking area) influence development of back-of-town and lakefront into mid-20th century.
1832	Cholera epidemic kills thousands, particularly newly arrived Irish immigrants.

CHAPTER 9 THE UNPLANNED STREET PLAN

On a map of modern New Orleans, streets seem to emerge from a nebulous midcrescent origin and radiate outwardly toward the arching river, like the blades of a handheld fan.[1] Viewed from the perspective of the river, the shape resembles the skeleton of a sinuous snake. Deeply influential in the experience of the city, the radiating pattern happened neither by chance nor by plan. Its antecedent is a cadastral (land parceling) system developed in north-central Europe around the end of the first millennium.

The logic behind the system is compelling. Given a valued linear resource at one end (usually a waterway or a road), unproductive land at the other end (marshes or mountains), and arable land in between (natural levees or valley bottoms), a surveyor can maximize the number of farms enjoying access to the valued linear resource by perpendicularly delineating the arable land into narrow strips. Excess width would diminish the number of farms created, while insufficient depth would deprive some farms of access to the waterway or road. The surveying of narrow, long parcels of land thus leads to the optimal allocation of two scarce resources: accessibility and arability.

It was primarily the French who introduced this tradition to the New World. The long-lot system arrived officially in Louisiana when the Crown, exasperated with overly generous land concessions granted to certain colonists, stipulated in the Edict of October 12, 1716 that land delineation occur "in the proportion of two to four arpents front by forty to sixty in depth."[2] To measure the cadasters (parcels), surveyors used the unit arpent, which equals 180 French feet (191.835 American feet) lineally and 0.845 American acres superficially. Settlers were granted riverside or bayouside land usually spanning two to eight arpents de face

Above and below: uptown New Orleans's breathtaking canopy of oaks. *Photographs by Richard Campanella, 2004.*

(frontage arpents) and extending back to the swamp by 40 or 80 arpents, depending on the width of the natural levee.[3]

By the 1720s, most riverine land near New Orleans had been delineated into arpent-based long lots. Straight portions of the river yielded neat rectangular long lots. Meandering portions rendered diverging parcels on the convex side of the meander (for example, the West Bank) and converging units on the concave side (such as the East Bank), forming a radiating pattern of elongated triangles or trapezoids. One by one, over many years, owners of those plantations contemplated whether to continue another season in agriculture or sell out for residential real estate. Eventually nearly all made the decision to develop and hired surveyors to design and lay out street grids. Of course, those grids had to conform to the limits of their client's property. The upper and lower limits of the plantation usually became the bordering streets of the new subdivision, the middle was often reserved for a grand avenue, and all other areas became side streets or house lots.

Where the river ran straight and the abutting plantations traced neat elongated rectangles, such as below Elysian Fields Avenue, orthogonal street grids fit snugly into the antecedent cadaster.[4] But uptown, where the river yawned broadly, surveyors were forced to squeeze street grids into wedge-shaped parcels. Odd angles, jogged and cut-off streets, multisized blocks, and slivers resulted from the mismatch.

Because of this piecemeal development and the lack of a central planning authority, the geometry of the colonial-era arpent system became burned into the expanding street network of the growing American city. Most long lots within the modern-day uptown New Orleans crescent transitioned from plantation to faubourg between 1788 and the Civil War, and most of those faubourgs—subdivisions such as Faubourg Plaisance, Faubourg Bouligny, Rickerville, Hurstville, Burthesville, Greenville, and Friburg, named for either their last plantation owner or first subdivision investor—reached full residential development by the early 1900s. Modern-day uptown represents a classic American streetcar suburb; replete with beautiful mansions as well as colorful shotgun houses, humble cottages, and vibrant commercial clusters, the leafy district ranks as one of the most splendid urban residential environments in the nation.

The ancient agrarian logic of the arpent system to this day defines the urban texture of uptown New Orleans. Clues to its influence abound; they are obscure at first but ubiquitous once discovered. The system explains why certain uptown streets suddenly terminate in a bewildering "T," forcing motorists to seek alternative routes to proceed. It explains why narrow grassy slivers split occasional streets and why structures built on them limn trapezoidal or triangular shapes, like New York's Flatiron Building. It also explains why driving in a straight line on a river-parallel street, such as St. Charles Avenue or Prytania, above Lee Circle, means you are driving within an old plantation, while turning your steering wheel ever so slightly means you're crossing an old plantation line: Most bends in river-parallel uptown streets correspond to old long-lot plantation lines. The wonder of the unplanned transformation from plantation system to urban system is that the resultant street network is distinctive, aesthetically appealing, and reasonably easy to navigate. The task of fixing those spots that proved problematic was among the first that the City Planning and Zoning Commission tackled after it formed in 1923.[5]

It may seem paradoxical that arbitrary and cryptic cadastral patterns often have a greater and longer-lasting impact on cityscapes than massive structures of bricks and mortar. But buildings are subject to the elements and the whims of their owners, whereas cadastral systems are inscribed in legal and political realms with deep roots in fundamental national philosophies. Excepting revolutionary changes of government, cadastral patterns usually endure under new administrations and continue their imprint upon the landscape. The French arpent system persisted even when Spanish dominion replaced the French, and American replaced the Spanish. Its geometry survived after plantation agriculture gave way to faubourgs, and faubourgs became city neighborhoods. It continues to affect residents' lives, from morning commutes to evening strolls.

48

TIME LINE, 1830s–1840s

1830s–1850s   Main era of Irish immigration to New Orleans; Irish settle in dispersed pattern throughout periphery of city, particularly along riverfront and back-of-town, while generally avoiding costly inner city. English-speaking Catholic churches are founded to serve this population.

1830s–1930s   Sugar handling and trading lead to creation of "sugar landing" on upper French Quarter batture, on the riverside of present-day North Peters, from Toulouse to Iberville. Area develops into Sugar District in 1870s, with high-rise processing plants, storage sheds, shipping facilities, and exchange. Sugar processing moves to St. Bernard Parish in 1910s, but industry continues to use French Quarter riverfront until 1930s. Most facilities have since been demolished; area, now occupied by parking lots, is often eyed for new development.

1830s	Captain Henry Shreve and State of Louisiana alter hydrology of Mississippi–Red–Atchafalaya rivers region in central Louisiana, not foreseeing consequences. Shreve cuts off meander loop near Red–Mississippi juncture (1831) to aid navigation; severed section (Old River) silts up in one part and sends Red River into Mississippi River in another portion. Immense logjam prevents water from escaping down Atchafalaya distributary and also retards navigation and development in south-central Louisiana. Shreve and state clear logjam during 1830s, unknowingly providing Mississippi with shorter path and steeper gradient to sea. Cleared logjam sends steadily increasing flow down Atchafalaya rather than Mississippi. Fearing catastrophic channel jump, engineers build Old River Control Structure in 1950s and 1960s to preserve lower Mississippi River channel—and New Orleans.
1834	First successful gas company brings new fuel to city for lighting and other purposes. Gasworks are soon constructed near present-day Superdome, illustrating how back-of-town was used for operations too sprawling and objectionable to be located in front-of-town. Gasworks remain in this area for over a century.
1835	New Orleans and Carrollton Rail Road installed on Nayades Street, now St. Charles Avenue. Streetcar plays important role in developing uptown New Orleans and guiding the surveying of new streets. Now oldest continually serving rail line in the world (except for two-year post-Katrina interruption), St. Charles streetcar represents first component of an urban rail system that would grow steadily until the 1920s, then decline back down to its original line after 1964.
1836	Anglo displeasure with Creole political control and related ethnic tensions lead to creation of essentially three separate cities within New Orleans: First and Third municipalities are mostly Creole and immigrant; Second Municipality is mostly Anglo and immigrant. Municipality system is inefficient and divisive but influential in ethnic geography of city, producing perception of Canal Street as dividing line between Creole and American cultures. City reunifies in 1852.

49

New Orleans ▪ The Unplanned Street Plan

1836–38	City's market system for vending of fruits, vegetables, meat, prepared food, and dry goods begins steady expansion. Public markets open above Old City (Poydras Market, St. Mary's Market) and below it (Washington Market), while original French Market, established by Spanish administration, enjoys its own expansion. City oversees 34 separate markets by 1911, largest such system in nation.
1837	Strong hurricane hits New Orleans, damaging structures and flooding marshes adjacent to Lake Pontchartrain.
1837–42	Opulent "exchange hotels" are built in First and Second municipalities; they combine lodging, dining, banking, and conference space under one roof. St. Louis Exchange Hotel opens in predominantly Creole First Municipality; domed St. Charles Exchange Hotel opens in predominantly Anglo Second Municipality. They become nuclei for competing Creole and Anglo interests. Described as among most splendid hotels in America, both cater to extended-stay guests during wintertime business season.
1830s–1840s	New American aesthetics affect built environment: Creole architecture peaks and begins to decline in French Quarter; replaced by Greek Revival, which first arrived there in 1808 from Northeast. Stylistic shift reflects larger cultural changes in local politics and society, from Creole to American.
1840	New Orleans's population reaches 102,193 (59,519 whites, 23,448 black slaves, and 19,226 free people of color, although that last figure may represent an error in the census, as the true figure is probably closer to 9,000–10,000). City is third largest in nation, highest ranking it has ever achieved; port is rated "the fourth port in point of commerce in the world, exceeded only by London, Liverpool, and New York."[6]

New Orleans ▪ The Unplanned Street Plan

CHAPTER 10 ANTEBELLUM FLOOD CONTROL

French and Spanish colonial administrations, weak and undersupported as they were, held plantation owners individually responsible for constructing and maintaining the levees fronting their riverine parcels.[1] The new American administration generally continued this tradition of localism, which, incidentally, prevailed also in drainage, sewerage, potable water distribution, firefighting, and other services. Most such efforts floundered. Localized flood control was no exception, rendering the rural delta's levee "system" vulnerable to overtopping and breaching.

The urbanized delta fared little better. In New Orleans, the City Council gradually gained control over the waterfront and, in 1810, set standards for levee construction. The dikes had to be at least three feet above the river at normal stage, one foot above the high-water line, and five to six feet wide at the base for each foot in height. The effort at this time fell under the direction of City Engineer Jacques Tanesee, who designed embankments that, unlike today's trapezoidal berms, fronted the river with a wall of wooden pilings reinforced by an earthen backslope, which doubled as a wharf. Levees in the provinces rarely conformed to those standards, thereby reducing the system's overall effectiveness to that of the weakest link.

On May 6, 1816, one particular link broke: The levee on Barthelemy McCarty's plantation in present-day Carrollton developed a crevasse, filling the backswamp until water reached the rear flanks of the city five miles downriver. "One could travel in a skiff from the corner of Chartres and Canal streets," read one account, "to Dauphin, down Dauphin to Bienville, down Bienville to Burgundy, thus to St. Louis Street, from St. Louis to Rampart, and so throughout the rear suburbs."[2] The damage to the built environment, however, came with a benefit to the natural environment: "The receding water," noted one historian, "filled the low terrain with alluvial deposits enriching the soil as well as elevating the swamp sections."[3] It also granted an epidemiological dividend, as that summer proved to be unusually healthy for the population. Only 651 deaths occurred in New Orleans in 1816, compared to 1,252 in 1815 and 1,772 in 1817, probably because the freshwater flushed out the stagnant, mosquito-breeding back-swamp.[4]

Levees of varying standards expanded upstream at a rapid pace throughout the antebellum era. Whereas late-colonial-era levees lined the river from English Turn up to the German Coast, by 1812 they extended up to Old River and by 1844 to Greenville, Mississippi.[5] A visitor during 1819–21 described the region's "artificial embankment" as

> thirty or forty yards from the natural bank of the river, four to six feet high, and six to nine feet broad at the base, [extending] 130 miles on the eastern, and about 170 on the western side of the river. . . . The law imposes on every individual to maintain in good repair that part which is before his own land . . . enforced by commissioners who are appointed to inspect and direct repairs.[6]

Fifteen years later, Joseph Holt Ingraham described New Orleans's system in his travelogue *The South-West by a Yankee*:

> [The levee] extends, on both sides of the river, to more than one hundred and fifty miles above New-Orleans. This *levée* is properly a dike, thrown up on the verge of the river, from twenty-five to thirty feet in breadth, and two feet higher than high-water mark; leaving a ditch, or fossé, on the inner side, of equal breadth, from which the earth to form the levée is taken. Consequently . . . when the river is full . . . the surface of the river will be *four feet higher* than the surface of the country.[7]

It took another disaster to rethink the wisdom of localism. In early May 1849, a levee deteriorated on Pierre Sauvé's plantation in what is now the River Ridge section of Jefferson Parish. The erosive torrent widened the crevasse to 150 feet long and six feet deep,

New Orleans ■ Antebellum Flood Control

slowly filling the hydrological basin between the river's natural levee and the Metairie Ridge. The deluge surpassed the New Basin Canal on May 8, reached Rampart Street on May 15, and peaked from May 30 to June 1 at the intersection of Bourbon and Canal streets.[8] A few days later, a *Daily Picayune* journalist described the view from the 185-foot-high cupola of the St. Charles Hotel. Far away in Carrollton and up to the Sauvé crevasse, the country was "one sheet of water, dotted in innumerable spots with houses . . . barns, out houses, lofty trees and brushwood." The streets in the Second Municipality were "so many vast water courses, or aquatic highways, issuing as it were from the bosom of the swamp." He observed: "Indeed, there is no place with which we can compare New Orleans . . . that would give the absent traveller so correct an idea of its topographical features, as the city of Venice."[9]

Volunteers heroically plugged the crevasse on June 20, but not before 220 city blocks, 2,000 structures, and 12,000 residents were flooded up to 17 miles away. Within a few days, water receded from most city streets (though not yet from the backswamp or rural Jefferson Parish) by draining out through the New Basin Canal and Bayou St. John, or evaporating in the summer sun. Displaced citizens returned home to clean up and rebuild; pavements, gutters, and city structures suffered enough damage to warrant a special tax to fund repairs. The deluge left behind a "deposit of alluvion [with] vegetable and animal matter," leading officials to fear that "an active agent of disease—the *materies morborum*" might threaten the population. Only months earlier, cholera had killed 3,176 New Orleanians. But heavy rains washed away the filth, and, as in 1816, death rates actually declined after the flood.[10]

Sauvé's Crevasse ranked as the city's worst flood for the next 156 years. It occurred in an era when the federal government reconsidered its role in overseeing lower Mississippi River flood control. Washington responded by offering federally owned swamplands to states in the Mississippi Valley in exchange for their commitment to build levees, drain the swamps, sell the land, and recoup their investment. The Swamp and Overflow Land Act of 1850 spurred more levee construction but fell short of expectations. The federal government also pursued its interest in improving the navigability and control of the Mississippi by funding

53

two landmark—and competing—surveys. One, led by Andrew Atkinson Humphreys, recommended a "levees only" policy to prevent the river from overtopping and channel jumping. The other, by Charles Ellet, suggested a comprehensive approach that included levees to constrain the river but also outlets and reservoirs to accommodate it should the levees prove insufficient. Humphreys's research would later lead to total federal emphasis on levees only in the closing decades of the century, a policy decision that would come to be regretted and reversed.[11]

The state also entered the picture. In 1854, the Louisiana state legislature formed four flood districts and a Board of Swamp Land Commissioners to oversee levee building. In time, this entity would evolve into the "levee district," a consortium of governmental bodies managing the engineering, construction, and maintenance work.[12] The age of localism was ending; flood control responsibility began to shift from landowners and local entities to state and federal hands. But mounting tension between state and federal authorities would derail progress for years, as war clouds gathered on the horizon.

TIME LINE, 1840s–1850s

1840s

Destrehan Canal dug to connect Mississippi River with Bayou Barataria and Barataria Bay. Waterway helps development of West Bank; is expanded as Harvey Canal with modern locks in 1907 and widened in 1924.

1845

War with Mexico breaks out. City plays prominent role as jumping-off point for troops and munitions; *Daily Picayune* becomes major source of war news for nation. Involvement symbolizes era (particularly 1830s–1850s) when New Orleans serves as favored site for launching campaigns of adventurism and intrigue into Latin America.

1840s–1850s

Main era of German immigration to New Orleans. Like Irish, Germans settle in dispersed pattern throughout city periphery, particularly in Lafayette and Third Municipality. Somewhat better educated than Irish but burdened by language barrier, Germans instill rich cultural and institutional traditions into New Orleans society.

1840s–1850s

Retailers migrate from narrow Royal and Chartres streets to spacious Canal Street, until now a mostly residential thoroughfare. Canal Street becomes South's premier downtown shopping destination for over a century.

1840s–1860

Canal excavation and railroad construction emanating from great northeastern population centers, starting with Erie Canal in 1825, tap into trans-Appalachian West, offering western farmers additional routes to deliver produce to market. New Orleans, which once monopolistically controlled western exports via its strategic position on the Mississippi, increasingly must compete for its commerce. Having once controlled more than 99 percent of Mississippi Valley shipments into the 1820s, New Orleans fights to handle only half that percentage by 1860. Yet because western production grows so dramatically in absolute terms, city leaders and commercial interests fail to diversify New Orleans's economy, relying instead on lucrative river trade. While city continues to grow in population, its relative ranking among nation's largest cities, which peaked at third largest in 1840, begins to drop. Seeds of New Orleans's decline are sown even as city enjoys meteoric rise.

Mid–1840s

After seven failed attempts since Louisiana Purchase, New Orleans launches a professionally staffed Board of Health to understand and improve city's terrible public-health crisis. Hard data and honest assessments of deplorable conditions are finally documented, yet death rate increases in ensuing decade, in part because of official complacency.

1846–56

Decaying Place d'Armes and surrounding buildings are renovated magnificently: St. Louis Cathedral and twin Pontalba Buildings constructed; Cabildo and Presbytère renovated with mansard roofs and cupolas; Andrew Jackson statue installed; newly fenced and landscaped plaza renamed Jackson Square. Outstanding work transforms dusty commons into place of splendor, completely intact today. Cast-iron galleries on Pontalba Buildings instigate local fashion craze and forever change streetscape of French Quarter, as iron-lace galleries are added to numerous town houses and storehouses.

1847–58

Yellow fever outbreak in 1847 claims lives of over 2,300 New Orleanians; commences era of terribly costly epidemics killing at least 22,500 in 12 years, disrupting nearly every aspect of city life. High death tolls are a product of large numbers of vulnerable residents, particularly immigrants, living near cisterns and other sources of stagnant water, perfect habitats for invasive *Aedes aegypti* mosquito.

1848   Illinois and Michigan (I & M) Canal is completed across hundred-mile-long Chicago Portage, providing waterborne passage between Great Lakes and Gulf of Mexico watersheds. New transportation option fuels development of Chicago, while diminishing New Orleans's once-monopolistic control of Mississippi River shipping traffic. The I & M Canal is supplanted in 1900 by larger Chicago Sanitary and Ship Canal.

1849   Crevasse in levee at Sauvé Plantation in Jefferson Parish fills backswamp and inundates city from rear, submerging 220 blocks, damaging 2,000 structures, and displacing 12,000 residents. City infrastructure is rebuilt with funds from special tax. Sauvé's Crevasse ranks as New Orleans's worst flood until Hurricane Katrina–induced levee failures of 2005.

New Orleans ■ Antebellum Flood Control

CHAPTER 11 POPULATING THE ANTEBELLUM CITY

Travelogues testify to the extraordinary ethnic diversity of early-19th-century New Orleans. "No city perhaps on the globe," wrote one visitor in 1816, "presents a greater contrast of national manners, language, and complexion, than does New Orleans." Marveled another in 1835, "Truly does New-Orleans represent every other city and nation upon earth. I know of none where is congregated so great a variety of the human species." Another visitor gushed, "What a hubbub! What an assemblage of strange faces [and] distinct people!"[1]

Prior to the early 1800s, the ethnic geography of New Orleans was relatively simple. Locally born French-speaking Catholics (Creoles), from various Francophone and Hispanic regions and racial backgrounds, spatially intermixed throughout the city, with the enslaved population living in close proximity to the enslavers. The few foreign-born residents, including Anglo-Americans, numbered too few to form significant ethnic clusters. In 1809, over 9,000 refugees from Saint-Domingue doubled New Orleans's population, revived its Francophone and Afro-Caribbean culture, and reinforced its intermixed settlement patterns.

This began to change in the 1810s. Anglo-American emigrants seeking opportunities in the Mississippi Valley frontier brought to the Old World–oriented, French-speaking Catholic city the external influences of American commerce and culture, English, Protestantism, and new concepts in everything from jurisprudence to architecture to race relations. Anglos gravitated to the uppermost blocks of the old city or the adjacent Faubourg Ste. Marie. By the 1830s, Anglo surnames outnumbered French ones in that suburb, known by that time as St. Mary or the American Quarter.[2] Economic, religious, political, and cultural institutions arose among the uptown Anglos, further reinforcing the trend. The pattern of an Anglo-dominant upper city versus a Creole lower city would deeply influence the cultural geography of New Orleans for generations to come.[3]

Racial geographies in antebellum New Orleans resembled those in other Southern cities. The domestic nature of urban slavery drove a spatially heterogeneous racial distribution pattern, in which enslaved blacks usually lived adjacent to their enslavers, often in appended quarters. This so-called "early Southern," "back alley" pattern of low-density intermingling has been documented in Charleston, South Carolina, Washington, D.C., Baltimore, and elsewhere.[4] But New Orleans's Creole and Anglo ethnic geography affected that dispersion in an unusual manner, particularly since many Creoles were *gens de couleur libre* (free people of color). Many members of this somewhat privileged mixed-race caste—making up roughly one-third the total African-ancestry population of antebellum New Orleans—excelled in professions, studied abroad, and gained middle- or upper-class status. Some even owned slaves. Throughout most of the antebellum era, more free people of color called New Orleans home than any other Southern city, and occasionally more than any American city, in both relative and absolute terms. A product of the city's Franco-Afro-Caribbean heritage, this caste helped distinguish New Orleans and Louisiana society from the national norm.

Free people of color clustered in the lower French Quarter, Bayou Road, the faubourgs Tremé, Marigny, New Marigny, Franklin, and those making up the present-day neighborhood of Bywater. Why there? This was the Francophone, Catholic, locally descended (Creole) side of town, a social environment largely created by free people of color (as well as white Creoles) and more conducive to their interests. Not only was the mostly Anglophone Protestant world on the upper side of town culturally foreign terrain, but its white inhabitants were often more hostile to the very notion of a person of color being free.

The antebellum geography of black New Orleans, then, consisted of slaves intricately intermixed citywide—"scattered through the city promiscuously,"[5] as the *Daily Picayune* put it in 1843—and free people of color predominating in the lower neighborhoods. With the minor exception of the back-of-town, where very poor manumitted blacks and others lived in squatter huts, there were no expansive, exclusively black neighborhoods in antebellum New Orleans. People of African ancestry lived next door to whites and others of various ethnic origins—locals and immigrants.

For most of the years between 1837 and the Civil War, more immigrants arrived at New Orleans than any other Southern city. Nationally, New Orleans routinely ranked second only to New York in immigrant arrivals.[6] Understanding how the various immigrant groups dispersed themselves across the deltaic cityscape requires a discussion of the city's physical, economic, and urban geography.

Although urbanization occurred almost entirely on the higher, better-drained natural levee abutting the Mississippi River, not all sections of that feature were equally valued. Those closest to the river boasted transportation and elevation advantages but suffered environmental nuisances associated with wharves and shipping activity. While ideal for commerce and replete with low-skilled employment, areas along the immediate riverfront were less desirable for residential living and attracted housing stock accordingly.

Areas farthest from the river were lowest in elevation and closest to the muddy, mosquito-infested, flood-prone swamp. Land in this so-called back-of-town suffered environmental risks and primitive infrastructure, cost the least, and inspired the development of the humblest housing stock. But it was not without opportunity: Canal excavation, railroad construction, stockyard, and other hard-labor jobs, which could not be found in the costly city center, abounded here.

Desirability of land also varied with distance from the urban core. Lack of mechanized transportation made life on the urban periphery inconvenient and thus cheap. Inner-city land, on the other hand, was convenient but scarce and therefore valuable. The lower classes therefore tended to occupy the periphery, while the upper classes predominated in the inner core—precisely the opposite of late-20th-century American cities. The pattern, in fact, is an ancient one—"in many medieval cities in Europe, the city centres were inhabited by the well-to-do, while the outer districts were the areas for the poorer segments of the population"[7]—and persisted in most New World cities.

Desirability of land thus varied directly with distance from the river and from the backswamp (the farther, the better) and indirectly with distance from the city center (the closer, the better). Areas that lay farthest from sources of nuisance and risk, *and* closest to amenities and opportunities, commanded the highest prices and attracted the best infrastructure and housing. These areas—the middle of the natural levee near the inner city—now compose the modern-day historic neighborhoods of the central French Quarter through the Central Business District and Coliseum Square and into the Garden District. St. Charles Avenue bisects the natural levee perfectly, equidistant from both the riverfront nuisances and the backswamp risks. It comes as no surprise that St. Charles ranks to this day as the city's grand avenue of elegance and affluence.

Encircling those highly desirable, convenient, low-nuisance, low-risk zones was an annulus of middle- and working-class neighborhoods. Farther out lay a periphery of low-density village-like developments, to which gravitated the disenfranchised, the marginalized, and the poor. During the first great wave of 19th-century immigration to New Orleans, from the 1820s to 1850s, laborer families mostly from Ireland and Germany settled throughout this semirural periphery. Here they found both affordable housing and low-skill employment at the flatboat wharves, warehouses, slaughterhouses, and tanneries, and in public-works projects for canals, drainage, and railroads. They established social networks and religious institutions that attracted and served additional brethren. Befitting a low-density periphery, Irish and German settlement patterns formed a galaxy-like pattern of greater and lesser concentrations, with no intense clusters and no complete absences. Ethnic intermixing prevailed markedly over segregation. It is for this reason that, to this day, the location of the legendary Irish Channel remains a hotly debated subject locally and why no particular neighborhood claims a German sense of historical place. It is difficult to pin down the exact location of a dispersed phenomenon.

Although certain overriding geographical patterns prevailed, spatial heterogeneity—that is, people of all backgrounds living next door to one another—characterized the residential settlement patterns of this urban delta during the antebellum era.

TIME LINE, 1850–65

1850   New Orleans's population reaches 119,460 (91,431 whites, 18,068 black slaves, and 9,961 free people of color). Despite growing population and booming economy, city drops in rank from third largest in nation in 1840 to fifth largest in 1850.

1850   New telegraph lines speed city's communication links with adjacent cities and areas downriver.

1850s   As slavery becomes most divisive issue in nation, racial tensions increase locally, and rights of free people of color are curtailed. City's traditional Caribbean-influenced three-tier racial caste system begins to give way to two-tier (white and black) notion favored in rest of nation. Some free Creoles of color respond by departing for Mexico, further diminishing city's nonwhite population in late antebellum years.

1851   New Orleans sees influx of 52,011 immigrants, almost equal to number arriving at Boston, Philadelphia, and Baltimore combined. City is primary immigration port in South and second in nation (behind New York) for most years between 1837 and 1860.

1852   Municipality system (1836) is abandoned; Lafayette annexed by New Orleans. City emerges from municipality era with new Anglo-American ethnic domination and momentum toward upriver expansion. City's political and economic epicenter, including City Hall, is relocated from old city to Faubourg St. Mary. Old house-numbering system and ward boundaries are updated.

1850s   Local publishing industry shifts its base from Chartres Street in Old City to Camp Street in Faubourg St. Mary, reflecting increasing influence of American side of town. "Newspaper Row" remains in and around 300 block of Camp Street until 1920s.

1853   City's worst yellow fever epidemic claims at least 8,000 lives, probably closer to 12,000 (one-tenth of the city). Irish and German immigrants suffer disproportionately; city streets are nearly deserted during late summer and early autumn. Subsequent epidemics in 1854–55 continue to devastate city's underclass.

1856   Hurricane strikes coastal Louisiana, soaking New Orleans and destroying famed hotel on Isle Dernière ("Last Island"). Death toll of over 200 includes many prominent New Orleanians.

1857
Krewe of Comus formed by men from Mobile; helps transform celebration of Mardi Gras from private balls and disorganized street mayhem into public parades, fanciful royalty, and elaborate civic rituals. Mardi Gras, celebrated in Louisiana since 1699, soon develops into premier outward cultural trait distinguishing New Orleans from other American cities.

1858
Another 4,800 New Orleanians perish by yellow fever, in city's second-worst plague. "Yellow jack" death toll declines nearly to zero during Civil War years, due in large part to sanitation efforts under federal occupation.

1860
New Orleans's population reaches 174,491 (approximately 149,063 whites, 14,484 black slaves, 10,939 free people of color). Despite growing population, New Orleans's rank among American cities declines from fifth largest in 1850 to sixth largest in 1860. Last antebellum year also marks city's highest ratio of whites to blacks: nearly six-to-one.

1861
Louisiana secedes from Union; local Gen. P. G. T. Beauregard fires opening shots at Fort Sumter. Civil War begins.

1862
New Orleans, weakly defended by Confederacy, succumbs peacefully to federal troops executing Anaconda Plan to encircle South by seizing Mississippi River. War ends early for Louisiana's deltaic region as federal warships penetrate lower Mississippi River and troops occupy New Orleans by late April. South loses premier metropolis and critical grip on lower river. Region's slave-based plantation economy, which enriched white New Orleanians since colonial times, collapses forever during subsequent months and years; era of human slavery in New Orleans draws to a close after more than 14 decades.

1862–65
South and Southern agriculture devastated; shipping commerce to New Orleans interrupted; federal presence and postwar racial tensions alter social landscape.

New Orleans ■ Populating the Antebellum City

CHAPTER 12 POPULATING THE POSTBELLUM CITY

After the Civil War, New Orleans's demographics and human geography changed.[1] The black population surged by 110 percent between the censuses of 1860 and 1870, which bracketed the trauma of the conflict and the ensuing emancipation. It rose another 54 percent by the turn of the century. Caught up in its own woes, the unwelcoming city nevertheless offered better opportunities to freedmen than the sugarcane fields. In 1870, black men, who made up one-quarter of the labor force, worked 52 percent of New Orleans's unskilled labor jobs, 57 percent of the servant positions, and 30 to 65 percent of certain skilled positions.[2]

Where were these impoverished newcomers to settle? Unaffordable rents and racially antagonistic neighbors prevented the freedmen from settling in most front-of-town areas. The town houses in the inner city, recently vacated by wealthy families, had since been subdivided into low-rent apartments, but these hovels were more likely to be leased to poor white immigrants than to poor emancipated blacks. Nor could the freedmen easily take refuge in the downtown neighborhoods of the former free people of color, who generally scorned the freedmen as threats to their once relatively privileged but now rapidly diminishing social status.

Destitute and excluded, most freedmen had little choice but to settle in the ragged back-of-town, where urban development petered into amorphous low-density shantytowns and eventually dissipated into deforested swamps. The back-of-town offered low real estate costs because of its environmental hazards, urban nuisances, inconveniences, and lack of amenities and city services. Together with many local ex-slaves who also found themselves, for the first time, seeking their own shelter, the freedmen began to form the city's first large-scale, exclusively black neighborhoods. Concurrently, emancipation diminished the "back-alley" inter-mingling pattern of black residency in quarters behind white abodes. (Irish and German servants had already replaced many domestic slaves in the 1850s, turning slave quarters into servant quarters.) The city's back-of-town grew increasingly black in both absolute and relative numbers, while the front-of-town became more white. There were exceptions: Some working-class black families settled along the immediate riverfront, which afforded low-priced housing and dock jobs, and in blocks with vernacular housing within walking distance of mansion-lined grand avenues, where many worked as domestics.[3]

Creoles of color generally remained in their historical lower-city location. Creole cultural influence by this time was declining, and old Creole notions of a gradient between white and black polarized into the American notion of strict racial distinction. *Plessy v. Ferguson* (1896) formally sealed the fate of Louisiana's complex racial caste system and replaced it with the carefully policed racial exclusivity practiced throughout the South.

As urban social structure changed in the postbellum era, so did urban form. Industrialization, telephony, electricity, mechanized transportation, and the rise of centralized high-rise business districts effected massive transformations upon urban America in the late 19th century. The change coincided with the second great wave of immigration to the United States, mostly from southern and eastern Europe. Ethnic urban residential distributions would transform accordingly, driven in New Orleans by three factors.

First, as streetcar networks were installed, gentry departed the inner city and resettled in what had previously been the inconvenient semirural periphery. These once-poor areas of market gardens and municipal projects developed as trendy streetcar suburbs, particularly in Uptown and along Esplanade Avenue.

Second, the exodus of the wealthy from the inner city, which began as early as the 1830s to 1850s but was mostly a postbellum trend, opened up hundreds of spacious town houses in the inner city as potential tenement housing for immigrants.

Third, jobs for the unskilled poor shifted from the periphery, where they were located in the agrarian days before the war, to the urban core. Neighborhood municipal markets provided much of them. The Poydras and Dryades street markets attracted Orthodox Jewish vendors from Russia and Poland, the French Market drew Sicilians, the Irish dominated the Suraparu and St. Mary's markets, and the Chinese created a series of shops on Tulane Avenue that became known as Chinatown.

Thus, unlike immigrants from antebellum times, those of the late 1800s settled in a concentric zone immediately around the inner core. This "immigrant belt" offered enough advantages (convenience, work, housing, and social networks) to make life easier for impoverished newcomers but suffered enough nuisances (crowding, noise, crime) to keep rents affordable.[4] The immigrant belt ran loosely from the lower French Quarter (nicknamed "Little Palermo") and Faubourg Marigny ("Little Saxony"), through Faubourg Tremé and the Third Ward ("Chinatown"), around Dryades Street ("the Jewish neighborhood"), and toward the riverfront in what is still today called the Irish Channel.

New Orleans prides itself on its uniqueness, sometimes to the point of extolling peculiarities where none exists. In fact, the Crescent City's ethnic distributions

Ethnic and racial geographies of New Orleans in the early 1900s. *Analysis and map by Richard Campanella.*

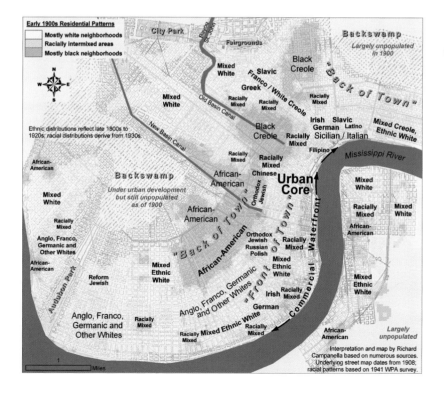

mimic those of other American cities, from antebellum times to today. The expression of immigrant enclaves, wrote one social geographer, commonly "takes the form of a concentric zone of ethnic neighbourhoods which has spread from an initial cluster to encircle the CBD"[5]—very much what occurred in New Orleans. In *Cities and Immigrants: A Geography of Change in Nineteenth Century America*, David Ward stated that researchers are "generally able to agree that most immigrants congregated on the edge of the central business district, which provided the largest and most diverse source of unskilled employment."[6] The concentric-ring phenomenon is standard material in urban-geography literature, where it appears diagrammatically as Ernest W. Burgess's classic Concentric Zone Model, part of the so-called Chicago School of urban sociology, which first viewed cities as social ecosystems in the 1920s. According to Burgess's model, a theoretical city's central business district was surrounded first by a "zone in transition," then a "zone of workingmen's homes," a "residential zone," and finally a "commuters' zone." In that transitional zone could be found "deteriorating... rooming-house districts" and "slums," populated by "immigrant colonies" such as "Little Sicily, Greektown, Chinatown—fascinatingly combining old world heritages and American adaptations." Burgess added: "Near by is the Latin Quarter, where creative and rebellious spirits resort." In the zone of workingmen's homes, Burgess predicted Germans, German Jews, and other second-generation immigrants would settle, and in the residential and commuter zones, he foresaw restricted residential districts and bungalow suburbs.

Burgess had Chicago in mind when he devised his Concentric Zone Model, but to a remarkable degree, he could have been describing circa-1900 New Orleans. Little Palermo, Chinatown, the Greek area, and the Orthodox Jewish neighborhood all fell within Burgess's transitional zone, which I am calling the "immigrant belt." Germans, German Jews, Irish, and other earlier immigrants and their descendants settled in the workingmen's zone (former Lafayette, the Third District, and other areas of the old semi-rural periphery). And Burgess's restricted residential zone and commuter zones describe the leafy garden suburbs (also known as trolley or streetcar suburbs, for the developmental role played by that conveyance) of uptown, Esplanade Avenue, Lakeview, and Gentilly—right down to the bungalows. Even his Latin Quarter model found local representation: "Creative and rebellious spirits" have long gravitated to the French Quarter.[7]

Postbellum New Orleans, then, saw its residential settlement pattern shift from the spatially heterogeneous toward one of greater spatial homogeneity (clustering). The change did not happen in a vacuum but rather reflected massive transformations in the urban environment, occasioned by technological breakthroughs and an emerging civic spirit that came to be known as the Progressive Era.

TIME LINE, 1865–1880s

1865–71	Nine tropical storms and hurricanes batter Louisiana coastal region, causing varying amounts of damage.
1866	Violent riot breaks out at Mechanics Institute, in which mostly ex-Confederate white Democrats and their allies engage black Radical Republicans and their supporters, assembled for Louisiana Constitutional Convention. Tragedy claims dozens of lives (mostly black), injures over 100, and presages heightened racial tension and violence in Reconstruction-era Louisiana.
1866–67	With city back under civilian control and no longer subject to military-enforced sanitation, public health troubles return. Cholera strikes twice in 1866; yellow fever outbreak in following year claims more than 3,000 lives.
1867–71	Sugar planters, seeking replacements for emancipated slaves, import Chinese workers from Cuban plantations. Effort fails but brings small number of Chinese to city.
1868	New state constitution, inspired by educated Creoles of color and their allies, is among most progressive in nation, extending suffrage to blacks while calling for integrated public schools and accommodations. But entrenched racial order from antebellum times eventually trumps constitution's aims, as racial tensions increase and federal troops depart in subsequent decade.

1869

State legislature takes action against public health nuisance created by city's livestock and meat-processing industry. New law treats butchering as public utility, creating monopoly and centralizing and isolating slaughterhouse activities away from city population. Outraged independent butchers sue; "Slaughterhouse Case" arrives at U.S. Supreme Court, which decides in favor of state monopoly in 1873. Locally, court's decision consolidates stockyards and slaughtering to Orleans–St. Bernard parish line; nationally, it sets controversial precedent limiting interpretation of Fourteenth Amendment.

1860s–1870s

Railroads are built across eastern marshes, connecting city with Rigolets, St. Tammany Parish, Mississippi Gulf Coast, Mobile, and points east. Speedy new transportation option unites New Orleans with coastal areas and diminishes passenger steamboat traffic to Port Pontchartrain on Elysian Fields Avenue lakefront. Recreation spots, summer escapes, fishing camps, and bedroom communities for early commuters develop along railroad, particularly in Bay St. Louis area.

1870s

International architectural styles begin to modernize cityscape. Creole architecture disappears almost entirely, as do antebellum American styles, particularly Greek Revival. Italianate facades, in New Orleans since 1850s via English Picturesque movement, rise in popularity.

1870

New Orleans population reaches 191,418, ninth largest in nation. Emancipated slaves migrate to city in droves, almost doubling 1860 black population to 50,456 (26 percent of total 1870 population). Most settle in back-of-town, a demographic pattern that survives today, even though backswamp does not.

1870s

New Orleans annexes Jefferson City, on uptown east bank, and Algiers, across from French Quarter on West Bank, in 1870. Carrollton joins city in 1874. Wards and municipal districts are adjusted to incorporate new city land. By 1880s, modern shape of Orleans Parish emerges.

1870s

Sugar planters start recruiting peasants from Sicily to work on Louisiana plantations in place of emancipated slaves. Sicilians, long part of New Orleans's tropical fruit trade, come by thousands between 1870s and 1900s. Most soon abandon field work and settle in lower French Quarter ("Little Palermo"), where they predominate in and near French Market until after World War II.

New Orleans ■ Populating the Postbellum City

1871	Crevasse at Bonnet Carré sends river water into Lake Pontchartrain; June winds prevent lake's normal outflow to gulf, allowing water levels to rise in adjoining New Basin navigation canal. On June 3, levee breaches at Hagan Avenue and inundates area between Old Basin and New Basin canals up to Rampart Street. Worst flood since Sauvé's Crevasse, the Bonnet Carré flood illustrates how man-made navigation canals threaten population by introducing lake and gulf water into heart of city.
1871–73	Mississippi and Mexican Gulf Ship Canal Company digs 36 miles of outfall canals across lakeside marshes in attempt to drain backswamp; project fails when company goes out of business. Canals are later incorporated into successful municipal-drainage effort of 1896–1915 and are widened. They remain in service today as the 17th Street, Orleans, and London Avenue outfall canals. All three waterways contributed to catastrophic flooding following Hurricane Katrina in 2005.
1872	Metairie Cemetery is laid out on former racetrack; becomes most famous of numerous cemeteries on Metairie and Gentilly ridges. Those topographic features also host parks, fairgrounds, and other large-scale public land uses that require well-drained land and proximity to city population but need too much acreage to be located in city proper.
1874	Violent riot between Democratic White League and Republican Metropolitan Police at foot of Canal Street represents flashpoint of postwar racial tensions. Conflict involves thousands and produces over 100 casualties. Monument to Battle of Liberty Place later dedicated at site becomes controversial reminder of racial discord in modern times; obelisk is eventually relocated and covered over with message of racial reconciliation.
Late 1800s	Emancipation and postwar racial tensions polarize Louisiana's historically fluid sense of racial identification into exclusive white and black categories. Creole identity is redefined by white narrative historians as exclusive domain of white descendants of French and Spanish colonials, despite ample historical use of term for Franco-African-American community. Writers of the "local color" tradition romanticize city's history and Creole society; New Orleans mythology is born and survives to this day.

69

New Orleans ■ Populating the Postbellum City

1875–79	With sedimentation of river channel delaying shipping traffic at mouth of Mississippi, Capt. James Eads constructs parallel jetties at South Pass. Structures constrain water flow, increase velocity, mobilize sediment, and deepen channel, allowing ocean-going vessels to enter river promptly. Coupled with development of barges, growth of local railroad network, and improving economic conditions, Eads's jetties help city rebound from postwar slump. But engineering effort also diverts sediment away from Louisiana coast and onto edge of continental shelf, rather than building up marshes of birdfoot delta.
1877	Federal troops withdraw; New Orleans's turbulent occupation and Reconstruction era ends.
Late 1870s	Garbage, waste, and excrement, traditionally dumped into Mississippi at various "nuisance wharves" along riverfront, are now loaded onto barges and dumped in the middle of river below city limits. Service is provided not by city but by private voluntary Citizens' Auxiliary Sanitary Association (1879), which also installs river pumps and pipes to flush out city streets.
1878	Worst yellow fever outbreak since 1850s claims more than 4,000 lives.
1878	T. S. Hardee and Auxiliary Sanitation Association publish "Topographical and Drainage Map of New Orleans and Surroundings," finest city map of the era. The 1879 version includes first comprehensive elevation measurements of city, at one-foot contour intervals.
1879	Federal government creates Mississippi River Commission, ending era of local and state levee projects and commencing modern era of federal authority over flood and navigation control of Mississippi River.
1880	New Orleans's population reaches 216,090; black population 57,617 (27 percent). By one account, city's ethnic mix comprises "some 70,000 French and Creoles, 30,000 Germans, 60,000 Negroes and mulattoes . . .10,000 Mexicans, Spanish and Italians [and] 80,000 or 90,000 . . . Anglo-Americans," including Irish.[8] City is now 10th largest in nation, dropping steadily from rank of third in 1840.

1880   Growing city boasts 566 miles of streets, of which only 94 miles are paved. Of those, cobblestones cover 35 percent, pulverized oyster shells overlay 25 percent, stone paving blocks cover 24 percent, and the remainder are treated with stone fragments or planks.

1880   Railroads now link New Orleans to: Cairo, Illinois, and points upriver; Mobile and points north and east; Morgan City and points west; and Donaldsonville across river (via ferries). Network of tracks complements city's shipping industry but pales in comparison to those connecting emerging Midwestern cities with northeastern metropolises.

1882   Chinese Mission, founded on South Liberty Street, draws Chinese immigrants to Third Ward back-of-town; Chinatown forms around 1100 block of Tulane Avenue and survives until 1937. Other Chinese immigrants start family-owned laundries dispersed widely throughout city.

1884–85   World's Industrial and Cotton Centennial Exposition held at Audubon Park. Exposition fails commercially but succeeds in helping transform semirural uptown into prosperous streetcar suburb with outstanding urban park and university campuses. Event also provides national and international venue for Louisiana artists and writers, who gain prominence afterward.

71

New Orleans ■ Populating the Postbellum City

CHAPTER 13   DRAINING THE DELTAIC CITY

Civic spirit and technological advancements enabled dramatic changes in New Orleans's municipal services during the Progressive Era, from the 1880s to the 1920s.[1] New infrastructure investments introduced municipal water treatment and distribution, modern sewerage service, street paving, and new parks and playgrounds. New technologies brought telephony, electrification, the internal combustion engine, and steel-frame high-rise construction. As a modern American city emerged, its footprint expanded upon deltaic lands readied for urbanization by the premier environmental alteration of the turn-of-the-century era: municipal drainage.

New Orleans had tried repeatedly since colonial times to drain runoff and groundwater from its soggy soils. By the late 1850s, engineers guided by a drainage plan envisioned by city surveyor Louis H. Pilié had built four steam-powered paddle wheels to push water through brick channels toward Lake Pontchartrain. The system fell into disrepair when war broke out in 1861. A more serious attempt occurred 10 years later, when the Mississippi and Mexican Gulf Ship Canal Company dug 36 miles of drainage canals (predecessors of today's 17th Street, Orleans, and London Avenue outfall canals) before it, too, went bankrupt. Failed private initiatives had placed the formidable task of drainage back into municipal hands by the 1880s, at which time the city's inadequate system could remove at most only 1.5 inches of rain per day.

A public consensus, driven in part by uptown women of means, finally arose during the 1890s in support of a serious drainage effort. The New Orleans City Council responded in February 1893 by directing the newly formed Drainage Advisory Board to gather data and design a solution, funding it with $700,000. No lethargic bureaucratic committee, the Drainage Advisory

Board assembled the best and brightest in the city: "successful engineers, international experts on public health . . . men who believed New Orleans's history of inconclusive skirmishes with . . . nature could end in a rousing victory for the city."[2]

The engineers' findings, presented in January 1895, included a summary of past drainage attempts, a new large-scale topographic map, and fresh meteorological and hydrological data. Their proposed solution: Use natural topography to drain runoff from within the various hydrological sub-basins to low points therein, then install pumps to propel the water through outfall canals and into adjacent lakes. A network of canals would facilitate the intricate dendritic drainage system: Street gutters would collect surface flow and direct it into covered branch drains; branch drains would flow into main drains; main drains would flow into gravity-fed branch canals; branch canals would flow into a central main canal at the lowest spot in the city, where pumping stations would speed the draw of water into it. Another set of pumps would then propel the water through the outflow canals (already in place since the 1870s) and finally into adjacent lakes Pontchartrain and Borgne.[3] What the engineers failed to understand at the time was that by locating the pumps in the bottoms of New Orleans's various hydrological sub-basins, rather than along their lakeside perimeters, the resultant soil subsidence—coupled with the inevitable expansion of residential neighborhoods into those drainage-targeted areas—would eventually create outfall canals that flow *above* the rooftops of people's houses.

Construction of the drainage system, which commenced in 1896, received an additional boost in June 1899 when voters—including women, who had the suffrage in this special municipal-bond referendum and enthusiastically supported municipal improvements—overwhelmingly approved a two-mill property tax to fund waterworks, sewerage, and drainage. This important moment in local democracy launched the Sewerage and Water Board of New Orleans, then and now the organization responsible for these Herculean tasks.

By 1905, workers had completed 40 miles of canals, hundreds of miles of pipelines and drains, and six pumps draining 22,000 acres by up to 5,000 cubic feet per second. This effort represented only 44 percent of the original plan, but it already transformed the landscape. Wrote George Washington Cable,

There is a salubrity that could not be when the mosquito swarmed everywhere, when the level of supersaturation in the soil was but two and half feet from the surface, where now it is ten feet or more. . . . The curtains of swamp forest are totally gone. Their sites are drained dry and covered with miles of gardened homes.[4]

A victim of its own success, the drainage system abetted urbanization and increased impermeable acreage and thus runoff, forcing the Drainage Advisory Board to reconvene in 1910 and expand the system—a reoccurring theme throughout the early to mid-20th century. What originally was a *wet* drainage system, in which acres of open land absorbed a fair amount of runoff, gradually grew into a *dry* system incapable of storing the accumulation of sudden intense rainfalls, thus forcing up the pumping capacity and giving the system zero leeway in pumping that water out.

Among the board employees was a quiet young Tulane engineering graduate named Albert Baldwin Wood, a descendant of the prominent Bouligny family. In 1913, Wood presented his design for a "screw pump," an enormous impeller that would draw water out of the suction basin and into the discharge basin rapidly and efficiently. Eleven "Wood pumps" were installed by 1915; many are still in use today. The brilliant and modest Wood devoted his career to New Orleans's drainage challenge; his patented Wood screw pumps and other inventions were adopted in China, Egypt, India, and the Netherlands. While

Opposite page: London Avenue Canal viewed from city toward lake, with pumping station in foreground (top); and from lake toward city, with gate and bypass pumps, installed in 2006, in foreground (bottom). Originally excavated in the 1870s and incorporated into the modern drainage system 30 years later, the London Avenue and other outfall canals paradoxically flow above the rooftops of the neighborhoods they drain, because the very success of the drainage system led to the subsidence of swampy soils and encouraged their subsequent urbanization. Because designers decided to locate the pumps at the heads of the outfall canals rather than at their lakefront mouths, the runoff is lifted early in its journey to the lake and thus must remain high, requiring levees and floodwalls to prevent the outfall from inundating adjacent neighborhoods. Hurricane Katrina's surge penetrated the London Avenue Canal and ruptured its floodwall in two locations, flooding nearly all areas visible in these photographs. Since then, temporary gates and bypass pumps have been installed at the mouths of the canals to keep surges out while still draining the city of runoff during storms. A consensus has emerged to relocate the pumps permanently to the lakefront (as in the suburbs), but funds are lacking to execute this costly option. *Photographs by Jaap van der Salm/David Waggonner,* Dutch Dialogues, *2009.*

Wood is often credited with draining New Orleans, he actually made an existing system faster and more efficient.

New Orleans's homegrown drainage technologies seemingly neutralized the city's age-old topographical and hydrological constraints. A land rush from the old riverside city into trendy, new lakeside suburbs ensued; assessed property value citywide grew during 1900–14 by 80 percent, to $250 million. Annual death rates that ranged around 7 percent in the late 1700s (70 deaths per 1,000 population) and 4.3 percent in the 1800s declined to 1.8 percent in the two decades following the installation of the drainage system.[5] Malaria and typhoid deaths decreased tenfold, and yellow fever disappeared forever after one last epidemic in 1905. The city's new water treatment plant and distribution system (also installed by the Sewerage and Water Board in this same era) played an even greater role than the drainage system in improving public health and ending yellow fever, particularly by eliminating the perfect habitat that *Aedes aegypti* mosquitoes found in cisterns.

By 1925, the New Orleans drainage system served 30,000 acres with a 560-mile network of canals, drains, and pipes and a total pumping capacity of 13,000 cubic feet per second. Neighborhoods with names such as Lakeview and Gentilly Terrace arose in the spacious style of suburban California, a world apart from the traditional local cityscapes three miles away. Pumps that were originally located behind the city's old neighborhoods were now in front of its new ones. The city's morphology shifted from a compact riverside crescent in the late 1800s to a sprawling nebula in the early 1920s and eventually to a spread-eagled triparish conurbation by the late 1900s. Municipal drainage preceded every expansion.

The Sewerage and Water Board in modern times drains over 61,000 acres in Orleans and neighboring Jefferson Parish of nearly 13 billion cubic feet of water annually. Ninety miles of covered canals (many beneath neutral grounds), 82 miles of open canals, 20 East Bank pumping stations, two West Bank stations, and 10 underpass pumps combine to siphon rainwater into neighboring water bodies at 45,000 cubic feet per second, 10 times the 1915 capacity and "enough to fill the Louisiana Superdome in 35 minutes."[6] Most of New Orleans, from uptown to the French Quarter to Gentilly and Lakeview plus Hoey's Basin in Jefferson Parish, drains northward through the 17th Street, Orleans, and London Avenue canals into Lake Pontchartrain. Bywater and the Upper and Lower Ninth wards, once a single natural hydrological basin until it was bisected by the Industrial Canal, drain into that man-made waterway. New Orleans East drains mostly northward into the lake, except for the area south of Chef Menteur Highway, which flows into the Intracoastal Waterway and out to the gulf. Algiers, also its own basin, drains into the man-made Algiers Canal and southward into Bayou Barataria.

Drainage of the "old city" (west of the Industrial Canal) is dependent on the immediate action of engineers to power up the pumps and propel runoff through the outfall canals and into Lake Pontchartrain as soon as possible, before it accumulates "in the bowl." There are no substantial retention ponds for temporary water storage. More recent systems, such as in New Orleans East, were wisely designed to incorporate water-storing lagoons and open canals into the cityscape, which retain a certain amount of heavy rainfall. As a result, less pump capacity is needed, and response time is extended. One of the reasons why the suburban systems can store runoff on the landscape is that their pumps (unlike those in the old part of New Orleans) are located at the perimeter of their respective hydrological basins and thus lift the water out at the last moment. This means the outfall canals that feed the pumps can flow below grade in open air, which not only enables the collection of rainfall and storage of runoff but also eliminates the levees and floodwalls that are required for above-grade canals. Below-grade drainage canals, however, must be excavated deeper and may increase subsidence rates because they do a more effective job of draining groundwater. This may explain why New Orleans East lies lower in some spots—10 feet below sea level—than the old city west of the Industrial Canal.

The draining of the New Orleans backswamp radically altered nearly every imaginable geography of New Orleans, from patterns of urban infrastructure and architectural style to spatial distributions of ethnicity, race, and class. It reworked hydrology and topography by slashing open the marshes with canals and lining them with earthen berms, creating new sub-basins and dangerously penetrating the city's heart with surge-prone waterways. It changed New Orleans vertically, allowing freshly drained hydric soils to subside by as many as 10 feet. It may have also affected local climate: Temperatures in New Orleans increased by eight degrees in summer and dropped by four in winter between 1900 and 1918. The

Weather Bureau attributed the polarization to the recent swamp drainage, which reduced surface water and its stabilizing effect on air temperature.[7]

Municipal drainage represented the single most dramatic transformation of the New Orleans cityscape, delivering many blessings but also creating the circumstances that led to the Hurricane Katrina catastrophe. The brilliant engineering solution that "drained dry" the dreaded backswamp and allowed it to be "covered with gardened homes" had indeed created scores of beautiful neighborhoods and thousands of happy home owners. But the drainage system, together with the levee system, also enticed people into harm's way with a fatally false sense of security. Call it "the levee effect," in which flood-control structures paradoxically increase flood damage by encouraging floodplain development. "Floods are 'acts of God,'" observed geographer Gilbert F. White in 1942, "but flood losses are largely acts of man."[8]

TIME LINE, 1880s–1900

1880s	Merchants become early adopters of electricity, making city's retail corridors among the best illuminated in nation—even as potable water, sewerage, and other municipal services lag. Electrification is introduced to streetcar system in 1890s and residential neighborhoods in 1900s–1910s.
1888	Strong hurricane, worst since 1837, strikes New Orleans; causes extensive structural damage, floods some areas with rainfall, and downs recently installed telephone and electrical lines.
1890	New Orleans's population reaches 242,039, 12th largest in nation. Black population is 64,491 (27 percent).
1890–91	Murder of Police Chief David Hennessy blamed on Sicilian mobsters; 11 Sicilians held at Parish Prison are lynched in retaliation. Incident leads to international crisis between Italy and United States; leaves deep scars in Sicilian community, contributing to its social isolation in "Little Palermo" (lower French Quarter) at turn of century.
1890s–1900s	Arabi subdivision develops upon old Le Beau plantation immediately below New Orleans, bringing upper St. Bernard Parish area into urbanized area.

1890s–1920s	Former Foucher tract and Allard Plantation landscaped into Audubon Park and City Park, respectively.
1891–1909	Residential parks created uptown along St. Charles Avenue. Rosa Park, Audubon Place, and other exclusive residential streets represent early form of zoning and gating of communities.
1893	Extremely powerful hurricane devastates coastal Louisiana and Gulf Coast, killing more than 2,000.
1894	Tulane University relocates uptown after 60 years downtown as antecedent public institutions. University area forms as Jesuits' Loyola University moves next door in early 1900s. Twin campuses impart vital character to uptown, helping form affluent neighborhoods with highly educated residents, many from out of town.
1894	Erratic 1852 house-numbering system is replaced with logical system in use today, in which addresses increment by 100 per block, with odd numbers indicating lakeside and downriver sides of streets. Effort reflects Progressive Era sensibilities about improved municipal services.
1890s–1900s	Research conducted at Audubon Park refines methods for purifying river water for residential use. Shortly after, purification and distribution plant is constructed in Carrollton, bringing city into modern age of municipal water systems. Carrollton site provides appropriate riverside location and elevation to draw water from Mississippi, remove sediment, add lime and sulfate of iron for softening, purify it with chloride gas, and store it. High-lift pumps then distribute water to city residents everywhere except Algiers, which is served through similar West Bank system.
1890s–1900s	Steel-frame construction and concrete pilings are introduced to New Orleans; first generation of high rises erected in CBD and upper French Quarter transforms city's skyline.
1893–98	Streetcar lines are electrified throughout city.
1895	Conflagration, last of great city fires, destroys much of Algiers. It is rebuilt in era of late Victorian architecture, giving modern-day Algiers Point neighborhood a quaint, turn-of-century ambience.

New Orleans ■ Draining the Deltaic City

1896	St. Augustine Catholic Church parishioner Homer Plessy tests post-Reconstruction Jim Crow laws by sitting in whites-only train car in 1892. Legal case regarding his arrest backfires in historic 1896 Supreme Court decision: *Plessy v. Ferguson* establishes "separate but equal" legal precedent, entrenching segregation in South for next half century. Public facilities in New Orleans, from streetcars to schools to department stores, are legally segregated by race. Case is viewed as the concluding chapter of the Americanization of New Orleans's Caribbean-influenced system of racial identity.
1897	Alderman Sidney Story sponsors ordinance to ban prostitution throughout city except in 15-block neighborhood behind French Quarter. Subsequent ordinance creates second zone along nearby Gravier Street. Laws succeed in controlling prostitution but inadvertently create vibrant and conspicuous red-light districts, dubbed Storyville and Black Storyville respectively. Storyville becomes nationally notorious and helps affirm New Orleans's reputation for debauchery, while also incubating some of city's musical genius. Storyville closes in 1917 by order of U.S. Navy; former "sporting houses" are demolished around 1940 for Iberville Housing Project.
1899	Sewerage and Water Board of New Orleans organized to oversee municipal sewerage, water distribution, and drainage.
1899–1902	Sicilian-born Vaccaro brothers and Russian-born Samuel Zemurray independently begin importing bananas from Central America through New Orleans. Vaccaros' firm grows into Standard Fruit; Zemurray's Cuyamel Fruit later merges with United Fruit. Banana companies tighten city's grip on nation's tropical fruit industry, attained in antebellum times via shipping routes with Sicily. Companies establish close ties between city and Central American republics, particularly Honduras, deeply influencing political and economic landscape of Central America for years to come. Hondurans immigrate to city in modest numbers throughout 20th century.
Turn of century	Jazz musical style emerges from myriad local and regional influences; soon diffuses nationwide and worldwide with help from Tin Pan Alley music industry and nascent recording technologies. Jazz becomes "sound track" of Western world from 1920s to World War II and is commonly recognized as New Orleans's most significant cultural contribution.

New Orleans ■ Draining the Deltaic City

CHAPTER 14   TURN-OF-THE-CENTURY FLOOD CONTROL

A complete chronology of floods in New Orleans resists easy compilation because no single agency kept consistent, detailed records until the late 1800s.[1] According to various sources, "partial inundations by the river" afflicted New Orleans in 1719, 1735, 1780, 1785, 1791, 1799, 1813, 1816, 1849, and 1862, while "partial inundations by Lake Pontchartrain or by this lake aided by the river" went undocumented prior to 1830 and were subsequently recorded in 1831, 1837, 1844, 1846, possibly in 1853 and 1854, 1855, 1856, 1861, 1868, 1869, 1871, 1881, and 1890. A recent Army Corps of Engineers source adds 1850, 1858, 1865, 1867, and 1874 to the list of flood years.[2] Another study found that from 1871 to the 1930s the river reached flood stage at New Orleans (but did not necessarily inundate the city) once every 4.07 years on average.[3]

Despite this hazard, the city continued to grow in population, economy, and urban extent. It did so by accommodating the effects of flooding through urban form, principally by building sturdy, raised structures in high density on elevated ground. Nearly all deluges mostly, if not entirely, inundated unpopulated swamps and fields. Destruction of homes and infrastructure was uncommon; deaths were rare.

The frequent flooding did, however, come at a serious economic cost and handicapped attempts to attract new investment and development in the city and region. Inadequate levees were seen as the culprit, and professionalizing them was seen as the answer.

Levees, like many other civil-engineering projects, came of age in the final decades of the 19th century. Locally, city engineers proposed in 1871—the year of the Bonnet Carré crevasse flood—an integrated system of protection levees and drainage networks,

Components of a Mississippi River levee: crest of natural levee at left; artificial levee with floodwall at center; concrete armoring on face of artificial levee; and willow-covered batture at right. The Mississippi flows about 150 feet beyond the batture. Levees are typically 25 to 35 feet above sea level in the New Orleans metropolitan area; the river typically flows between 5 and 15 feet above sea level but may range anywhere from 1 to 20 feet in extreme conditions. While the metropolis roughly straddles the level of the sea, it lies mostly below the level of the river, typically by 55 to 75 percent but up to 99 percent during high water. *Photograph by Richard Campanella, 2003.*

which eventually led to the excavation of today's 17th Street, Orleans, and London Avenue outfall canals. Statewide, in 1886, Louisiana created levee districts to begin coordinating levee maintenance efforts.[4] Federally, a new era dawned in 1879 when Congress created the Mississippi River Commission and directed it to work with the Army Corps of Engineers in controlling the lower Mississippi. With the Mississippi River Commission "offering advice, serving as a clearing house for technical data, and providing two thirds of the funding required for construction, levees in Louisiana reached a new level of sophistication."[5] In 1890, the state created the Orleans Levee District and the Board of Levee Commissioners, charging them with the "construction, repair, control and maintenance of all levees in the District, whether on river, lake, canal or elsewhere."[6] With the help of the Board of State Engineers and other organizations, the modern-day levee system on the lower Mississippi began to take shape. In New Orleans proper, within two years of the Orleans Levee Board's first meeting in 1890, a half-million cubic yards of soil were moved and sculpted to construct five miles of new levees and to strengthen 24 miles of existing levees. Over a million more cubic yards were added to the city's system in 1892–96. Earth-moving machines were introduced in 1907, reducing construction costs by half while speeding the work and improving quality. By the late 1920s, the Orleans Levee Board and its men had moved an additional 15 million cubic yards of soil to the New Orleans riverfront levees, to the exacting standards of the Mississippi River Commission.[7]

To tame the Mississippi, the commission and corps

adopted in 1885 a "levees only" policy, based on concepts advocated by Andrew Atkinson Humphreys and others since the 1850s. An 1873 document supporting the federalization of levees spelled out the reasoning behind relying on levees alone, without any backup mechanisms such as outlets, reservoirs, distributaries, and cutoffs:

> The channel of the river is made by the abrasive force of its waters. A greater force would produce a greater channel. . . . The greater the channel for a given quantity of water[,] the less the liability to overflow. Concentration of force increases abrasive powers, and diffusion of force reduces it. Levees confine and concentrate the waters, concentrate and increase the flow, therefore increase the abrasion, therefore increase and enlarge the capacity of the channel.[8]

"Outlets," the theory continued, "diffuse the waters, reduce the abrasive forces, and therefore reduce the capacity of the channel." During high water, a channel insufficiently scoured down through levee constraint would overtop and flood adjacent lands. Hence, levees must be erected quickly—and exclusively.

Humphreys and the levees-only advocates were right in that levees prevented inundations during most high-water events. But they proved wrong theorizing that levees could consistently do this job alone. Levee constraint did not "increase the abrasion" of the bottom of the river to the degree originally envisioned. Instead, it raised the top of the river. Water levels swelled, requiring higher levees, which allowed water to rise even higher and flow more powerfully. The vicious tiger-by-the-tail cycle would continue until extremely high flow would finally overpower a weak spot in the levee, breach it, and cause a catastrophic flood. That inevitability occurred in April 1927, when the Great Mississippi River Flood inundated a vast expanse of the lower Mississippi Valley and parts of the deltaic plain. Federal levees succeeded in sparing New Orleans, but commercial leaders nevertheless prevailed in legally dynamiting a section of levee below the metropolis to guarantee the safety of the prosperous city at the expense of poor, rural Plaquemines Parish. The controversial decision, which caused massive property loss and displacement and ultimately proved unnecessary, remains a bitter episode in local history to this day.

It also laid the groundwork for future levee-dynamiting conspiracy theories, which became gospel among certain communities in the wake of the breaches induced by hurricanes Betsy and Katrina.

The 1927 flood revealed the imprudence of the long-standing levees-only policy for river flood control and demonstrated the need to *accommodate* the will of the river. Afterward, spillways, which are essentially controlled crevasses, were installed at Bonnet Carré and Morganza to serve as safety valves during flood stage (officially defined as when the river flows at 17 feet above sea level or 1,250,000 cubic feet per second in volume at the Carrollton Gauge). The Mississippi River still potentially threatens New Orleans—the Bonnet Carré Spillway was opened in 1937, 1945, 1950, 1973, 1975, 1979, 1983, 1997, and 2008—but not in well over a century has Mississippi River water significantly impinged directly upon Orleans Parish. Yet the legacy of the old threat lingers, affecting urban growth, influencing residential settlement patterns, spooking investment, and diverting scarce resources.

Riverfront levees today form the single most influential man-made feature in the deltaic landscape, protecting people, creating value, and encouraging urban development even as they cause soil subsidence and coastal erosion. They held fast when Hurricane Katrina's residual Category 5 surge raised the river's stage from four feet to 16 feet above sea level. The same cannot be said of the slender levees and floodwalls lining the city's intricate network of drainage and navigation canals. Their failure formed the proximate, though not the ultimate, cause of the city's worst flood ever.

TIME LINE, 1900–1920s

1900   New Orleans's population reaches 287,104; black population 77,714 (27 percent). City remains 12th largest in nation.

1900   Race riot erupts following violent exchange between police officers and back-to-Africa advocate Robert Charles. Incident, which occurred in poor, isolated back-of-town area settled by emancipated slaves, is often described as city's last major race riot, attesting to relatively peaceful race relations there. But neighborhood, modern-day Central City, remains troubled today.

Early 1900s	Steam-powered riverboats are gradually replaced by tug barges and other petroleum-powered vessels for freight shipping. Sights and sounds of steamboats crowding riverfront disappear from Mississippi River, except for excursion vessels, many of which carry local jazz bands to interior cities.
1901–1920s	Dock Board modernizes port facilities, constructing riverside warehouses, grain elevators, canals, and new docking space.
1901	Louis Armstrong born in back-of-town, as jazz musical style emerges. New Orleans's most famous son greatly enhances city's image in eyes of world, but city fails to embrace Armstrong until years after his death, even demolishing his neighborhood in 1950s for new City Hall complex.
1904–20, 1926	Algiers resident Mayor Martin Behrman oversees important civic improvements, including modernization of drainage, sewerage, and water systems; expansion of city services and public education; and creation of Public Belt Railroad.
1905	More than 400 people die in city's (and nation's) last yellow fever epidemic. Poor Sicilian immigrants living in crowded conditions in lower French Quarter are blamed for outbreak. After *Aedes aegypti* is identified as vector, new drainage and potable-water systems that eliminate mosquito-breeding puddles and cisterns finally end century-old public-health threat.
1905–08	Sewerage and Water Board's Carrollton Water Works Plant opens as city's first full-scale modern municipal water treatment facility. System draws water from Mississippi through intake pipes, pumps it into head house, removes coarse particles, softens it with lime and sulfate of iron, sifts out fine particles, strains water through sand filters, treats it with small dosage of chloride gas, and finally stores and pumps purified water through distribution system to residences. Water mains, laid throughout city streets starting in 1905, extend 512 miles by 1910 and 700 miles by 1926, by which time nearly every household has municipal potable water. System ends era of cisterns, reduces yellow fever and other public-health threats, complements new drainage and sewerage systems, and furthers urban expansion toward lake.

85

New Orleans ▦ Turn-of-the-Century Flood Control

Urban geographies of New Orleans. *Montage and most photographs by Richard Campanella, 1999–2009.*

1905–10	New home construction commences in recently platted Lakeview subdivision, drained from marsh only a few years earlier. Lakeview develops mostly during 1910s–1940s, becoming comfortable and stable middle-class inner suburb. Deed covenants restrict home ownership to whites only, affecting city's racial geography, as middle-class white families leapfrog over black back-of-town to settle in drained marshes.
1906	Continuing spirit of municipal improvements ongoing since 1890s, Olive Stallings establishes city's first playground for neighborhood children. Stallings leads new Playgrounds Commission in 1911 and eventually wills a portion of her estate to city's public playgrounds and pools, leading to birth of New Orleans Recreation Department.
1910	New Orleans's population reaches 339,075; black population 89,262 (26 percent). City drops to 15th largest in nation.
1910s	Architectural styles change: Creole cottages and shotgun houses decline in popularity, replaced by Craftsman, City Beautiful, and California-style bungalows. Three-bay town houses give way to "catalog" frame houses, villas, and other structural types and styles.
1910s–1940s	Gentilly is developed on and near Gentilly Ridge in Seventh and Eighth wards. New suburb, with non-native architectural styles and spacious green surroundings, expands city's footprint toward newly drained lakefront. Deed covenants in many areas restrict sales to whites only.
1910s–1960	New Orleans continues to grow in population, while stabilizing in rank relative to other American cities at around the 15th-largest city in United States. Shipping and industrial activity relating to two world wars helps explain suspension of city's steady decline in national ranking.
1911	City's 34th municipal market opens but proves to be last, as competition from ubiquitous corner grocery stores takes toll on old centralized stall markets. Automobiles, supermarkets, franchises, suburbanization, and globalized food production and distribution render municipal market system obsolete by mid-20th century.
1914–18	World War I rages in Europe; city benefits from war-related increase in river traffic. Local German community is devastated by stigma of enemy association; most German cultural institutions and public traditions in city are permanently silenced.

87

New Orleans ▓ Turn-of-the-Century Flood Control

Elegant simplicity: early 20th-century shotgun houses near Bayou St. John. *Photograph by Richard Campanella, 2008.*

1915
Hurricane strikes New Orleans region, damaging 25,000 structures, causing flooding, inflicting $13 million in expenses, and killing 275 Louisianians. Eleven major churches lose their steeples or towers. Antebellum landmarks Old French Opera House and former St. Louis Hotel are heavily damaged; latter is subsequently demolished.

1917
Xavier University founded. Nation's only black Catholic institution of higher learning reflects New Orleans's distinct Creole heritage.

1918–23
Dock Board excavates Inner Harbor Navigation Canal (Industrial Canal) on old Ursuline nuns' holding in Ninth Ward; canal and narrow lock connect river and lake, providing shortcut to gulf and opening up new deepwater private-sector wharf space. Much port activity shifts to Industrial Canal by mid-1900s but returns to river by turn of 21st century. Canal benefits port but isolates Lower Ninth Ward from rest of city, while dangerously introducing surge-prone waters into urban interior.

1919	Immense base for Army Quartermaster Corps is constructed at foot of new Industrial Canal, changing face of Ninth Ward riverfront and augmenting military presence in New Orleans. Base serves as port of embarkation during World War II. Army transfers base to Navy in 1966; Navy prepares to depart in 2009. Future of Naval Support Activity is currently under discussion.
1919	Old French Opera House burns. Demise of Bourbon Street landmark, built in 1859, symbolizes end of centuries-old cultural exchange between France and New Orleans; helps inspire appreciation for decaying French Quarter.
1920	New Orleans's population reaches 387,219, 17th largest in nation; black population is 100,930 (26 percent).
1922	New Orleans Public Service, Inc., gains control of all streetcar lines, electrical service, and natural gas distribution in city. Decade of 1920s marks apex for streetcar system, with over 220 track miles spanning from West End to Lower Ninth Ward and uptown on nearly every river-parallel street between Dryades and Tchoupitoulas. Ensuing 40 years see gradual transition to rubber-tire buses and termination of 90 percent of mileage.

CHAPTER 15 BUFFERING THE DELTAIC CITY

Five miles from the bustling quay of the Mississippi River lay historic New Orleans's "other" waterfront: the grassy shore of the semi-brackish inland bay known by the quasi-misnomer of Lake Pontchartrain.[1] Low, marshy, and remote, the lakeshore remained a wilderness in the early decades and a shantytown of fishing camps and jerry-built shacks into the early 20th century. The only exceptions were West End, Spanish Fort, and Milneburg, which served as lakefront resorts for city dwellers and mini-ports for the waterways and railroads that connected them with downtown.

The municipal drainage project of the early 1900s transformed those marshes into valuable real estate. As white middle-class New Orleanians eagerly moved out of old riverside neighborhoods and into the new lakeside suburbs, engineers turned their attention toward reinforcing the lakeshore against hurricane-induced storm surges. The Great Storm of 1915 illustrated the threat posed by incursions of saltwater into low-lying areas. At first, the Orleans Levee Board built a levee about 300 feet inland from the marshy shore (now Robert E. Lee Boulevard), but the high humus and water content of the soils resulted in shrinkage and subsidence. A more ambitious solution had been envisioned decades earlier, by city surveyor W. H. Bell, whose *Plan of Property Improvements for the Lake Shore Front of the City of New Orleans* (1873) first broached the idea of combining flood protection with residential and recreational land creation. Why settle for a flimsy levee when you could build a solid seawall and create high, dry, scenic real estate at the same time?

In 1924, chief engineer Col. Marcel Garsaud was commissioned to develop the concept, and within the year emerged with a plan so ambitious that the Levee Board needed additional constitutional authority

to approve it. A curving levee reinforced by a stepped concrete seawall over five miles long and a half-mile offshore would be built in the lake; bottom sediments would then be dredged and pumped into the bemired enclosure behind it, creating high, dry new land. Colonel Garsaud's plan also called for the improvement and sale of the new land to offset the original $27 million price tag.

Work on the Lakefront Improvement Project began in 1926. A temporary wooden bulkhead was constructed 2,500 to 3,500 feet offshore to an elevation of two feet above lake level. Lake-bottom sediment was then hydraulically pumped behind it until flush with the levee top. The bulkhead was then strengthened and raised by four feet, then filled again to the brim. The entire process took more than three years; the result was 2,000 new acres of lakefront land, averaging four to six feet above lake (sea) level, or roughly half the elevation of the natural levee. A stepped concrete seawall, designed after similar structures on the Florida coast, completed the project in 1930.

What to do with this scenic new land? One plan allocated most acreage to recreational use; another proposed lagoons and canals among parklands and

The Lakefront Improvement Project (1926–34) created 2,000 acres of new land with the intention of buffering the rapidly developing lakeside of the city from storm surges. The area today hosts attractive neighborhoods, recreational space, the University of New Orleans (foreground), an airport (upper left), and the mouths of Bayou St. John and three outfall canals. *Photograph by Peter Hermans/ David Waggonner,* Dutch Dialogues, *2009.*

residences. A compromise allowed for the public recreational development of lands between Lakeshore Drive and the lake, and residential and public-facility development (sans lagoons) of remaining areas. The sale of land to pay off the Levee Board's bonds spawned new residential neighborhoods such as Lake Vista, Lakeshore, Lake Terrace, and Lake Oaks, developed during 1939–60. The Lakefront also hosted Pontchartrain Beach (for whites only; blacks bathed at Lincoln Beach from 1955 to 1964), an amusement park, marinas, recreational facilities, a branch of Louisiana State University that became the University of New Orleans in 1974, and Southern University's New Orleans branch.[2] "Lakefront was and is an ornament to the city," wrote geographer Peirce Lewis, "one of the very few places where twentieth century city planning has truly improved a large area of an American city."

"It is some measure of the project's scale," continued Lewis, "that a municipal airport was added to the Lakefront scheme almost as an afterthought,"[3] through the efforts of politically connected Levee Board president Abe Shushan. Built between 1931 and 1933 on a triangular peninsula jutting into the lake, Shushan Airport required no real estate acquisition, did not interfere with existing infrastructure, provided obstruction-free approaches and departures, and allowed for inexpensive expansion farther into the lake.[4] At the time one of the finest airfields in the nation, Shushan Airport, along with the Naval Air Station, played an important role in preparation for the air war against Germany and Japan. Today, the 300-acre man-made peninsula, now Lakefront Airport, hosts a 6,879-foot-long airstrip and an Art Deco–style terminal, and is extensively used by corporate and private aircraft.

Now more than one-quarter the age of the city, the Lakefront pads the northern edge of New Orleans from the Jefferson Parish line to the Industrial Canal. In utter contrast to the old riverfront city, Lakefront New Orleans today is spacious, sprawling, suburban, relatively prosperous, and privy to expansive horizon-wide vistas of water and sky. It presents a subtropical coastal ambience associated more with modern-day Florida hundreds of miles away than with historic riverine New Orleans five miles away.

Despite its success in creating new residential land, the Lakefront Project was primarily designed to resist hurricane-induced surges of lake and gulf water.

It served this function well during Hurricane Katrina, remaining mostly dry while preventing 10-foot-high lake waters from spilling into eight-foot-low residential neighborhoods. The same cannot be said for the slender levees and floodwalls lining the city's outfall canals—the very canals that enabled urban expansion toward the lake, necessitating the Lakefront Project.

TIME LINE, 1920s–1940

1923–29

New Orleans forms City Planning and Zoning Commission (1923), in response to new state law and nationwide movement toward professional urban planning. Commission endeavors to integrate activities of "transit facilities, port and industr[ies,] railroads, agencies for public recreation, zoning, civic art and other [entities, with] plans of the Levee Board, Dock Board, Public Belt [Railroad], Sewerage and Water Board, City of New Orleans, and other agencies engaged in building for a larger, greater city."[5] Throughout 1920s, commission meets with agencies, gathers data, writes city survey, updates existing piecemeal land-use ordinances, and conducts public hearings. In 1929, Comprehensive Zoning Ordinance becomes law; New Orleans enters modern age of urban planning.

1926–35

With modern technology enabling road construction on deltaic plain, new Airline Highway antiquates historic River Road as main terrestrial connection between New Orleans and Baton Rouge. Highway soon draws old riverfront communities away from Mississippi but 40 years later is itself superseded by Interstate 10.

1927

Great Mississippi River Flood inundates 26,000 square miles from Cairo, Illinois, to gulf; kills hundreds, displaces half million, and threatens New Orleans. City is spared from river flooding, but controversial dynamiting of levee in St. Bernard and Plaquemines parishes to ensure metropolis's safety creates lasting ill will between city dwellers and rural neighbors. Nation's worst natural disaster transforms federal river-control policy (through Flood Control Act of 1928) from levees-only to one of massively augmented levees, floodwalls, spillways, control structures, reservoirs, canals, revetments, and other devices throughout Mississippi Valley. Profoundly influential act puts federal government in flood-control business, mandating federal financial and engineering responsibility for controlling Mississippi and other rivers but immunizing government from liability should these systems fail.

1920s–1940s	Old Basin (Carondelet) and New Basin canals, rendered obsolete by railroads, highways, and barges, are incrementally filled in, opening up valuable ingress/egress corridors to downtown. Bed of New Basin Canal later becomes Pontchartrain Expressway right-of-way.
Late 1920s	Highway 11 Bridge erected over eastern Lake Pontchartrain increases automobile access to Slidell and areas east. New bridges over Chef Menteur and Rigolets passes speed up trip to coastal Mississippi.
1929	St. Charles Avenue between Lee Circle and Jackson Avenue is zoned for light industrial use, leading to demolition of old homes. Twenty-four years later, area is rezoned to eight-story commercial district, encouraging construction of large-scale edifices. Zoning changes alter character of once-elegant lower St. Charles Avenue to motley mix of retailers and open lots amid occasional old homes.
1930	New Orleans's population reaches 458,762; black population 129,632 (28 percent). City is 16th largest in nation.
1930s–1941	Two New Deal agencies, Works Progress Administration and Public Works Administration, execute numerous projects citywide, renovating historic structures, rebuilding aging infrastructure, and documenting city's past.
1934–38	Public Works Administration renovates French Market, restoring circa-1813 Butchers Market, reconstructing Bazaar Market, remodeling Vegetable Market, demolishing Red Store, adding Fish Market, and razing Gallatin Street for new Farmers Market and Flea Market pavilions.
1935	Huey P. Long Bridge, first across lower Mississippi River, links east and west banks of Jefferson Parish. Built for both railroad and automotive traffic, bridge ends era of train ferries and sparks development in semi-rural Jefferson Parish. Hair-raising "Huey P" later proves inadequate for modern vehicular traffic; widening of lanes commenced in 2008.
1936	State constitution authorizes city to preserve French Quarter. Vieux Carré Commission guards nation's second legally protected major historic district (after Charleston); buildings deemed architecturally and historically significant are preserved and held to codified aesthetic standards. By saving city's iconic neighborhood, effort creates bedrock of future tourism industry and helps inspire protection of other historic areas.

New Orleans ▪ Buffering the Deltaic City

1937	Chinatown at 1100 Tulane Avenue is razed; small Chinese merchant community relocates to 500 block of Bourbon Street, where it survives in remnant form into 1980s.
Late 1930s–1940s	Gulf Intracoastal Waterway (GIWW) is excavated through eastern New Orleans and across West Bank. Completed in 1949, thousand-mile channel links rivers, bays, sounds, and canals to allow barge traffic to pass from Port Isabel, Texas, to Apalachee Bay, Florida, without venturing into open seas.
1940	New Orleans's population reaches 494,537; black population 149,034 (30 percent). City is 15th largest in nation, gaining slightly in rank due to Depression-era migration from rural regions, Works Progress Administration–related job opportunities, and employment in industries relating to impending war.

New Orleans ■ Buffering the Deltaic City

CHAPTER 16 TWENTIETH-CENTURY DELTA URBANISM

Transforming a natural landscape into a cityscape is a costly endeavor anywhere, but particularly in a subtropical deltaic environment with soft alluvial soils and a complex human history. A 1927 City Planning and Zoning Commission report contended that New Orleans's urbanization costs were "much higher than in other cities built on different terrain." Initial surveying, for example, was complicated by continued use of "the French system of measurements" and "the antiquity, inadequacy and inaccuracy of records," not to mention the difficult terrain. Clearing dense forest and underbrush proved more demanding in New Orleans than elsewhere, while excavating hydric soils often meant encountering enormous old cypress stumps lying layers-deep in the mucky earth. Then came the costly engineering challenges of keeping unwanted water out (flood control), removing unwanted water from within (drainage), guiding potable water into the city, and directing sewage out of the city. Finely textured soils loaded with organic matter and prone to sinkage made the grading and paving of streets and sidewalks that much more expensive. Constructing underground infrastructure—namely, sewer, gas, and water lines—also challenged engineers, and still does. Large structures must rest upon pilings hammered into the earth to keep from leaning, while high rises require specialized pilings penetrating into hard sub-alluvial Pleistocene clays to remain upright. The added effects of humidity, high rainfall, luxuriant vegetation growth, termites, mosquitoes, and occasional high winds and hard freezes further increase the costs of urbanization. In the 1920s, New Orleans spent more per capita on sanitation and streets than any major American city, not because it aspired to higher standards but because it had to overcome a far more challenging starting point. (Incidentally, it ranked at or near the bottom in per-capita expenditures on public health, hospitals, schools, and libraries.)[1]

How humans positioned themselves across the urban delta reflected the relative costs of delta urbanization. From the early 1700s to the early 1900s, nearly all New Orleanians lived on the higher natural levees close to the Mississippi River. Elevated, better drained, arable, and more convenient, these lands were vastly more attractive and cheaper to urbanize than the low-lying cypress swamps and saline marshes near Lake Pontchartrain.

This centuries-old relationship began to change after the municipal improvements of the Progressive Era began to have their effect. The installation of the drainage system starting in the 1890s and the addition of the Wood screw pumps in 1915 transformed the seemingly useless backswamp into developable real estate. Street, streetcar, potable water, sewerage, electrical, and telephone systems followed. The Lakefront Project of 1926 brought additional flood protection and recreational amenities to the lakefront, further ratcheting up land values. City officials, developers, investors, and the home-buying middle class all eagerly eyed the new land as an opportunity for 20th-century California-style suburban development, complete with bungalows, lawns, driveways, and modern amenities. "The entire institutional structure of the city was complicit" in the ensuing urbanization of the lowlands, wrote local historian John Magill. "Developers promoted expansion, newspapers heralded it, the City Planning Commission encouraged it, the city built streetcars to service it, [and] the banks and insurance companies underwrote the financing."[2] New Orleanians, convinced that the topographical and hydrological factors that once constrained them to the natural levee had now been neutralized by technology, migrated enthusiastically off the natural levee and settled into trendy new suburbs with names such as Broadmoor, Fontainebleau, Gentilly, and Lakeview. Popping up along the new orthogonal street grids and spacious suburban lots were thousands of California bungalows, Spanish Revival villas, English cottages, Midwestern ranch houses, and other non-native architectural styles. Into those abodes moved thousands of families: Between 1920 and 1930, nearly every census tract lakeside of the Metairie–Gentilly Ridge at least doubled in population. Low-lying Lakeview saw its population increase by

97

Juxtapositions: St. Louis No. 2, second oldest of New Orleans's famous above-ground cemeteries, lies between the Iberville Public Housing Project and the I-10 Claiborne overpass in the historic neighborhood of Tremé. *Photograph by Richard Campanella, 2004.*

about 350 percent, while parts of equally low Gentilly grew by 636 percent. Older neighborhoods on higher ground, meanwhile, lost residents: Historic faubourgs Tremé and Marigny dropped by 10 to 15 percent; the French Quarter declined by 25 percent. The high-elevation Lee Circle area lost 43 percent of its residents, while low-elevation Gerttown increased by a whopping 1,512 percent.[3] Similar figures could be cited for the 1910s and 1930s–1950s.

The radical new urban geography affected the social fabric of the city—and vice versa. What resulted might be described as *racial spatial disassociation*. From the 1910s to 1940s, middle-class white families, formerly residents of the historical front-of-town, leapfrogged over the black back-of-town and settled in the low-lying lakeside subdivisions, where deed covenants often expressly forbade sales or rentals to black families. The intricately intermixed racial geography of old New Orleans had further disassociated; in the two generations since emancipation, white and black New Orleanians had moved away from each other en masse. The trend would only strengthen.

Tremendous social transformations forged new racial relationships in mid- to late-20th-century New Orleans. Chief among these were *Brown v. Board of Education* (1954); integration of public schools starting in 1960–61; the Civil Rights Act of 1964 and the ensuing desegregation of public facilities; and overall increased opportunities in education, employment, and housing for African Americans. Jim Crow disappeared with less violence and resistance here than in other Southern cities; black and white New Orleanians subsequently found themselves working, shopping, and dining together in increasing numbers. Yet *living* together did not necessarily follow; in fact, residential integration diminished. Suburban-style subdivisions in lakefront and eastern New Orleans, in Jefferson, St. Bernard, and St. Tammany parishes, and even as far as coastal Mississippi, drew white New Orleanians by the tens of thousands between the censuses of 1960 and 2000.

Suburban lifestyles also attracted the black middle class. Because this group historically comprised the downtown-based Creole community, its expansion into suburban-style subdivisions tended to occur in the drained backswamp adjacent to the old downtown Creole faubourgs, particularly the Seventh Ward. When white philanthropists funded the first modern suburban subdivision in which African-American families could buy homes—Pontchartrain Park, in 1955–58—it furthered the spread of the black middle class into this eastern area. Many whites in nearby Gentilly Terrace and adjacent neighborhoods responded in the 1960s–1980s by fleeing to Jefferson or St. Bernard parishes, opening up more fine housing stock for middle-class black families. The same was true for eastern New Orleans, the last major suburban development within Orleans Parish. Initially mostly white from the 1960s to the 1980s, New Orleans East swiftly became predominantly black in the 1980s–1990s with the oil bust and the rise of multifamily Section 8 housing. Areas west of City Park (Lakeview) were unattached to historically black source regions, particularly middle-class ones, and remained mostly white.

Suburban lifestyles beckoned also to immigrants. Central Americans and Vietnamese war refugees, who arrived in modest numbers in the late 20th century, tended to settle in distant suburbs such as Kenner, extreme eastern New Orleans, and the West Bank. Again, New Orleans's experience parallels national trends: Immigrants nationwide now regularly gravitate toward suburbia; popular notions of immigrant-

99

dominated inner cities and homogenous white suburbs are increasingly obsolete.

By century's end, the greater New Orleans metropolitan area had racially dichotomized into a predominantly white west and a black east, with some notable exceptions. We see this from mapping out census data and computing each group's population centroid—that is, the center of balance of a population's distribution. In 2000, whites throughout Orleans, Jefferson, and St. Bernard parishes were evenly distributed around a theoretical point near South Carrollton Avenue. Blacks were evenly dispersed around a point near St. Claude Avenue in the Upper Ninth Ward, fully five miles away. Greater New Orleans's racial geography by the early 2000s ironically formed more de facto segregated spatial patterns than it did in the early 1800s. "Two centuries of paradox" is how one researcher described the phenomenon.[4]

Perhaps the most pernicious driver of de facto racial segregation began as a progressive federal and city government program designed to help the poor. Following the U.S. Housing Act of 1937, the Housing Authority of New Orleans cleared a number of old neighborhoods, replete with 19th-century architectural gems but considered unsightly slums at the time, to make room for subsidized housing for poor families. Two- and three-story garden apartments, tastefully designed to reflect local architectural style and scale, were built in geometrical arrangements among grassy walkways and oak trees. In accordance with the Jim Crow laws of the day, each complex was racially segregated: Two white-only developments were located on higher ground in the front-of-town, while the four black-only projects occupied lower-elevation areas in the back-of-town. The complexes were expanded following the Housing Act of 1949.

After desegregation of the projects in the 1960s, whites promptly left the units for affordable-living alternatives in working-class suburbs, and poor blacks took their places. Within a few years, tens of thousands of the city's poorest African Americans became intensely consolidated into a dozen or so projects, all of which were isolated from adjacent neighborhoods and cut off from the street grid. With that concentrated poverty came the full suite of social pathologies, including fatherless households, teen pregnancy, government dependency, drug trading, gang activity, and incessant violent crime. (Whether the projects bred and exacerbated social ills or merely concentrated them is a matter of ongoing debate.)

So bad did matters get by the 1990s that the federal government, which had come to view public housing as warehouses of indigence and cyclers of dependency, intervened. The new philosophy, encapsulated in a controversial scheme named Project HOPE (Home-ownership and Opportunity for People Everywhere), called for the demolition of the most troubled projects and their replacement with mixed income new urbanist communities, in which subsidized rental units for the poor abutted market-rate rentals and purchasable homes aimed at modest-income families. The HOPE philosophy rested on two geographical notions: that a physically improved and aestheticized place fosters a better society, and that class intermixing restrains delinquency and dependency among the poor. While both concepts are subject to varying levels of debate, among geographers and the public in general, most agreed that the public-housing status quo could not continue.

In the early 2000s, amid vocal opposition but with the overwhelming support of the general population, the solidly built structures of the St. Thomas, Desire, Fischer, and other projects were demolished and re-developed with pastel-colored new urbanist designs. Opponents read bitter irony into the policy, noting that New Orleans's circa-1940 housing projects, with their modest scales, airy verandahs, and shady courtyards, seemed to embody new urbanist principles a half century before the term was coined. Paralleling Chicago's Cabrini-Green and Atlanta's East Lake experiments with mixed income public housing—which really did replace ugly, dehumanizing high rises—New Orleans's grand social experiment got under way. Its interruption by Hurricane Katrina and controversial continuation afterward is discussed in Chapter 21.

TIME LINE, 1940s–1970s

1946–61   Mayor de Lesseps "Chep" Morrison oversees postwar modernization of city's infrastructure. New city hall, courthouses, library, train station, airport, improved rail-street crossings, more buses, fewer streetcars, and bridges over river and lake are among the transformations of Morrison era.

1946   New York City urban planning czar Robert Moses submits "Arterial Plan for New Orleans" to guide modernization of city's transportation system. Most controversial component entails connecting points east with West Bank by running elevated expressway in front of French Quarter. Funding arrives for Riverfront Expressway in 1964, igniting bitter controversy among New Orleanians for remainder of 1960s over fundamental notions of preservation and progress.

1946   City's first modern supermarket, 40,000-square-foot Schwegmann Brothers Giant Supermarket, opens on St. Claude and Elysian Fields. More follow, encouraged by increasing automobile dependence and flight to suburbs. Trends eventually spell doom for most corner grocery stores, street vendors, and municipal markets. Food retail, once small-scale, locally owned, and spatially dispersed, becomes concentrated and less reflective of local food culture.

1947   Fourteen years after region's first offshore oil well is drilled, President Truman offers Louisiana all royalties and lease bids for near-shore wells and 37.5 percent of those farther offshore. State rejects offer in hope of more lucrative deal, which never comes. Decision costs state billions of dollars over next six decades and is only partially remedied when 2006 law directs 37.5 percent of future offshore royalties to four gulf states.

1947–65   Upturn in tropical storm activity produces eight hurricanes affecting Louisiana coast, including two serious strikes to New Orleans proper.

1947   Late summer hurricane strikes New Orleans region while on northwestern track toward Baton Rouge. Winds of over 100 miles per hour buffet city; small storm surge floods lightly developed eastern ramparts of metropolis as well as Jefferson Parish. Damages amount to $100 million; 51 people perish. Unnamed "Hurricane of 1947," as well as subsequent September 1948 storm, inspire additional levee construction along lakeshore and adjacent marshes.

1950	New Orleans's population reaches 570,445, 16th largest in nation; black population 181,775 (32 percent).
1950	Louisiana Landmarks Society is founded to preserve historically and architecturally significant structures; mission is later expanded to preserve historic neighborhoods and fight inappropriate development. Society saves many of city's famous buildings and instills appreciation for historical architecture among general public.
1950s	Isolated by Industrial Canal, low-lying eastern New Orleans remains mostly rural except for ingress/egress services along Chef Menteur Highway, citrus orchards, and recreational camps along Hayne Boulevard. First modern subdivisions appear along Dowman Road and Chef Menteur in the early 1950s, followed by aggressive development in the 1960s–1970s when Interstate 10 is built. Installation of drainage system precedes urbanization; unlike the circa-1900 system west of Industrial Canal, eastern system is designed to store runoff in lagoons and open canals, thereby requiring less pumping capacity to remove it to Lake Pontchartrain. Lakefront location of pump stations allows adjoining drainage canals to flow below-grade, without floodwalls and levees. Below-grade canals, however, drain groundwater more effectively and hasten subsidence rates.
1952–54	Orleans Parish Levee Board evicts squatters living on uptown batture from Burdette Street to Jefferson Parish line so that Army Corps of Engineers may realign levee and erect floodwall. Order ends tradition of living cheaply in raised camps and shacks along sections of riverfront not used by port. Last batture community remains today on Jefferson side of parish line.
1953	All but two streetcar lines—Canal and St. Charles—are discontinued in favor of rubber-tire buses.
1954	*Brown v. Board of Education* Supreme Court decision reverses locally originated 1896 *Plessy v. Ferguson* ruling on "separate but equal" public schools. Ruling sets legal stage for end of de jure segregation of schools and public accommodations in South. During next decade and particularly after Civil Rights Act in 1964, Jim Crow gradually disappears from streetcars, buses, department stores, schools, housing, restaurants, and facilities. Change is accompanied often by protests and tensions but rarely by violence.

103

New Orleans ▪ Twentieth-Century Delta Urbanism

Containerization radically altered the economics and geographies of the Port of New Orleans, concentrating activity in the uptown container facilities (shown here) and freeing up miles of old riverfront wharves. The ongoing "Reinventing the Crescent" effort seeks to reconnect city-dwellers with their river by converting areas once needed for shipping and warehousing to green space, recreational facilities, and promenades. *Photograph by Jaap van der Salm/ David Waggonner,* Dutch Dialogues, *2009.*

1954

Union Passenger Terminal opens near present-day Loyola Avenue. New station unifies (hence the name) numerous passenger lines and leads to closing of turn-of-century stations located throughout city, including two picturesque structures near French Quarter. Consolidation of railroad tracks within recently filled-in New Basin Canal right-of-way leaves many old rail corridors abandoned throughout city, many owned by railroad companies to this day.

1954–62

Old River Control Structure is built to regulate flow among Mississippi, Red, and Atchafalaya rivers, addressing circa-1830s intervention that aided navigation interests but inadvertently altered system's hydrology. One of world's great engineering projects, "Old River" ensures that Mississippi will not abandon channel and jump into Atchafalaya (leaving New Orleans on elongated brackish bay) by allocating flow at government-approved 70-to-30 ratio between the two rivers.

1955–Present

New technology that enables cargo to be packed into standardized containers and handled in mass-production mode, from ship to truck or train, rapidly transforms world's ports. Containerization ends centuries-old longshoremen culture in port cities, alters geography of urban waterfronts, and allows new small ports to compete with old major ports. With containerization, great ports no longer need great port cities. Port and city of New Orleans are deeply affected by new technology.

1955	Lincoln Beach, a lakefront recreational destination for black New Orleanians prohibited through Jim Crow laws from using nearby Pontchartrain Beach, opens along Hayne Boulevard. An integral childhood memory of a generation of African Americans, Lincoln Beach remains open until 1964, when Civil Rights Act prohibits discrimination at public facilities. A few vestiges of facility stand in ruins today.
1955–58	Pontchartrain Park subdivision, with its distinctive curvilinear street network and golf course, is built in lakeside Seabrook section of Ninth Ward, with funds from white philanthropists. First modern suburban-style development open for black New Orleanians draws middle-class families, many of them black Creoles, out of historical neighborhoods to settle in eastern lakeside section of parish. By end of century, black population generally occupies eastern half of metropolis, while whites gravitate toward western half.
1956	Federal Aid Highway Act is signed by President Eisenhower, commencing historic effort to build interstate highway system. Over next two decades, New Orleans is connected to nation via I-10 and I-610 plus nearby I-12, I-55, and I-59. One of world's longest causeways connects rural St. Tammany Parish with metropolitan Jefferson Parish, opening Florida Parishes to suburban expansion. "Across the lake" becomes "the north shore" in local parlance, particularly after second span is opened in 1965 and exodus increases. Region's first modern tunnels open on West Bank of Jefferson Parish, while now-infamous Carrollton Interchange is completed near Orleans–Jefferson Parish line. Most major modern transportation corridors are built in the 15 years following 1956, radically altering cityscape and urban geography of region.
1957	After a century at Lafayette Square, City Hall is relocated to new International Style Civic Center built upon recently demolished back-of-town neighborhood that included Louis Armstrong's birthplace. Five office, court, and library buildings—built between 1957 and 1959 around Duncan Plaza—give city government more space and aura of progressive modernity. Brasília-like complex unifies previously dispersed city functions and fosters growth of government services sector on expanded Loyola Avenue.

105

New Orleans ▪ Twentieth-Century Delta Urbanism

Downtown cityscape: Former Faubourg St. Mary, now the Central Business District and Warehouse District, viewed from the top of St. Patrick's Church on Camp Street toward the Crescent City Connection. *Photograph by Richard Campanella, 2006.*

1958

First downtown Mississippi River Bridge opens. Bridging of river furthers West Bank development but comes at expense of scores of historic structures in Lee Circle area. Second span is erected in late 1980s, creating Crescent City Connection and forming new iconic vista of downtown New Orleans.

1958

U.S. Navy relocates air station from East Bank lakefront to Belle Chasse, across river. Move encourages new development in bridge-accessed West Bank portions of Orleans and Jefferson parishes and brings upper Plaquemines Parish into metropolitan fold. Belle Chasse Naval Air Station–Joint Reserve Base is now major hub of military's presence in metropolitan area.

1959

Louisiana State University in New Orleans, created in 1956 in response to citizens' demand for public higher education, opens on lakefront site recently vacated by Navy. Parallel effort results in creation of Southern University at New Orleans (SUNO), only one mile away in Pontchartrain Park, for African-American students. Louisiana State University in New Orleans is renamed University of New Orleans (UNO) in 1974. Legacy of racial segregation permeates city's universities to this day, as Tulane, Loyola, and UNO serve predominantly white student bodies, and Xavier, Dillard, and SUNO have largely black enrollments.

1958–68

Mississippi River–Gulf Outlet Canal is excavated in St. Bernard and Plaquemines parishes. "MR-GO" gives ocean-going traffic shorter alternate route to Port of New Orleans and helps develop Industrial Canal–Gulf Intracoastal Waterway as new center of port activity. But 75-mile-long MR-GO also causes coastal erosion and saltwater intrusion, requires constant dredging, and provides pathway for hurricane-induced storm surges to reach populated areas. Guide levees are built of local soils laden with organic matter, which proceed to subside. Mississippi River–Gulf Outlet Canal plays role in flooding following Hurricane Betsy in 1965 and infamously during Hurricane Katrina in 2005, serving as a surge corridor, a "funnel," and a cause of widespread coastal land loss. "MR-GO Must Go" becomes battle cry of angry flood victims and environmentalists nationwide after 2005 catastrophe; waterway is finally closed to navigation by rock barrier in 2009.

1960

New Orleans's population peaks at 627,525, 15th largest among American cities; black population is 233,514 (37 percent). Suburban Jefferson Parish population grows from 103,873 in 1950 to 208,769 in 1960. Roughly half of New Orleanians in 1960 reside above sea level, down from more than 90 percent a half century earlier. After 1960, New Orleans declines in both absolute population and in relative rank among American cities.

1960–64

Civil rights movement, court orders, and Civil Rights Act of 1964 hasten end of de jure segregation in New Orleans. Long in process but now empowered by national movement, struggle for racial equality in New Orleans comes to head with initial integration of public schools. Ugly street protests garner national attention, but city generally avoids violence seen in other Southern communities. "White flight" begins in earnest, setting Orleans Parish on ongoing trajectory of population decline and de facto segregation in residential settlement patterns.

1960s–1970s

Hispanic immigrants, disproportionately from Cuba and Honduras, settle in working-class and middle-class areas of Irish Channel, Mid-City, and Ninth Ward.

1960s

Petroleum industry rises; port economy mechanizes. Coastal and offshore oil brings outside investment and professionals to New Orleans; triggers construction of downtown skyscrapers and "Houstonization" of city. Containerized shipping technology replaces many longshoremen and sailors; requires less waterfront space and frees up riverfront for recreational use. As oil industry rises, port-related employment declines.

1963–72	Coast-to-coast I-10 is constructed through New Orleans. Major new infrastructure gives birth to modern metropolitan area; fosters middle-class exodus and suburban growth in eastward and westward directions. Interstate also destroys famous forested neutral ground of North Claiborne Avenue (main street of black Creole New Orleans) and leads to decline of old ingresses/egresses, such as Airline Highway, Tulane Avenue, and Chef Menteur Highway.
1964	Civil Rights Act outlaws segregation in schools and public places. Blatant Jim Crow segregation disappears from public facilities, putting many integrated retailers out of business, particularly on South Rampart and Dryades streets. Housing projects, segregated de jure since their opening around 1940, soon integrate, but then resegregate de facto as whites leave for affordable housing elsewhere.
1964	Reflecting nationwide switch from rails to buses and from urban transit to autos, all remaining streetcars except historic St. Charles line are terminated. Next 25 years mark low point in city's long history of urban railways; 1964 decision is later regretted and reversed at century's end.
1964–69	Federal funding arrives to build Riverfront Expressway, connecting bridge and CBD traffic with points east via French Quarter riverfront and Elysian Fields Avenue. Bitterly controversial plan, originally recommended by Robert Moses in 1946, divides citizenry and motivates unprecedented and ultimately successful campaign of resistance over next five years.

This view of Arabi in St. Bernard Parish captures mixed riverfront land uses immediately downriver from New Orleans, including residential, commercial, intermodal transportation, light and heavy industry (Domino's sugar refinery, top left), and even the vestiges of agriculture. Two 19th-century plantation homes may be seen on either side of the open field at center right. *Photograph by Jaap van der Salm/David Waggonner,* Dutch Dialogues, 2009.

1965   Hurricane Betsy strikes New Orleans region in early September, causing extensive wind damage and flooding Ninth Ward, parts of Gentilly, Pontchartrain Park, and eastern New Orleans. Disaster kills 81 Louisianians, injures 17,600, and causes $372 million in damage, about one-third in New Orleans. Betsy prompts Congress to authorize Flood Control Act of 1965, which includes Lake Pontchartrain and Vicinity Hurricane Protection Project. Influential act puts federal government in the business of storm protection; entails improvement and construction of hurricane-protection levees, floodwalls, and gates to what would later be called Category 3 standards. Envisioned flood protection increases real estate values and inspires new home construction in the very areas that flooded. During subsequent oil-boom years, over 75,000 homes are built in eastern areas, most of them on concrete slabs at grade level. But inadequate funding, new environmental regulations, engineering challenges, and other factors derail original plans, which are only partially executed. Failure leaves New Orleans by century's end with inadequate system in face of deteriorating soils and rising seas.

1966   Effort to compete with Houston and other ascendant Southern cities inspires widening of Poydras Street as showcase corporate corridor. Numerous historic structures are razed on lower side of street. Plan foresees need for major traffic-generating anchors at each end of Poydras Street: Rivergate Exhibition Hall is built in 1968 at river end, Superdome in 1975 at lake end.

1966	Simultaneous erection of International Trade Mart and Plaza Tower, city's first modern skyscrapers, symbolizes increasing oil-related wealth and new piling technology. Project sites are selected to spark competing skyscraper development along Poydras Street and Loyola Avenue, respectively. Poydras Street ultimately prevails; Plaza Tower at Loyola and Howard avenues remains in isolation to this day.
1967	Saints NFL franchise brings professional football to New Orleans, making it a "big league city" mentioned in sports media in same breath as Dallas, Houston, Atlanta, and other competing cities. But with small market, declining population, and low per-capita income, city struggles to maintain "big league" perception. Team remains wildly popular locally, particularly after Hurricane Katrina, illustrating important role played by spectator sports in establishing regional identity and encouraging hometown loyalty.
1967	Standard Fruit and Steamship Company relocates its Thalia Street Wharf banana-importing operation to Gulfport, Mississippi, costing New Orleans hundreds of jobs and millions of dollars in lost wages.
1968	Rivergate Exhibition Hall is constructed at foot of Canal and Poydras streets. Bold, freeform design adds stunning new vista to city's premier intersection; nurtures convention trade and fosters development of skyscraper hotels on lower Canal Street in early 1970s.
1968	Congress creates National Flood Insurance Program, pricing coverage at below-market rates to encourage participation. Program creates bonanza for real estate interests by encouraging development of flood zones, including coastal areas popular with wealthy second-home buyers.
1960s–1970s	Ten blocks of historic Tremé, including many early-19th-century vernacular cottages, are leveled for Theater for Performing Arts and Louis Armstrong Park. Controversial urban renewal project, which displaces over a thousand residents, transforms Faubourg Tremé and is soon regarded by many as a mistake.
1968	Mississippi River–Gulf Outlet Canal, commenced a decade earlier, fully opens for port traffic. Waterway's economic benefits are disappointing; environmental toll proves catastrophic.

110

New Orleans ■ Twentieth-Century Delta Urbanism

1968–69	After holding steady at 40,000 annually since *Brown v. Board of Education* (1954), white student enrollment at New Orleans's public schools begins steady decline, while black enrollment doubles to 70,000. White exodus to suburbs and entrenchment of black underclass in Orleans Parish eventually lead to de facto resegregation of New Orleans's public schools. System that was one-to-one black-to-white in 1957 becomes five-to-one in early 1980s and nineteen-to-one in early 2000s.
1969	New hotels are prohibited in French Quarter, in attempt to balance tourist and residential use. Ban shifts new hotel development to Canal Street and later to CBD and Warehouse District.
1969	Federal cancellation of bitterly divisive Riverfront Expressway project saves French Quarter's Mississippi River frontage and makes New Orleans one of first American cities to defeat nationwide trend toward elevated expressways along downtown waterfronts.
1969	Category 5 hurricane Camille strikes coastal Mississippi, obliterating significant portion of historic Gulf Coast. New Orleans suffers some wind and flood damage but is mostly spared what could have been a catastrophe.
1970	New Orleans's population declines to 593,471; black population 257,478 (43 percent). Falls in rank from nation's 15th-largest city in 1960 to 19th largest in 1970, at the time the largest 10-year drop in its history.
1970	City Planning Commission's circa-1920s Comprehensive Zoning Ordinance is updated to modern planning sensibilities, discouraging mixed use in favor of suburban-style land use. Ordinance is regularly amended over subsequent decades, often in confusing and contradictory ways. Century's end brings strident calls for new master plan with force of law, complete with overhauled comprehensive land-use and zoning ordinance.

111

New Orleans ▪ Twentieth-Century Delta Urbanism

1970	Jazz and Heritage Festival is held at Congo Square. Created by Massachusetts-born George Wein, inventor of the modern music festival, event grows into annual New Orleans Jazz and Heritage Festival (Jazz Fest), now second only to Mardi Gras in the cultural-tourism economy. Festival provides important venue for local musicians and helps instill "New Orleans sound" as essential part of American roots music; performs similar service for Louisiana food. Event's location at Fairgrounds on Gentilly Boulevard helps expose traditionally French Quarter–bound visitors to non-tourist neighborhoods.
1971	Friends of the Cabildo publishes *New Orleans Architecture, Volume I: The Lower Garden District*. Study inspires new appreciation for historic architecture outside French Quarter and Garden District, sets scholarly tone for local historical research, and stirs modern preservation movement. Nomenclature and boundaries used in series—currently eight volumes strong and growing—help revive historical place-names and affect public's perceptions of place.
1971–72	Galvanized by construction of out-of-scale Christopher Inn Apartments and empowered by subsequent historic district zoning (first since Vieux Carré protection in 1936), residents establish Faubourg Marigny Improvement Association. Group participates in political process, with eye toward historic preservation and neighborhood improvement; inspires residents of other historic neighborhoods to mobilize similar efforts, leading to both revitalization and gentrification. Old French term *faubourg* is revived in neighborhood nomenclature and adopted by real estate industry and press. Faubourg Marigny begins transforming from mostly working-class neighborhood of natives to professional-class neighborhood of transplants; becomes city's premier gay neighborhood.
1972	One Shell Square—697 feet high and resting on 200-foot-long pilings—rises as tallest structure in city and lower Mississippi Valley. Skyscraper symbolizes apex of 1970s oil boom.

Mardi Gras on St. Charles Avenue represents the most famous and picturesque way New Orleans celebrates Carnival but is by no means the only way. The movable feast is enjoyed "under the bridge" (I-10 overpass) in Tremé, at elegant society balls, with Mardi Gras Indians and "second line" parades in downtown wards, at backyard barbecues, and on the streets and balconies of the French Quarter. *Photograph by Richard Campanella, 2009.*

1972   Last full-scale Mardi Gras parades roll through French Quarter. Increasingly elaborate Carnival celebrations, including new "super krewes" (starting 1969), create safety hazard in Quarter's narrow streets. St. Charles Avenue becomes new route for most parades; French Quarter is left to inebriated revelry and lewdness. Neighborhood krewes gradually abandon their local parade routes and centralize along standard St. Charles route, even as parading tradition diffuses to suburbs and beyond. Beads, doubloons, and other "throws" grow in popularity, practically forming a city industry (although they are mostly manufactured in China). City's Mardi Gras celebration enters modern age during 1970s, as a major tourism-driven civic ritual attracting a nationwide audience.

1973   Second-worst Mississippi River flood on record threatens region. Old River Control Structure is damaged and later enlarged; Bonnet Carré Spillway opened to relieve pressure on levees.

113

1973–74   Curtis and Davis architectural firm issues *New Orleans Housing and Neighborhood Preservation Study*. Landmark document identifies and delineates 62 official city neighborhoods, based on earlier demarcations in 1927 City Planning Commission study, natural geographical barriers and transportation arteries, social and economic patterns, and census tract boundaries. Effort influences perceptions of place, space, and nomenclature in city; marks modern era of city planning. Designation of national and local historic districts starting in 1970s furthers trend toward perceiving neighborhoods as discrete, bounded, officially named entities with mutually agreed upon characteristics.

CHAPTER 17 PERCEIVING THE DELTA CITY

Like city dwellers anywhere, New Orleanians perceive, delineate, and label their urban spaces in myriad ways — and argue about it endlessly.[1] The spatial perceptions vary complexly over time and within subsegments of the population. While some pedantic souls insist that neighborhoods are named absolutely and delineated officially, as if it is a matter of law or physics, such perceptions of place are more appropriately viewed as the human constructs they are, wonderfully individualized and wholly subject to interpretation. Therein lies their significance.

The subjectivity begins with the city's first neighborhood. *French Quarter, the Quarter, the Old City, Vieux Carré* (*Old Square*), and *Vieux Carré de la Ville* usually describe those blocks bounded by Iberville Street, North Rampart Street, Esplanade Avenue, and the Mississippi River. In informal contexts, they also include the 100 blocks between Iberville and Canal streets, although this strip did not fall within the original plat and remains today beyond the jurisdiction of the Vieux Carré Commission. Slivers of blocks along North Rampart and Esplanade also stretched beyond the original street grid and fortifications but are now officially in the French Quarter. The French Quarter fell within the First Municipality when the city experimented with semi-autonomous municipalities in 1836; after reunification in 1852, it became part of the new Second Municipal District, which in turn was sliced into the Fourth, Fifth, and Sixth wards, all of those designations remaining in use today. Some locals shrug off all of the above and refer generically to all quaint, historic neighborhoods below Canal Street as *the French Quarters* — plural — or simply as *da quarters*.

Faubourg or *fauxbourg* (literally "false town") is the French term for an inner suburb. Sometimes used syn-

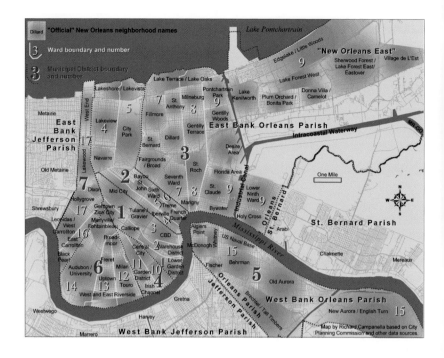

Map by Richard Campanella based on City Planning Commission and other data sources.

New Orleans ■ Perceiving the Delta City

New Orleanians subdivide their city in various—and oftentimes conflicting and contested—ways. Shown here are three official methods, all of which remain in use today: wards (1852–74), municipal districts (1836–74), and planning neighborhoods (1973–74 and later modified). National Register districts, local historic districts, planning districts, and neighborhood association limits offer additional methods of identifying neighborhoods. No one method, of course, is "right." Such perceptions of place are more appropriately viewed as the human constructs they are, highly individualized and subjective. *Map by Richard Campanella.*

onymously with the term *banlieue* ("outskirts" or "suburbs"), it described the subdivisions laid out within old plantations beyond the limits of the original city, starting in 1788. Both terms faded as French disappeared from local speech in the late 1800s, but *faubourg* was revived in the 1970s through the efforts of preservationists, neighborhood organizations, and real estate agents. The first neighborhood to re-embrace the term was the Faubourg Marigny, which many view as the quintessential New Orleans faubourg. The term is now commonly used as a synonym for "historic neighborhood" throughout New Orleans, except (by definition) the French Quarter. Popular with culturally aware history buffs—many of them transplants—the term *faubourg* is, ironically, uncommon among deeply rooted locals, particularly native-born elders, who came of age when the term was defunct.

Faubourg Ste. Marie, Faubourg St. Mary, St. Mary, Second Municipality, American Sector, American Quarter, Central Business District, and *CBD* all refer to the area loosely bordered by Canal Street (or Iberville Street); Claiborne or Loyola avenues; Howard Avenue or the Pontchartrain Expressway; and the Mississippi River. In certain historical contexts, the Canal Street corridor, between Iberville and Common streets, is considered separate because this swath remained a dusty commons for 20 years after the faubourg's 1788 platting. *Faubourg Ste. Marie* is generally used for discussions recounting the late 1700s and early 1800s, while *Faubourg St. Mary*, *St. Mary*, and the *American Sector* usually connote 19th-century contexts. *Second Municipality* implies exclusively the municipality era of 1836–52, while *Central Business District* and *CBD* refer to the area in modern times. Today, the CBD falls within the First Municipal District and (mostly) the Third Ward. One real estate investor is currently spearheading an effort to redesignate and market the CBD as the American Sector, recognizing the role of Anglo-Americans in developing the area in the early 1800s and playing off the world-famous cachet of the French Quarter.

Everyone has their own feel of where downtown becomes uptown in New Orleans and, relatedly, whether the words are common nouns or capitalized proper nouns. Many people today divide the two places-of-mind along the Pontchartrain Expressway, which roughly separates the harder, congested streets of the commercial sector from softer, leafier residential environs. Others refer exclusively to the Garden District or the University area as uptown, and the French Quarter and Central Business District as downtown. Years ago, Canal Street would have been seen as the demarcation—a notion still held by many New Orleanians, despite the fact that most local usage of *downtown* and *uptown* implies otherwise. Understanding the two distinctive yet nebulous regions is enabled by embracing their various and adamantly defended definitions, rather than by dogmatically attempting to reject all but one.[2]

The term *Garden District*, in use at least since the 1850s, connotes the wealthy historic neighborhood initially laid out as the inland portion of the former Jefferson Parish city of Lafayette. Now bounded by Magazine Street and Jackson, Louisiana, and St. Charles avenues, this area earned its name as wealthy families of predominantly Anglo-American stock built spacious mansions (1830s–1850s) set back from the streets and surrounded by greenery. The result was an urban environment strikingly different from that of the Old City. Exact limits of the Garden District depend on whether one is referencing official city neighborhood delineations, local historic districts, or national historic districts. Even then, many locals and most visitors use

117

Garden District to mean all prosperous, leafy uptown historic neighborhoods.

Wards as political-geographical units were introduced with the 1805 chartering of the city, replacing a Spanish equivalent from colonial times. Serving as voting districts, as demographic units for censuses, and other municipal purposes, wards were delineated and redrawn four times over the following 47 years. After the city's unsuccessful 16-year experiment with semi-autonomous municipalities, in 1852 the reunified city government redrew ward lines for a fifth time. Because Felicity Street had for many years marked the Jefferson–Orleans parish line, the new wards were enumerated starting from Felicity Street (First Ward) and continuing consecutively downriver to the Orleans–St. Bernard parish line near today's Jackson Barracks (Ninth Ward). Each ward extended perpendicularly from the highly populated riverfront straight to the uninhabited backswamp. To equalize populations within wards, the high-density French Quarter was sliced into the narrowest wards—Fourth, Fifth, and Sixth—while the lower-density upper and lower faubourgs were cut into broader wards. The lowermost outskirts of the city were so unpopulated that a single megaward—the Ninth—enveloped the entire area, all the way out to the eastern marshes. City fathers then swung around above Felicity Street and demarcated newly annexed Lafayette as wards 10 and 11. The enumeration continued upriver as more Jefferson Parish communities merged with New Orleans: Jefferson City became wards 12, 13, and 14 in 1870, then Algiers on the West Bank was annexed as Ward 15. Upriver expansion concluded when the city annexed Carrollton, which became wards 16 and 17. As development spread toward the lake, old ward lines that once projected neatly off the sinuous Mississippi were extended and angled awkwardly to intersect the smooth west-to-east arc of the lakeshore. The modern-day map of New Orleans's wards, unchanged since the 1880s, thus reflects the city's piecemeal growth since 1852.

An additional adjustment in ward geography came in the 1920s, when the newly excavated Industrial Canal severed the Ninth Ward into upper and lower sections—a reference to the direction of the river's flow, not topographic elevation. By the late 20th century, the riverside sections of the Upper and Lower Ninth wards had become respectively known by the more

118

appealing monikers of Bywater and Holy Cross, while areas behind St. Claude and Claiborne generally remained anonymous. Why? Higher degrees of historical and architectural significance brought Bywater and Holy Cross greater attention from preservationists and planners, thus subjecting them to specialized naming and treatment. This attests to the significance of place-names. All things being equal, more people would probably rather live in a neighborhood called the Faubourg Bouligny than the 13th Ward.

Place perceptions and labels inform on nativity, race, and other social dimensions. New Orleans natives with deep local roots often use the ward system in perceiving and naming urban space, probably because it formed the premier space-delineation option prior to the era of urban planning and historic districting that began in the 1970s. Recent transplants, many having specifically moved to the city for its historical and cultural charms, tend to recognize space vis-à-vis recently revived historical names, such as Faubourg St. John, the Marigny, and Faubourg Tremé. Because nativity rates are much higher among black residents than whites, wards are particularly popular as a spatial reference in the African-American community. Elderly natives of any race are often unfamiliar with the trendy revived faubourg names; conversely, many recently arrived transplants and college students are at a loss when asked what ward they live in. Native-born New Orleanians, who tend to be culturally traditional and family oriented, are more likely to identify landmarks and regionize the city by churches, church parishes, and school districts, a spatial lexicon that does not work for many young, secular, childless transplants. What is the Seventh Ward to a native-born black Creole may be Faubourg New Marigny or the "Jazz Fest neighborhood" to a white transplant; what is the Upper Ninth Ward to the working class may be Bywater to artists and bohemians. Older members of the black community still speak of the back-of-town and front-of-town, even though the swamps and marshes that gave meaning to those ancient spatial perceptions have long been drained away.

Spatial references often reveal subtle (or not-so-subtle) social, racial, and political narratives. Politicians in New Orleans cleverly deploy localized spatial references—to wards, uptown, downtown, or the back-of-town—to certify their "authenticity," establish their

119

New Orleans ■ Perceiving the Delta City

"street cred," or allude to racial dynamics. When Mayor Ray Nagin famously assured black residents that post-Katrina New Orleans will remain a "chocolate" city, he pointedly shrugged off "what people are saying in Uptown," implying that residents of that urban region bear other racial designs.[3] The adjectives *inner-city* and *suburban*, which originally carried geographical meaning, are now widely and openly used as race and class euphemisms—despite the fact that many inner cities are gentrifying while suburbs grow increasingly diverse. Sometimes prejudices are revealed when observers unconsciously describe the same area differently, depending on context. "When something bad happens," lamented one New Yorker, "[this] neighborhood is called Harlem. When something good happens, it is the Upper West Side."[4]

New Orleanians also break down space via landmarks such as favorite restaurants, stores, places of worship, and nightspots. Gangs a century ago often identified themselves by referencing neighborhood landmarks: the St. Mary's Market Gang and Shot Tower Gang, for example, were named for two prominent features in the Irish Channel area. Gangs today often spatialize their identity by ward—for example, 10th Ward Posse—something regularly seen in graffiti and on commemorative T-shirts sold at gangster funerals. Curiously, some gangs based in housing projects pre-Katrina adopted ward-based names that did not reflect the actual ward locations of their home turf. Wards often pop up in rap lyrics; one rapper in 2005 dubbed himself Fifth Ward Weebie.

Government agencies and advocacy groups eschew nuanced and contested perceptions of place, preferring instead bureaucratic and cartographic clarity. Toward this end, authorities periodically impose rigid boundaries and official monikers upon the ambiguous cityscape. The first attempt at planner-driven neighborhood delineation appeared in the 1929 *Handbook to Comprehensive Zone Law for New Orleans, Louisiana*. Its compilers borrowed census tract delineations devised by the U.S. Census Bureau as part of its experiment to aggregate population data at more detailed levels.[5] The bureau officially adopted census tracts for the 1940 enumeration of New Orleans, making those semi-arbitrary tract lines increasingly useful for local urban-planning applications. Federally devised and locally adopted census tracts thus drove bureau-

cratic perceptions of neighborhood geography in subsequent decades. Residents' perceptions of where
they lived, however, generally remained nebulous and
subjective—with the exception of the French Quarter,
the Garden District, Carrollton, Algiers, and a few other
places.

That began to change after 1973–74, when the architectural firm Curtis and Davis modified those extant
delineations vis-à-vis natural barriers, transportation
arteries, and socioeconomic patterns. The Curtis and
Davis report, published as the *New Orleans Housing
and Neighborhood Preservation Study*, created 62 "official" city neighborhoods, each a carefully drawn poly-
gon with a name that was sometimes familiar, sometimes completely invented. Later studies increased the
number to 73. Planners and researchers have widely
adopted the Curtis and Davis neighborhood map (particularly after Katrina, when out-of-town observers
seeking spatial clarity embraced the system), lend-
ing credence to what are, for the most part, arbitrary
squiggles and subjective subdivisions. Most New Orleanians would be at a loss to identify three-quarters of
their city's "official" neighborhoods.

The 1970s also saw the rise of the preservation
movement, which in its quest to bring attention to historic neighborhoods relied heavily on inscribing charac-
ter into otherwise nameless places. Their tool of choice
was the "historic district." New Orleans came to earn
some of the largest urban National Register Historic
District designations in the nation, a process that is
ongoing to this day. Inclusion in the U.S. Department
of the Interior's National Register of Historic Places
is largely honorary; the only material benefits involve
certain tax credits and special consideration in relation to federally funded projects. Yet these delineations
have proven highly influential in the perception of the
city because the Preservation Resource Center, New
Orleans's largest historic-protection advocacy group,
embraced them in a widely distributed map and web-
site. Local historic districts, on the other hand, span
far less acreage and are less familiar to the public but
have more power in protecting architecturally and historically significant structures from demolition. They
are overseen by the city's Historic District Landmarks
Commission, with involvement from the City Planning
Commission and other groups.

Neighborhood   perceptions   are   consequential

121

New Orleans ■ Perceiving the Delta City

because, arbitrary as they are, the resultant delineations drive statistical aggregations of everything from population to crime rates, real estate values, and post-Katrina recovery metrics. They therefore influence policy and resource allocation—as well as the formation of neighborhood associations and their respective levels of civic clout. At a deeper level, neighborhood perceptions drive residents' mental maps and spatial awareness of their city and become highly personalized and defended forms of identity.

New Orleans's most distinctive spatial perception involves not place but direction. Cardinal directions only serve to confuse in this crescent-shaped city, so *lakeside*, *riverside*, *upriver* (or *uptown*), and *downriver* (or *downtown*) are widely used as surrogates for *northward*, *southward*, *westward*, and *eastward*. Confusing at first, the delightful vernacular system works well—and makes more sense locally than allusions to distant poles and stars.

TIME LINE, 1970s–1990

1970s	Renovation transforms historic French Market from local food market to "festival marketplace" primarily oriented to visitors.
1970s	Post-Betsy flood control, Interstate 10, Industrial Canal, NASA Michoud plant, and new subdivisions make eastern New Orleans hot new real estate market, led by New Orleans East land development scheme.
1970s	Zoning ordinances dating from 1920s are updated to 1970s sensibilities but prove to be inappropriate for a mixed use, pedestrian-scale historical city. Projects proposed in subsequent decades routinely seek zoning variances through political means, creating inconsistent and confusing environment for sustainable urban and economic development. After numerous false starts, effort commences in 2008 to overhaul city's land-use and zoning ordinances through new master-planning exercise.

1974	Preservation Resource Center is founded. Local nonprofit group injects preservationist and "livable city" philosophies into civic discourse; becomes most influential group advocating adaptive reuse of historic structures and revitalization of old neighborhoods.
1975	Moratorium is imposed on demolitions in CBD, after scores of 19th-century storehouses are razed for skyscrapers or parking lots.
1975	Louisiana Superdome is completed, marking peak of city's competition with Houston. Spectacular domed stadium transforms skyline and breathes new life into CBD. Superdome serves as venue for high-profile events, publicizing city and its attributes to nationwide audiences on a regular basis.
Late 1970s	Vietnamese refugees from postwar communist Vietnam arrive at New Orleans on invitation of Catholic Church. Archdiocese settles hundreds of mostly Catholic refugees in Versailles apartments in eastern New Orleans and in spots on West Bank. Versailles settlement forms unique neighborhood, one of city's most isolated and purest ethnic enclaves, known for elaborate multitiered market gardens and open-air Saturday market. Neighborhood functions as nerve center for Vietnamese community dispersed throughout central Gulf Coast region.
1976	Riverfront promenade Moonwalk—honoring progressive Mayor Moon Landrieu—opens in front of French Quarter. Signifies change of riverfront land use from port activity to recreation, as containerization and Industrial Canal docks concentrate and relocate shipping facilities off Mississippi River.
Late 1970s	New suburban subdivisions encounter unwelcome problem in former Jefferson Parish backswamp: soil sinkage. Subsidence of recently drained hydric soils causes structural damage to thousands of new ranch houses built on concrete slabs; issue makes headlines throughout late 1970s, particularly after some houses explode when gas lines break. New piling-based construction standards are subsequently adopted, but soils continue to sink.

123

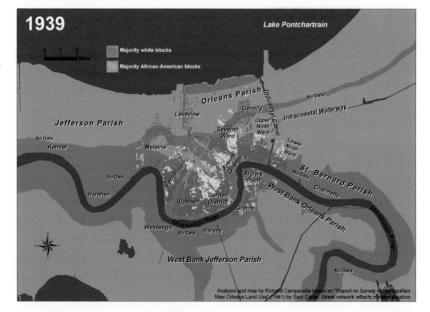

Human geography of New Orleans throughout the 20th century. *Research and maps by Richard Campanella.*

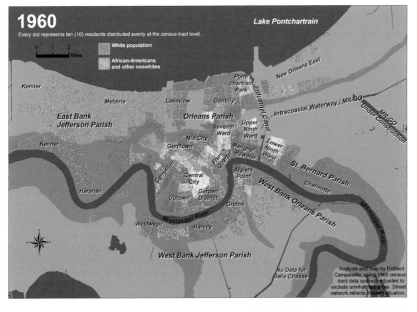

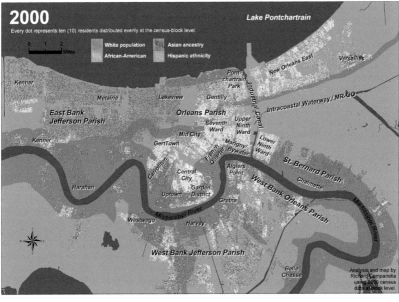

1977   Lawsuit filed by environmental group successfully prevents Army Corps of Engineers from building gates at mouth of Lake Pontchartrain, a flood-control measure envisioned in 1964 to keep storm surge from entering lake. Corps later agrees to raise levee heights instead. Such an apparatus theoretically would have prevented Katrina-driven breaches on lakeshore outfall canals, though not those on eastern navigation canals.

1977   City, now majority black for first time since 1830s, elects first black mayor, Ernest N. "Dutch" Morial, a descendant of Creoles of color, like many city leaders today. Mayor Morial serves from 1978 to 1986.

Late 1970s   Audubon Zoo, constructed mostly during 1920s and 1930s and considered an out-of-date "animal prison" by modern standards, is redesigned and expanded into national-class zoological attraction and research facility.

1980   New Orleans's population declines to 557,515; black population 308,149 (55 percent). City is now 21st largest in nation.

1983–84   Worldwide oil crash hits city; devastates Gulf Coast and other petroleum-based economies. Bust costs New Orleans thousands of white-collar jobs in subsequent years and initiates dark era of job loss, middle-class exodus, and increasing crime rates, which endures until mid-1990s. Louisiana's oil- and gas-related employment plummets from nearly 95,000 jobs in 1981 to about 41,000 in 2005.

1984   Louisiana World Exposition is held along what is now Convention Center Boulevard, on 100th anniversary of World's Industrial and Cotton Centennial Exposition at Audubon Park. Like its predecessor, it fails financially but succeeds in terms of cultural promotion and urban development. Historic Warehouse District is revitalized into convention, hotel, condominium, and arts district in subsequent years, as former fair structures are converted into Ernest N. Morial Convention Center and expanded to more than 1 million square feet. Residential population of CBD and Warehouse District climbs from less than 100 in 1980 to more than 1,300 in 2000.

126

New Orleans ▪ Perceiving the Delta City

Mid- to Late 1980s	Army Corps of Engineers raises heights of city's levee system but neglects to account for new research on increased storm strength, surge height, coastal erosion, and soil subsidence. Concrete floodwalls are erected along riverfront and outfall canal levees, but some are built with insufficiently long sheet piling. Corps' plans for "butterfly gates" to prevent surge from entering outfall canals are opposed by New Orleans Sewerage and Water Board and Orleans Parish Levee Board, because they would reduce ability to pump rainwater out of city. Shortfalls of flood-protection system are revealed 20 years later during Hurricane Katrina.
Mid-1980s	Festival marketplaces like those pioneered by James Rouse open along Mississippi River. Jax Brewery and Riverwalk further recreational and retail utilization of downtown riverfront, once reserved for maritime use. Riverfront Streetcar (1988), first new line in decades, connects French Quarter with new attractions and Ernest N. Morial Convention Center.
1985	Unusual late-October hurricane Juan floods coastal region, including portions of West Bank. Incident leads to raising of levees along metropolis's southern fringe.
1985–86	New Orleans East land development company, poised to urbanize over 20,000 acres of wetlands in eastern Orleans Parish, fails amid oil bust. Land is transferred to federal government and becomes Bayou Sauvage National Wildlife Refuge, reflecting new appreciation for once-scorned marshes and wetlands. Had area developed as envisioned, Hurricane Katrina's toll in lives and property would have been even higher.
1980s–1990s	Numerous generations-old downtown department stores and restaurants—Holmes, Krauss, Maison Blanche, Godchaux's, Maylie's, Kolb's, and others—go out of business due to middle-class exodus, growth of suburbs, crime concerns, parking crunch, and rise of tourism. Buildings are often converted to hotels for growing hospitality industry.

127

New Orleans ▪ Perceiving the Delta City

1989	CNG Tower is constructed next to Superdome. Twenty-three years after erection of first modern high rises, New Orleans's last office skyscraper to date (later named Dominion Tower) symbolizes declining petroleum-related wealth.
1990	New Orleans's population drops below half-million mark to 496,938, ranking as 24th-largest city in nation; black population is 307,728 (62 percent). Jefferson Parish population declines for first time, from 454,592 residents in 1980 to 448,306 in 1990, due in large part to oil crash.

CHAPTER 18   ENVIRONMENTAL CONSEQUENCES OF DELTA URBANISM

Modern levee construction and municipal drainage effectively ended the occasional flooding—from river, lake, or sky—that frustrated New Orleanians in historical times.[1] These interventions also inadvertently eliminated incoming freshwater and sediment, removed the water component from the soil body, and allowed organic matter to decompose. Fine sand, silt, and clay particles settled into the resultant air cavities, compacting the soil and lowering its elevation. The result: soil subsidence.

Soil subsidence had been observed in New Orleans for many years in many places. A document submitted to Congress in 1860 reported that the "St. Charles Hotel [had] sunk 36 inches; St. Patrick's Cathedral even more; the St. Louis Hotel about 24 inches [and the] Custom House [by] 20 inches."[2] This type of sinkage was caused by overburden: heavy structures compressing the soft soils on which they rested. What was happening in the early 20th century, however, was different; it was systematic and widespread, like a geological disease rather than a localized wound. Vast acreages with zero overburden began to subside annually by multiple millimeters or centimeters. By 1935, roughly 30 percent of the urbanized land surface had fallen below sea level.[3] Subsidence worsened even as more and more people moved into subsiding areas. While the vast majority of New Orleans's 300,000 residents lived above sea level in the early 1900s, only 48 percent remained above sea level in 1960, when the city's population peaked at 627,525. Fully 321,000 New Orleanians in that year resided in the 20th-century subdivisions built on lakeside lowlands—which had already dropped vertically by one to two *meters* below sea level.

Subsequent years saw tens of thousands of New Orleanians migrate *horizontally* as well. They departed

Orleans Parish neighborhoods for social and economic reasons, not for any sense of environmental hazard. The Crescent City's population dropped by 23 percent from 1960 to 2000, representing a net loss of 143,000 mostly middle-class whites to adjacent Jefferson, St. Bernard, and St. Tammany parishes or beyond. Within the remaining Orleans Parish population, 121,000 New Orleanians—many of them middle-class blacks—internally migrated from higher historic neighborhoods to low-lying subdivisions east of City Park and into New Orleans East, which offered suburban-sized lots, modern housing, less congestion, and an ample inventory of multifamily housing accepting Section 8 government-subsidized rent vouchers. By the end of the 20th century, half of the city proper and the metropolis south of Lake Pontchartrain had sunk below sea level, in some areas by two to three meters, while 62 percent of New Orleanians lived below sea level. Convinced that infrastructure and technology had neutralized historical hydrological hazards, hundreds of thousands of New Orleans–area residents unknowingly increased their exposure to environmental hazard.

Falling below sea level is hazardous because incoming water that ordinarily would drain off a tapered surface now becomes impounded by a collapsed surface and must be pumped out. The municipal drainage system utilizes enormous screw pumps for precisely this purpose, lifting and ejecting runoff through outfall canals and into adjacent water bodies. Where those pumps are located is critical. A planning decision made when the system was being designed in the 1890s positioned the pumps directly behind the urbanized area, along the edge of the backswamp. It seemed to make sense: Runoff would be collected at low spots behind the city, at which point the pumps would mobilize the water through the canals and over the levees into Lake Pontchartrain. What the engineers failed to appreciate was that the very success of their project would cause soils to subside and encourage urbanization on the newly dried former swampland *beyond* the pumps. Within a few decades, thousands of people lived all around the pumping stations and among the outfall canals, which had to be lined with levees and, later, floodwalls. Their neighborhoods subsided to the point that the canals now flowed above their rooftops, because the pump-enabled lifting of the water occurred at the canals' inner-city headwaters rather than at their

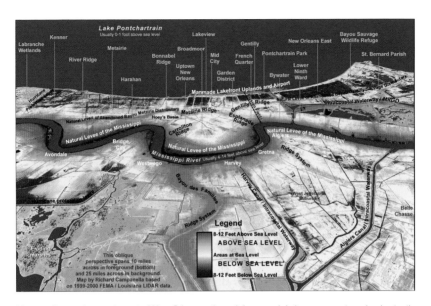

Human efforts to keep water out of New Orleans—through levee and drainage apparatus—inadvertently reduced the organic matter and water content of the soil body, allowing roughly half the deltaic metropolis to subside below sea level. As recently as the 1890s, the entire city lay at or above sea level. The 1895 and 2000 Elysian Fields Avenue elevation profiles (bottom) show that subsidence is worse in the former saline marshes and cypress swamps near Lake Pontchartrain than on the natural levee of the Mississippi River. *Map and profiles by Richard Campanella based on 2000 Louisiana/FEMA LIDAR data and 1895 Drainage Advisory Board elevation surveys.*

131

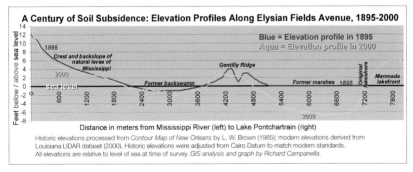

lakeside discharges. Making matters worse was the fact that the outfall canals communicated openly with the surge-prone waters of Lake Pontchartrain, which was not controlled by floodgates. Federal proposals to install such gates were resisted locally because they would reduce the capacity of the drainage system to pump out runoff.

The circa-1890s siting of the pumping stations

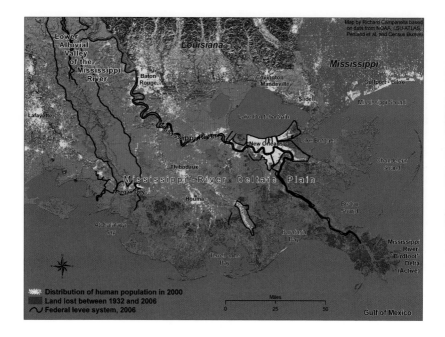

Map by Richard Campanella based
on data from NOAA, LSU-ATLAS,
Penland et al. and Census Bureau

Lower
Alluvial
Valley
of the
Mississippi
River

Louisiana

Mississippi

Baton
Rouge

Covington
Mandeville

Gulfport · Biloxi

Lafayette

Slidell

Mississippi Sound

Lake Pontchartrain

Mississippi River

New Orleans

Lake Borgne

Chandeleur
Sound

Thibodaux

Mississippi River Deltaic Plain

Morgan City

Houma

Breton
Sound

Atchafalaya
Bay

Barataria
Bay

Mississippi
River
"Birdfoot"
Delta
(Active)

Terrebonne
Bay

Distribution of human population in 2000
Land lost between 1932 and 2006
Federal levee system, 2006

Miles

0   25   50

Gulf of Mexico

132

Human manipulation of the Mississippi Delta has essentially transformed this river-dominated deltaic system into one dominated by wave action. The region now confronts what will soon be a global crisis. In this map, yellow represents the population distribution in 2000; green is land; and the heavy black line shows the levee system. Red shows land lost in the past seven decades, and blue represents gulf waters, which are predicted to rise by one meter by the end of this century. *Map by Richard Campanella based on data from NOAA, LSU-Atlas, Penland et al., and U.S. Census Bureau.*

proved to be a dreadful planning oversight. Fortunately, however, planners in Jefferson Parish and eastern New Orleans learned from the mistake when they designed their systems in the 1950s–1960s. They positioned their pumps along the lakeside periphery, *expecting* that the basins they drained would subside and populate. For this reason, outfall canals in the suburbs flow below street-grade level and do not require levees or floodwalls because the runoff is lifted at the last moment, just prior to being ejected into the lake. This explains why there are no levees intruding into the Jefferson Parish and eastern New Orleans hydrological basins but three such levees intruding into the "old Orleans" basin. The suburban drainage canals caused no significant problems during Hurricane Katrina; those in old Orleans caused catastrophic problems. Below-grade canals do, however, come at a cost: They increase subsidence rates because they more effectively remove groundwater. Some of the lowest spots in the urban delta—10 to 12 feet below sea level—are in eastern New Orleans and Jefferson Parish.

Subsidence alone constitutes a tolerable urban problem. In the face of eroding coasts and rising seas, however, it can be deadly. A century of environmental manipulation brought those rising gulf waters closer and closer to the subsided metropolis. Three major navigation canals—the Industrial Canal (1918–23), the Gulf Intracoastal Waterway (GIWW, 1930s–1940s), and the Mississippi River–Gulf Outlet Canal (MR-GO, 1958–68)—allowed saltwater to intrude into the ragged edges of the deltaic plain. Wave action eroded saline marshes, and salinity killed freshwater cypress swamps, allowing more saltwater to intrude and repeating the cycle of ecological destruction until it brushed against the levee-lined perimeter of the million-person conurbation.

An extensive network of oil and gas canals instigated the same cycle throughout the Louisiana coastal region: intrusion, wave action, swamp die-off, erosion. Worse yet, the canals' attendant guide levees and spoil banks served to channelize storm surges and funnel them inland, then impound those same waters when they tried to flow back to the sea. Additionally, the control of the Mississippi through artificial levees—commenced in the 1720s but augmented dramatically in the late 1800s and again after the Great Mississippi River Flood of 1927—starved the deltaic plain of replenishing freshwater and floodborne sediments. Invasive nutria (*Myocastor coypus*) devoured marsh grasses and exacerbated land loss, while global climate warmed and sea levels rose.

As a result of all these factors, Louisiana has lost roughly 2,000 to 2,300 square miles of coastal wetlands—about one-third of the Louisiana deltaic plain—since the 1930s. During the 1970s and 1980s, annually 25–35 square miles of marsh disappeared, a pace of loss well over 20 times swifter than the Mississippi River took to build those wetlands in the previous 7,200 years. The rate slowed somewhat in the 1990s and 2000s, not because the problem had been in any way solved, but because so little land remained to be lost. Three hundred years of environmental alteration, particularly in the past century, have essentially shifted the source of the New Orleans flood threat from the Mississippi River to the Gulf of Mexico. It has also partially transformed the Mississippi Delta from a river-dominated system to one dominated by coastal wave action.

Coastal wetlands protect New Orleans because they buffer hurricane-induced gulf surges and help prevent them from reaching the bowl-shaped city. Any

133

New Orleans ■ Environmental Consequences

form of friction and impedance that can be inserted between open water and populated areas—barrier islands, marshes, swamps, vegetation, ridges—serves to reverse a certain level of incoming surge. Centuries of environmental manipulation have greatly diminished the delta's ability to build that buffer and undermined the buffer it *had* built during previous millennia. Scientists debate the exact relationship and ratio between coastal wetlands and storm surge, but everyone agrees that more of the former means less of the latter.

New Orleans's extraordinary geophysical problems overshadow its numerous routine environmental hazards. For example, high levels of soil lead, associated with lead-based paint, occur where automobiles and wooden housing stock are concentrated. The nearby River Road industrial corridor, between Baton Rouge and New Orleans, is described by many as "cancer alley." Atrazine, arsenic, total coliform bacteria, and other contaminants have been detected in the city's Mississippi River water source. Old industries and municipal dumps left behind numerous brownfields and other potentially hazardous areas, such as the Agriculture Street Landfill, where residential populations later settled. Combined with deeply rooted social, educational, and economic vulnerabilities, the delta's myriad geographical hazards set the city on a tenuous footing and heightened its urban risk. A sufficiently strong tropical storm was all that was needed to cause catastrophe.

134

New Orleans ■ Environmental Consequences

TIME LINE, 1990–2005

1990–91
Coastal Wetlands Planning and Protection Act ("Breaux Act") brings federal funds to Louisiana for coastal restoration; Caernarvon Freshwater Diversion opens below city, first major effort to divert river water into eroding wetlands to push back intruding saltwater and rebuild wetlands.

Early 1990s
Race relations deteriorate amid troubled economic times. Tensions are also a product of gubernatorial candidacy of former Klansman David Duke, Mardi Gras krewe integration controversy (which motivated three old-line krewes to cease parading), protests at Liberty Place monument on Canal Street, and record high crime rates. Lag time between late-1980s decline of oil industry and mid-1990s rise in tourism and service economy exacerbates problems.

1990s
Hurricane evacuation planning is transformed radically. Coastal erosion, subsiding soils, rising seas, and an upswing in hurricane frequency end traditional notion of evacuating to sturdy schools and shelters within city limits. Now citizens are urged to evacuate entire deltaic plain in their own automobiles; rural coastal residents who once evacuated to New Orleans are now directed farther inland. Plans to evacuate the poor and others without cars are never fully articulated—a tragic oversight that would cost hundreds of lives during Katrina in 2005.

1990s–2000s
Declining population forces archdiocese to close or reduce services at numerous historic Catholic churches, some of which are partially converted to homes for aged. Many religious elements of historical cityscape fall silent as local families relocate to suburbs and young, secular transplants move into old neighborhoods.

1992
Category 5 hurricane Andrew, first of wave of megastorms in 1990s and 2000s, pulverizes southern Florida and south-central Louisiana. New Orleans is spared but begins to recognize growing threat of storm surges as coast erodes. Light winds in city cause surprisingly heavy damage to live oaks, leading to discovery of extensive Formosan termite damage.

135

New Orleans ■ Environmental Consequences

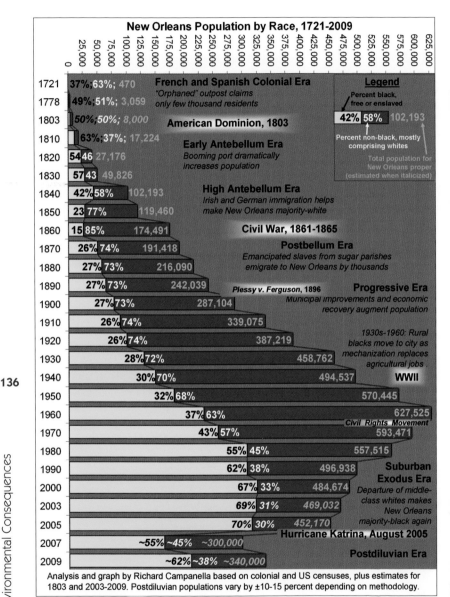

New Orleans Population by Race, 1721-2009

Year	Black %	Non-black %	Total	Era / Notes
1721	37%	63%	470	**French and Spanish Colonial Era** "Orphaned" outpost claims only few thousand residents
1778	49%	51%	3,059	
1803	50%	50%	8,000	**American Dominion, 1803**
1810	63%	37%	17,224	**Early Antebellum Era** Booming port dramatically increases population
1820	54	46	27,176	
1830	57	43	49,826	
1840	42%	58%	102,193	**High Antebellum Era** Irish and German immigration helps make New Orleans majority-white
1850	23	77%	119,460	
1860	15	85%	174,491	**Civil War, 1861-1865**
1870	26%	74%	191,418	**Postbellum Era** Emancipated slaves from sugar parishes emigrate to New Orleans by thousands
1880	27%	73%	216,090	
1890	27%	73%	242,039	*Plessy v. Ferguson,* 1896 **Progressive Era**
1900	27%	73%	287,104	Municipal improvements and economic recovery augment population
1910	26%	74%	339,075	
1920	26%	74%	387,219	1930s-1960: Rural blacks move to city as mechanization replaces agricultural jobs
1930	28%	72%	458,762	
1940	30%	70%	494,537	**WWII**
1950	32%	68%	570,445	
1960	37%	63%	627,525	**Civil Rights Movement**
1970	43%	57%	593,471	
1980	55%	45%	557,515	
1990	62%	38%	496,938	**Suburban Exodus Era** Departure of middle-class whites makes New Orleans majority-black again
2000	67%	33%	484,674	
2003	69%	31%	469,032	
2005	70%	30%	452,170	**Hurricane Katrina, August 2005**
2007	~55%	~45%	~300,000	**Postdiluvian Era**
2009	~62%	~38%	~340,000	

Legend
Percent black, free or enslaved
42% 58% 102,193
Percent non-black, mostly comprising whites
Total population for New Orleans proper (estimated when italicized)

Analysis and graph by Richard Campanella based on colonial and US censuses, plus estimates for 1803 and 2003-2009. Postdiluvian populations vary by ±10-15 percent depending on methodology.

Population and racial composition of New Orleans proper (Orleans Parish), from early colonial times to post-Katrina. *Research and graphic by Richard Campanella based on U.S. Census data and other sources.*

New Orleans ▪ Environmental Consequences

1992–Present   Formosan termite infestations explode across city and region. Accidentally imported on shipping pallets from East Asia during World War II, termites threaten housing stock, particularly historical structures, and urban trees; cost city hundreds of millions of dollars annually in control and damage costs. Threat leads to increased use of steel and aluminum in new construction and renovation.

1994   U.S. Environmental Protection Agency lists Upper Ninth Ward neighborhoods of Gordon Plaza, Press Park, and Liberty Terrace as Superfund sites. City's garbage dump from 1900s to 1960s, Agriculture Street Landfill was covered with topsoil, developed, and populated with working-class, mostly black, families. High levels of lead and other contaminants in soil force school closures and extensive clean-up during 1990s–2000s; many residents resist remediation in favor of more costly solution of buyouts. Controversy garners attention of nationwide environmental justice movement.

1995   May 8 storm dumps up to 18 inches of rainfall on metropolitan area; some areas get 12 inches in single hour. City's worst rainfall floods 56,000 homes and businesses and causes $761 million in damage throughout 12-parish area; leads to half-billion dollars of mostly federal funding for new drainage projects. With installation of new pumps, canals, culverts, and backup generator, New Orleans increases pumping capacity from three inches to five inches of rain every five hours.

137

1995   Amid protests, architecturally significant Rivergate Exhibition Hall is demolished for Harrah's Casino at foot of Canal Street. Opened in 1999 after turbulent construction period, Harrah's is predicted to transform downtown but eventually settles into modest niche between traditional French Quarter tourism and emerging Warehouse District convention trade. Gambling in New Orleans falls well short of exuberant expectations of early 1990s, indicating that visitors are more interested in enjoying city's unique attributes than increasingly ubiquitous gaming opportunities.

1995–Present   Upturn in tropical storm activity makes hurricanes a matter of nearly constant public apprehension during summer months. Storm threats causing partial or total evacuations occur at pace of nearly every other year during this era. Persistent sense of uncertainty leads many to ponder city's long-term viability.

138

Roofscapes of the French Quarter, in summer sun, winter twilight, and rare snowfall. *Photographs by Richard Campanella, 2003–09.*

1996	*Brightfield* vessel collides with Riverwalk Mall, causing no fatalities but demonstrating risk of converting shipping wharves to public recreational and commercial uses.
Late 1990s–Early 2000s	Hotel capacity, mostly in CBD and Warehouse District, skyrockets to 37,000 rooms, to accommodate nearly 10 million annual visitors. Numerous historic structures in CBD and Warehouse District are remodeled into boutique hotels.
Late 1990s	New subdivisions and gated communities around Eastover Golf Course in eastern New Orleans attract wealthy African-American families. Trend reflects preference of many upwardly mobile black families to depart inner city in favor of suburban lifestyles but without leaving Orleans Parish.
1998	City narrowly avoids Hurricane Georges. Reminder of inevitability of "the Big One," Georges teaches lessons on evacuation planning and street flooding in Mid-City area.
1999	New Orleans Arena opens, aiming to accommodate events too big for other venues but too small for nearby Superdome. With 16,000 to 19,000 seats, indoor arena succeeds in attracting Charlotte, North Carolina, NBA franchise Hornets to city in 2002, plus numerous other entertainment and sports events.
2000	New Orleans's population declines to 484,674, making it 31st-largest city in nation. Black population is 325,947 (67 percent). Census in 2000 finds that metropolitan area's most ethnically diverse census tract is Fat City in suburban Metairie, while least diverse tract is inner-city Lower Ninth Ward—exact opposite of earlier times. Thirty-eight percent of New Orleanians now reside above sea level, down from about half in 1960 and more than 90 percent in 1910.
2000	D-Day Museum opens June 6, creating critical mass of cultural venues near Lee Circle. Museum District now comprises Ogden and Civil War museums, Contemporary Arts Center, and Julia Street art galleries. The highly successful attraction, renamed National World War II Museum, undergoes massive expansion during 2007–09.

139

New Orleans ▦ Environmental Consequences

2000	One of largest mapping efforts in state history entails measurement of topographic elevation through light detection and ranging (LIDAR) technology. High-resolution elevation maps of city and region, released to the public incrementally throughout the 2000s, dramatically illustrate effects of subsidence and coastal erosion. Data sets prove crucial in measuring depth of Hurricane Katrina flooding in 2005.
2000	Jazzland amusement park, built entirely on raised wooden boardwalk, opens in eastern New Orleans marshes. Venture struggles financially and soon changes hands to Six Flags, only to be flooded during Hurricane Katrina in 2005 and closed.
Early 2000s	Popularity of downtown condominiums grows, triggering conversion of numerous historical structures and launching proposals for new Sunbelt-style condominium towers. Out-of-town buyers help drive up local real estate prices and intensify gentrification pressure on adjacent neighborhoods. Post-Katrina woes and cooling of national housing market temper condo trend in 2006–09.
2001–05	Lower Garden District riverfront sees radical landscape alteration. Saulet apartment complex, reengineering of Tchoupitoulas and Religious streets, demolition of St. Thomas Housing Project, new Wal-Mart and River Garden development, and renovation and demolition of old warehouses make area one of nation's most transformed inner-city riverfronts. Projects reflect city's ongoing "rediscovery" of river.
2003	New Orleans's population drops to Depression-era level of 469,032, representing loss of over 15,000 since 2000 (greater drop than during entire decade of 1990s). Fastest-growing parish in region is St. Tammany on north shore, which surpasses 200,000 for first time.
2003	Tourists spend more than $4 billion a year in Orleans Parish, generating over 61,000 jobs. Visitors to New Orleans account for 44 percent of state's tourism economy. Oil and gas sector fares much worse: City's Exxon-Mobil office relocates to Houston, continuing 20-year trend of petroleum industry forsaking New Orleans and Louisiana.

140

New Orleans ■ Environmental Consequences

2004   New Orleans's population declines to 462,269, barely ahead of Jefferson Parish's 453,590. City proper is now home to only 35 percent of seven-parish metro-area population, down from 80 percent a century earlier. New Orleans as a whole, which was majority white from 1830s to 1970s, declines from peak population of 627,525 in 1960 to 462,269 in 2004, of whom over two-thirds are black. Wealthier whites predominate in higher-elevation swath from French Quarter through uptown and in low-lying Lakeview; while middle-class African Americans, including those of Creole ancestry, predominate in eastern half of city, an area intersected by navigation canals connecting with the Gulf of Mexico. Poorer African Americans settle here, too, but otherwise remain in the historical back-of-town and immediately along the high riverfront. Poorest citizens, nearly all black, reside in high-density subsidized projects. Most immigrants live in suburban fringe, with Latinos predominantly in Metairie and Kenner, and Vietnamese in eastern New Orleans and West Bank.

2004   Success of 1988 Riverfront line inspires reintroduction of streetcars to city's transportation system. Major new routes are installed on Canal Street (starting 1997) and Carrollton Avenue, designed to circulate tourists throughout city and foster rail commuting. Much-anticipated Canal line opens in April 2004 and succeeds in invigorating Mid-City businesses. Additional lines are foreseen to reinvigorate neighborhoods elsewhere. Hurricane Katrina derails most efforts, as floodwaters damage new streetcars and rearrange priorities.

141

2004   Major new containerized shipping facility at Napoleon Avenue wharf, combined with environmental problems on MR-GO and bottleneck lock on Industrial Canal, return river to position of prominence in local port industry. Exact opposite was foreseen in 1970s, when Centroport was planned to shift most port businesses to MR-GO, GIWW, and Industrial Canal wharves. New uptown facility also concentrates port activity and frees up antiquated downtown wharves for other uses.

New Orleans ■ Environmental Consequences

2004

Category 4 hurricane Ivan spares city but devastates coastal Alabama. New contraflow plan, devised after Hurricane Georges in 1998, opens up incoming interstate lanes to outgoing evacuees. Horrendous traffic jams lead to refinement of evacuation planning. Ivan's sideswipe brings additional attention to urgency of coastal restoration; in retrospect, serves as dry run for following year's Hurricane Katrina.

2004–05

City holds "riverfront charrette" to gather ideas for new land uses from Poland to Jackson avenues. With port activity now concentrated in uptown containerization facilities, city and developers eye abandoned wharves for new recreational uses. Plan emerges in which Port of New Orleans would relinquish its maritime servitude of riverfront to city in exchange for percentage of land sales and leases. If enacted, agreement would open up more than four miles of riverfront, from Bywater to Lower Garden District, for massive redevelopment. Rejuvenated in 2007–09 as "Reinventing the Crescent," effort now proposes $300 million from state, local, federal, and private coffers to fund new public green space.

2005

Pentagon recommends closure of Naval Support Activity in Algiers and Bywater. Twin locations straddling Mississippi made military sense when installation was created but prove to be costly obstacle in modern times. City's loss of up to 2,700 jobs may be mitigated by growth of Naval Air Station in Belle Chasse and creation of federal agency office complex, cruise terminal, and other facilities and amenities in vacated riverfront properties.

2005

Following Hurricane Ivan traffic-jam debacle, new contraflow evacuation plan is unveiled. Strategy involves evacuating most vulnerable areas first, then diverting outbound traffic onto inbound lanes at four carefully policed crossovers, giving evacuees six different escape routes to safety.

July 2005

New Orleans's population estimated at 452,170, down by 10,000 in a year and 32,000 since the 2000 Census.

New Orleans ▪ Environmental Consequences

CHAPTER 19   DEVASTATING THE DELTAIC CITY

On Tuesday, August 23, 2005, tropical air fueled by unusually warm ocean water spiraled in an upward, counterclockwise direction over the southeastern Bahamas. The westward-edging column of low pressure sucked increasing quantities of heated air into the system, growing it sufficiently for the National Hurricane Center to classify it as Tropical Depression 12, and by the next morning as Tropical Storm Katrina. By late Thursday afternoon, Category 1 hurricane Katrina approached the metropolis of southern Florida with 75-mile-per-hour winds. The system and its heavy rains killed nine people in the north Miami area overnight, then, surviving the jaunt over the Florida peninsula, entered the Gulf of Mexico.[1]

Although the 2005 hurricane season had been accurately predicted as an extraordinarily busy one, tropical activity had disarmingly abated during July and August, and most New Orleanians only passively noted the seemingly weak and distant storm. But awaiting Katrina in the gulf was a gigantic source of storm fuel: a loop current of deeply layered warm water, pulsating in from the Caribbean between Cuba and the Yucatán and breaking off into eddies through the Gulf of Mexico before exiting into the Atlantic between Cuba and Florida. With sea surface temperatures around 90 degrees and without the reprieve of cooler subsurface waters, a system that made it into the gulf at this particular time would strengthen dramatically.

Computer models at first forecasted storm tracks up the Florida peninsula, then westward over the panhandle, then further westward to the Alabama border, where so many storms had landed during the preceding 10-year surge in tropical activity. The farther west Katrina crept, the more energy it drew from the warm loop current, and the more seriously it threatened coastal communities.

Yet as schools and offices closed down in New Orleans on Friday afternoon, most conversations and e-mails concerned weekend plans and next week's business, not evacuations and possible closures, much less national calamity. It was not until that evening, by which time the forecast tracks started pointing to the Louisiana–Mississippi border and Governor Kathleen Blanco declared a state of emergency, that citywide attention turned to the heightening threat.

With Katrina a strengthening Category 3 storm and the notoriously divergent computer models now all ominously concurring on a Louisiana landfall, the central Gulf Coast population finally mobilized on Saturday. Emergencies were declared at the state level in Mississippi and the federal level in Louisiana, something rarely done before a disaster strikes. Officials activated the complex contraflow evacuation plan, allowing motorists to utilize incoming interstate lanes to flee the New Orleans metropolitan area. Many departed Saturday; more left Sunday, August 28, when the system strengthened to Category 4 and Category 5 levels within five hours.

By late Sunday morning, with Katrina's winds hitting 175 miles per hour, nearly all qualified observers confirmed a New Orleans–area landfall. Mayor C. Ray Nagin ordered a mandatory evacuation of the city, though no one seemed to know exactly what that meant and many could not comply even if they wanted to.

The evacuation window had all but closed by Sunday night, as the initial feeder bands whisked over the city; the only choices now were to ride it out at home or take refuge in the Superdome. Roughly 100,000 New Orleanians—one in every four to five—remained in the city, and of those approximately 15,000 lined up outside the Superdome, expecting at least a safe if uncomfortable night in this shelter of last resort. A solemn and profoundly troubled air prevailed among the reporters and authorities on the local news stations that evening. No one could believe that the proverbial Big One, the topic of endless planning scenarios and stern authoritative admonitions, the butt of countless doomsday jokes and glib clichés, was finally upon New Orleans, all within a summer weekend.

Overnight, Hurricane Katrina's low barometric pres-

New Orleans ■ Devastating the Deltaic City

sure and high winds sucked up a dome of gulf water and blew it north and northwestward into the Mississippi Gulf Coast and Louisiana deltaic plain. Shallow coastal depths reverberated the vertically churning water upward, further heightening the dome-shaped, landward-moving surge. Under natural conditions, hundreds of square miles of wetlands would have absorbed or spurned much of the intruding tide. But a century of coastal erosion cost the region precious impedance, while a labyrinth of man-made navigation, oil, gas, and drainage canals served as pathways for the surge to penetrate inland. The funnel formed by the Gulf Intracoastal Waterway (GIWW) and the Mississippi River–Gulf Outlet (MR-GO) allowed Katrina's surge to swell waters 16 feet above normal levels in the circa-1920 Industrial Canal. Pressure built on the floodwalls and levees and upon the high-organic-matter soils beneath them. Seepage began to trickle into the topographical bowls on the other side.

As dawn broke and the system approached shore, waters began to overtop the GIWW guide levees in the undeveloped eastern flanks of the city and the MR-GO guide levees behind the Bayou Bienvenue marshes north of St. Bernard Parish and the Lower Ninth Ward. Shortly after, a breach—that is, a structural failure, as opposed to overtopping—formed in the western floodwall of the Industrial Canal, sending saltwater into the streets of the Upper Ninth Ward. A similar leak developed on the 17th Street Outfall Canal, wetting adjacent streets in Lakeview.

Hurricane Katrina made landfall at 6:30 a.m. over Louisiana's Barataria Basin, between Grand Isle and the mouth of the Mississippi. The eye's center passed over the river towns of Empire and Buras, then the eastern St. Bernard Parish community of Hopedale, about 25 miles east of downtown New Orleans. The coiling mass of storm clouds spanned from central Louisiana to western Florida; the outermost feeder bands stretched from the Texas hill country to the Georgia coast, from the Yucatán to the Appalachians.

Although Katrina's wind speeds had abated to Category 2 levels and lower, its storm surge retained momentum from the earlier Category 5 status. Gulf waters swelled 10 to 30 feet above normal sea level, inundating 200 miles of coastline across four states. Lake Pontchartrain's waters swelled to almost nine feet above normal, while the Mississippi River, which had been gauged at a typically low late-summer stage of about four feet above sea level, rose to nearly 16 feet and spilled over laterally into lower Plaquemines Parish.

Pressure mounted on the soft marsh soils beneath the Industrial Canal's floodwalls. The concrete-encased steel sheet pilings did not penetrate the earth deeply enough to curtail the seepage. Finally, between 7:00 and 7:30 a.m., two gigantic sections on the Lower Ninth Ward side, spanning more than 200 and 800 feet respectively, caved in from below. A torrent of saltwater 14 feet above normal levels gushed into a neighborhood that lay as low as four feet below sea level. High-velocity rapids knocked houses off their pilings, blew down walls, and sent residents scrambling to their attics or roofs if they could—or else to a terrifying death drowning in their own homes.

What the Lower Ninth Ward experienced first, St. Bernard Parish experienced moments later: Both communities—despite the racial and class tensions that had divided them for a generation—shared the same hydrological basin and the same sad fate. Floodwaters deepened when overtopping from MR-GO, as well as widespread disintegration of its worthless guide levee, delivered additional water into the basin from the north. Levee failures had turned a weakening, off-target storm into an unfurling catastrophe, and it was not yet midmorning.

The same combination of multiple overtopping and breaching that flooded basins south of the GIWW and MR-GO navigation canals proceeded to occur on their north side. By 9:00 a.m., most of low-lying New Orleans East and its vast acreage of circa-1970s subdivisions—built almost entirely at grade level—lay under saltwater. Around the same time, breaches multiplied and worsened on the outfall canals connected to Lake Pontchartrain: at two spots on either side of the London Avenue Canal, at a preexisting low spot on the Orleans Avenue Canal, and at the two-hour-old leak on the 17th Street Canal, which widened into a 458-foot-long catastrophic collapse. Now Lakeview experienced the same high-velocity blast that the Lower Ninth Ward suffered earlier. The multiple failures meant that all three of Orleans Parish's major east-bank hydrological basins—the Lower Ninth Ward, New Orleans East, and the city's heart between the Industrial Canal and the Jefferson Parish line—were now filling with saltwater. St. Bernard Parish to the east fared even worse, while Jefferson Parish to the west saw rainwater and spillover from the lake accumulate in low spots because its pump operators had been evacuated for fear of their lives. Neighborhoods in Jefferson Parish's Hoey's Basin, hydrologically connected to Orleans's drainage system, suffered deep flooding as well. Swollen gulf waters would continue to pour into the metropolis's gravely compromised levee "protection" system for hours and days to come.

By late morning, Hurricane Katrina had made its second landfall near the mouth of the Pearl River along the Louisiana–Mississippi border. The Mississippi Gulf Coast towns of Waveland and Bay St. Louis, positioned in the northeastern quadrant of the storm's track, bore the full strength of Katrina's hundred-mile-per-hour winds and the maximum 29-foot-high storm surge (recorded off Biloxi, the highest ever in the region). Communities within a half mile of the coast were wiped off the face of the earth. In New Orleans, winds peeled off the white surface coating of the Superdome and broke two six-foot holes in the roof, terrifying the thousands of frightened evacuees within the darkened and sweltering interior. Denizens of higher ground who rode out the storm at home experienced the same moment-to-moment apprehension of winds rocking their houses and rattling roofs, windows, and doors. What few realized, of course, was that their fellow citizens faced not only these same fierce gusts but also deadly rising water.

The southern Mississippi landmass deprived Katrina of its warm-water fuel source, weakening the system to tropical-storm levels as it pushed inland, but not before it buffeted the southern half of the state as well as the eastern Florida parishes of Louisiana. Winds, now from a westerly direction, died down by late afternoon in New Orleans.

Many journalists, overly focused on Katrina's east-of-the-city track and diminishing intensity, mistakenly reported Monday afternoon that New Orleans, as the infamous cliché had it, "dodged the bullet." Many residents, evacuated and otherwise, went to bed prepared to return home, pick up branches, fix roofs, and resume their lives. It was not until Tuesday that they learned a jolting new truth—one that, in fact, was as

147

New Orleans ■ Devastating the Deltaic City

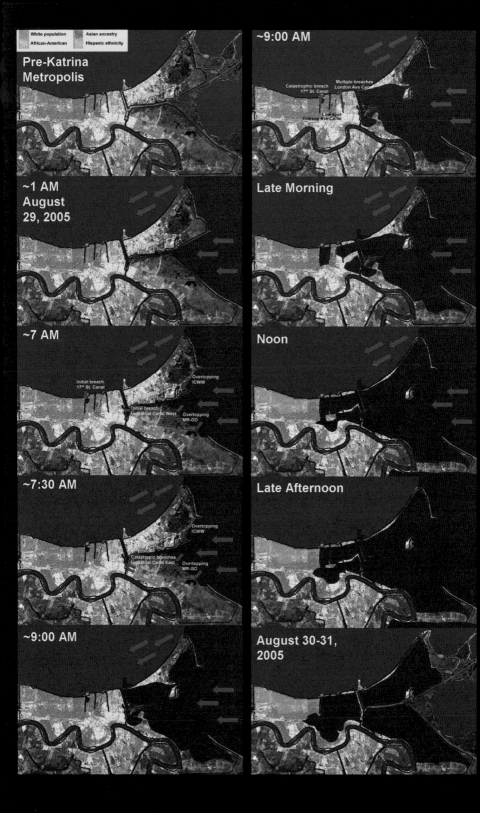

Opposite page: Chronology of Hurricane Katrina's surge, levee over-
toppings, breaches, floodwall failures, and flooding of New Orleans,
August 29–31, 2005. *Graphic by Richard Campanella based on
studies by TU-Delft (Kok, Aalberts, Maaskant, and de Wit), U.S. Army
Corps of Engineers, and NSF Independent Levee Investigative Team,
2005–09.*

old as the city itself. The flood-protection and drainage
system had not neutralized hydrology and topography;
New Orleans's ancient geographies of hazard, suppos-
edly subjugated by technology generations ago, revealed
their obscured relevance. Centuries of manipulating the
deltaic plain had allowed the enemy to get too close to
the fort. Decades of subsidence had turned the fort into
a vulnerable bowl. And years of under-engineered, cava-
lierly inspected, and poorly maintained levees—with cul-
pability at federal and local levels—had turned the bowl
into an impending catastrophe.

Social unrest fomented among the trapped, thirsty,
hungry citizenry. Looting—sometimes out of genuine
need for food and water, other times for opportunistic thievery or sheer vandalism—became so rampant
that already overwhelmed police chiefs and politicians
generally paid it lip service or ignored it entirely. Officials called for the immediate evacuation of the tens of
thousands of people who remained in the city, but no
mechanisms were in place to do so, nor were any immediately on the way. Crowds of the poorest citizens
swelled to as many as 45,000 at the damaged Superdome and at the Morial Convention Center, both
of which were completely unprepared for the crush.
Scenes stereotypical of Haiti or Bangladesh, with all
the ugliest of connotations, played out in downtown
New Orleans and were broadcast worldwide. Elders,
the infirm, and children suffered the most; some
youths exploited the chaos by looting, brawling, and
allegedly shooting at rescue workers.

Efforts to plug the 17th Street Canal breach with
helicopter drops of sand failed utterly. Only when Lake
Pontchartrain's high waters drained sufficiently back
into the Gulf of Mexico on Wednesday and Thursday did water cease entering the city, allowing for the
makeshift repair of the levees.

With Katrina's winds long gone and the floodwaters no longer rising, New Orleans now grappled with
another crisis: social disintegration. Police had to be
called off search-and-rescue missions to control pil-

New Orleans ▪ Devastating the Deltaic City

laging and chaos. Stranded crowds suffering deplorable conditions at the Superdome and later the convention center started making their way up exit ramps and onto interstates and bridges in search of any alternative to the hell below. The line between victim and perpetrator blurred in the eyes of overstressed authorities, occasionally leading to ugly confrontations and injustices. Buses to evacuate the desperate masses were few and slow in coming; the very first were able to depart for Houston on Wednesday. The shocking spectacle of a modern First World society coming apart at the seams within the borders of the wealthiest and most powerful nation on Earth led news broadcasts worldwide, repeatedly, for days and weeks.

Crises multiplied and intensified; what started as a disaster that turned into a catastrophe was now starting to look like an apocalypse. Bandits and authorities engaged in shoot-outs. Gas bubbled up from floodwaters and burned, like scenes from hell. Fires broke out citywide, and firefighters could neither reach nor douse them. Plumes of smoke rose across the skyline. An anguished Mayor Nagin, his city at the darkest moment of its history and seemingly abandoned by the nation, issued a "desperate S.O.S." to the world via an emotional interview on WWL radio. "Don't tell me 40,000 people are coming here," he raged. "They're not here. It's too doggone late. Now get off your asses and do something, and let's fix the biggest goddamn crisis in the history of this country!" Federal responses in the form of armed troops, supplies, buses, medical attention, and, most importantly, communication and coordination finally began to trickle in late Thursday. It would take a full two to three days before they could stabilize the degenerate human conditions in the ravaged city, 80 percent of which was underwater, and evacuate the stranded to Houston or elsewhere.

By this time, pundits and the national press had started to remark openly about what had been silently obvious to television viewers: The vast majority of the people stuck in the cauldron of the calamity were poor and black. A national conversation, conducted in tones ranging from cautious explanation to righteous indignation, ensued about race, poverty, history, and New Orleans society. The disaster-turned-catastrophe-turned-apocalypse was now becoming a troubling commentary about America.

The "Lost September" of 2005 will be remembered by New Orleanians—scattered nationwide and humiliatingly dependent on the kindness of strangers—as among the most difficult times of their lives. Unknowns haunted every aspect of life, from food, clothing, and shelter in the near term, to the whereabouts of loved ones, to housing, finances, education, and employment in the long term. Backdropping this angst was the greatest unknown of all: the very survival of the metropolis. Once among the most diverse and colorful assemblages of humanity on the continent, regularly predicted to rank among the world's great cities, New Orleans in September 2005 stewed in its own filth, empty, broken, moldy, and silent.

New Orleans ■ Devastating the Deltaic City

TIME LINE, SEPTEMBER–OCTOBER 2005

September 2005

With a million citizens of southeastern Louisiana and coastal Mississippi scattered nationwide, ghost city of New Orleans begins long, slow process of recovery. Waters are pumped out faster than expected, electricity returns to selected unflooded areas, and some residents return at end of month, even as rescue squads discover more dead. Impromptu morgue is set up in town of St. Gabriel; Katrina's fatalities eventually total in the 1,400–1,600 range (plus more than 200 in the rest of Mississippi). Damage to historic district on high natural levee is mostly wind driven and repairable; water-caused damage to 20th-century neighborhoods near lake and eastward into St. Bernard Parish is utterly devastating. New Orleanians, many of them now homeless and unemployed, contemplate their future and that of their crippled city.

September 23–24, 2005

Hurricane Rita, second "storm of century" in one month, strikes Louisiana–Texas border region, destroying communities on southwestern Louisiana coast and raising gulf and lake levels in New Orleans area. Some hastily repaired levees breach again, reflooding Lower Ninth Ward and adjacent areas. Nearly half of Louisiana's population is directly affected by storms; state economy and infrastructure are in shambles.

October 5, 2005

Residents are permitted back into city everywhere except Lower Ninth Ward, although only those in higher areas near river have basic utilities and services.

Mid-October 2005

Army Corps of Engineers pumps out last traces of Katrina's and Rita's surges.

Late October 2005

Hurricane Wilma, third Category 5 gulf storm in two months and most intense hurricane ever recorded in region, strikes Florida and Mexico. Together with Katrina and Rita, Wilma lends dramatic credence to emerging worldwide discourse on global warming.

152

New Orleans ■ Devastating the Deltaic City

CHAPTER 20 "PLANDEMONIUM"

Three-quarters of New Orleanians, plus nearly all residents of St. Bernard and Plaquemines parishes and some of Jefferson Parish, remained scattered nationwide in the months after the deluge, forming what became known as the New Orleans Diaspora.[1] For the lucky 100,000 or so who returned to unflooded homes, life in the postdiluvian city during that memorable autumn of 2005 proved extraordinary. Citizens realized the history they were both living and making, and moved about with a sense of purpose. Citizens worried about their neighbors and established new bonds with former strangers. They learned new lessons about their city's history, geography, and what exactly happened during the storm—including the scandalous realization of how their flood-protection infrastructure failed them. What initially appeared to be a case of an overwhelmed system proved in fact to be an under-engineered system, with insufficiently long sheet pilings beneath the floodwalls, excessive organic matter and inconsistent soil texture in levee soils, cursory inspections, and delayed improvements—all in the face of sinking soils, eroding coasts, rising seas, and seemingly more powerful storms. Scientists and policy makers nationwide began to question openly the wisdom of rebuilding a city so damaged on a deltaic plain so deteriorated. "New Orleans is one of America's great historic cities, and our emotional response . . . is to rebuild it grander and greater than before," wrote one geologist in a *Boston Globe* editorial, which later earned him an interview on CBS's *60 Minutes*. "However," he continued, "this may not be the most rational or scientifically sound response and could lead to even greater human catastrophe and financial loss in the future." His advice: "Time to move to higher ground."[2]

Such talk motivated outraged New Orleanians to engage passionately in defending their city and debating plans for the future. Everyone seemed to become a policy wonk, a disaster expert, an engineer, a geographer, and above all, an urban planner. While full-scale urban abandonment and relocation ranked as utterly unthinkable, many stakeholders embraced the notion of conceding certain low-lying neighborhoods to nature in the interest of creating a more sustainable urban core. "Shrinking the footprint," as the concept came to be called, quickly became the single most controversial urban-planning option on the table. Should the city's urban footprint, particularly its 20th-century sprawl into low-lying areas adjacent to surge-prone water bodies, be shrunk to keep people out of harm's way? Or should the entire footprint be restored, on the understanding that everyone had a right to return to their homes and that federal levee failure, not nature, ultimately caused—or rather, failed to prevent—the deluge?

That question, and others concerning flood protection, soil contamination, health, education, justice, economic recovery, and coastal restoration, drove energized public discourse in the autumn of 2005. To address these issues, Mayor C. Ray Nagin formed on September 30 the Bring New Orleans Back (BNOB) Commission, inside what the *New York Times* described as "the heavily fortified Sheraton Hotel on Canal Street, a building surrounded [by] beefy private security guards armed with weapons."[3] Committees and subcommittees tackled a wide range of topics, but it was the footprint question that inspired the most passionate debate. *Are they going to close down my neighborhood?* Subsequent public meetings with capacity crowds and long lines of testifiers indicated how heavily that question weighed on everyone's mind. The BNOB Commission brought in members of the Urban Land Institute (ULI) to study the matter, hold a public hearing, and issue recommendations. "In a city that has seen a resurgence of civic activism" since Katrina, wrote *The Times-Picayune*,

> more than 200 people attended the [ULI] meeting to voice their opinions about what shape New Orleans should take in the future. The resounding refrain: Learn from our history. Many residents told the 37-member Urban Land Institute panel to use the original footprint of the city—along the Mississippi river and its high ridges—as a guide for land use.[4]

Those 200 people, however, mostly resided on those same high ridges they recommended for prioritization. Residents of low-lying areas, which mostly flooded, numbered few at the meeting, but nevertheless they managed to engage through their city council representatives. Their stance, shared by many in higher areas, was firm: Everyone has a right to return; the entire city will come back; the urban footprint will remain precisely as before the storm.

When the ULI finally issued its recommendations to the BNOB Commission—via a long PowerPoint presentation that was at once wordy and carefully worded—it gently advocated footprint shrinkage through the allocation of recovery resources first to the highest and least-damaged areas, and only later to the depopulated flooded region. The news hit the front page of *The Times-Picayune* in the form of an intentionally confusing map of three purple-shaded "investment zones," in which Investment Zone A, despite its optimistic label, was recommended for, at best, delayed rebuilding, and possibly for conversion to green space.[5]

The word-smithing and map-smithing fooled no one. "Don't Write Us Off, Residents Warn; Urban Land Institute Report Takes a Beating," scowled the headlines after the recommendations sunk in. The article continued, "Elected officials and residents . . . responded with skepticism and, at times, outright hostility to a controversial proposal to eliminate their neighborhoods from post-Katrina rebuilding efforts." Even Mayor Nagin, the newspaper noted, said he was reserving judgment on whether to abandon some of the lowest-lying ground, though he "reiterated his intention to ultimately 'rebuild all of New Orleans.'"

> [City Council member Cynthia] Willard-Lewis spoke with particular disdain for ULI's "color-coded maps" which divide the city into three "investment zones:" areas to be rehabilitated immediately, areas to be developed partially, or areas to be re-evaluated as potential sites for mass buyouts and future green space. Those maps, she said, are "causing people to lose hope" and others to stay away.[6]

Indicating the reductionist power of maps—a reoccurring theme in the footprint debate—another councilwoman, "noting that she was wearing a pink blouse . . . said sarcastically that she should have worn purple,

155

the map color used by ULI for sections of the city that suffered the worst flood damage."[7]

Mayor Nagin found himself in a dilemma of his own, since the ULI offered its advice specifically for the benefit of his BNOB Commission. He assured agitated citizens that "once the recommendations are finalized . . . it will be up to the commission members and the community to 'evaluate it, kick the tires, say we like this and we don't like this.'"[8]

Kick it they did. The ULI report ratcheted up civic engagement in postdiluvian New Orleans markedly. It, as well as a similar consultation from the Philadelphia-based design firm Wallace, Roberts & Todd (WRT), became grist for further rounds of highly attended and increasingly polemical BNOB Commission meetings during December and January.

Finally, on January 11, 2006, the Urban Planning Committee of the BNOB Commission unveiled its final recommendations. Like the ULI, the group (sometimes referred to as the Land Use Committee) communicated its findings through a hefty PowerPoint presentation, rather than traditional printed methods. Entitled "Action Plan for New Orleans: The New American City," the 69-page presentation's dizzying array of proclamations, factoids, bulleted lists, graphics, and platitudes seemed eager to placate all sides while sacrificing lucidity in the process. Audience members hungry for a clear answer to the footprint question grew agitated at the recommendation of a moratorium on building permits for certain heavily damaged neighborhoods until May 2006. During those four months, residents themselves would have to demonstrate their neighborhood's "viability"— a requirement that cleverly placed the burden of proving neighborhood wherewithal on the backs of the most vocal full-footprint advocates. Further insight on the BNOB Commission's position on the footprint question came halfway through the presentation, in the form of a map entitled "Parks and Open Space Plan." It depicted Orleans Parish with the usual cartographic overlays of street networks and water bodies. At the bottom of its legend was a dashed-green-line symbol indicating "Areas for Future Parkland," which corresponded to a series of six large perforated circles sprinkled throughout certain low-lying residential neighborhoods.[9]

The next morning, The Times-Picayune featured the map on its front page. The newspaper's adaptation transformed the dashed circles, which cartographically suggested a certain level of conjecture and abstraction, into semi-opaque green dots labeled as "approximate areas expected to become parks and greenspace." The green dots spanned so much terrain with such apparent cartographic confidence that many readers interpreted them to represent discrete polygons, rather than dimensionless abstractions merely suggesting the possibility of some new neighborhood parks. *If my house lies within those green dots*, readers reasoned, *it will be "green spaced" into wetlands.*

Just as citizens in November seized upon the ULI's "purple investment zone" map as the parapraxis of that organization's underlying footprint philosophy, they now pointed to the "Green Dot Map" as the Freudian slip of the BNOB Commission. The response was livid. Said one man to committee chairman Joseph Canizaro, whose day job as a major real estate investor was not viewed as coincidental by skeptical citizens, "Mr. Joe Canizaro, I don't know you, but I hate you. You've been in the background trying to scheme to get our land."[10]

"4 MONTHS TO DECIDE," blared *The Times-Picayune* headline, "Nagin panel says hardest hit areas must prove viability; City's footprint may shrink."[11] The infamous Green Dot Map entered the local lexicon, even as it motivated residents of heavily damaged neighborhoods to commence demonstrating viability and saving their neighborhoods. *Green space*, a benign notion elsewhere in urban America, became dirty words in postdiluvian New Orleans.

What ensued, starting in late January 2006, was one of the most remarkable episodes of civic engagement in recent American history. Scores of grassroots neighborhood associations and civic groups formed organically, sans professional expertise and usually with zero funding. Websites went online, e-mails were circulated, impromptu venues were arranged, and signs popped up on once-flooded lawns: "Broadmoor Lives!" "I Am Coming Home!" "I Will Rebuild!" "I Am New Orleans!" One association in the heavily flooded Lake Bullard neighborhood, lacking a decent venue but not an ounce of determination, demurely asked attendees to "bring their own chairs" to the group's next meeting.[12] Despite their tenuous life circumstances and other responsibilities, New Orleanians by the thousands joined forces with their neighbors and volunteered to take stock of their communities; document local history, assets, resources, and problems; and plan solutions for the future.

So many grassroots neighborhood planning groups formed that umbrella associations arose to coordinate them. One, the Neighborhood Partnership Network, listed at least 70 fully active neighborhood organizations within Orleans Parish alone, while others in poorer areas strove to coalesce.[13] Their names formed a veritable "where's where" of famous New Orleans places—French Quarter Citizens Inc., Audubon Riverside Neighborhood Association, Bouligny Improvement Association, Faubourg St. Roch Improvement Association, Algiers Point Association—but also included less-famous modern subdivisions more likely to occupy lower ground and suffer higher flood risk: Lake Bullard Homeowners Association Inc., Venetian Isles Civic and Improvement Association, Lake Terrace Neighborhood Property Owners Association. In some cases, such as the stellar Broadmoor Improvement Association, professional help arrived from outside (Harvard University), and funding aided the planning process. Many associations eventually produced fine neighborhood plans and, perhaps more importantly, empowered people to meet their neighbors and learn about their environs to degrees unimaginable a year earlier.

158

One crude way to measure New Orleanians' intense new interest in planning is to compute the number of times the terms *civic association* and *neighborhood association* appeared in *Times-Picayune* articles or announcements, as queried through the LexisNexis news database. Before the storm, when roughly 450,000 to 455,000 people lived in the city, those keywords appeared at a steady pace of 40 to 45 times per month. That rate dropped to zero during the Lost September of 2005 but returned to normal by early 2006, despite the dramatic drop in population. After January 2006— when the Green Dot Map inadvertently kick-started the grassroots planning effort—the terms appeared over 100 times per month before stabilizing by summertime at around 70 per month. When normalized for population differences, neighborhood associations were literally making news in post-Katrina New Orleans at least four times, and up to seven times, the rate of antediluvian times—*despite* the new hardships of life in the struggling city.[14] A statistical sampling of 362 meeting announcements posted in *The Times-Picayune* between November 2005 and April 2007 (from a total of more than a thousand) revealed that fully 48 percent represented neighborhood association meetings, and another 19 percent came from planning-oriented civic groups unaffiliated with specific neighborhoods.[15]

In an editorial on "the Curse of the Green Dot," *Times-Picayune* columnist Stephanie Grace reflected on the episode. "You know the Green Dot," she reminded her readers.

> In a move that will go down as one of the great miscalculations of post-Katrina planning, [the ULI and BNOB Commission] designated the off-limits areas with green dots. [Residents] saw, for the first time, that their neighborhoods could be slated for demolition. To say they didn't take the news well is an understatement. "People felt threatened when they saw the green dot," LaToya Cantrell, president of the Broadmoor Improvement Association, would say months later. "All hell broke loose." . . . City Councilwoman Cynthia Willard-Lewis, who represents the hard-hit Lower 9th Ward and Eastern New Orleans, said the green dots made many of her African-American constituents flash back to the civil rights era, thinking they would need to fight for equal access all over again. *The maps, she said soon after they were unveiled, "are causing people to lose hope."*[16]

Ironically, the very recommendations that motivated grassroots associations to form—the Green Dot Map, the permit moratorium, and the threat of green spacing if neighborhood viability was not demonstrated by May 2006—ended up torpedoing the very commission that issued them. Mayor Nagin, embroiled in a nationally watched reelection campaign, rejected the politically volatile advice of his own BNOB Commission. Fatally undermined despite its worthwhile contributions beyond the footprint issue, the commission disbanded unceremoniously. Footprint shrinkage became a radioactive topic among the mayoral candidates; anyone who supported the concept risked losing the votes of tens of thousands of flood victims. Engaged citizens and their representatives had, for better or worse, yelled the footprint debate off the table.

After Mayor Nagin cinched reelection in the mayoral campaign, the great footprint debate largely disappeared

159

from public discourse. His laissez-faire repopulation and rebuilding stance, which was more of a default position than an articulated strategy, answered the footprint question by saying, in essence, *let people return and rebuild as they can and as they wish, and we'll act on the patterns as they fall in place.* Federal agencies bore responsibility as well: FEMA's updated Advisory Base Flood Elevation maps, which drive flood insurance availability and rates, turned out to be largely the same as the old 1984 maps. This seemingly communicated federal endorsement, as well as actuarial encouragement, to home owners deliberating on whether to rebuild in low-lying areas. Federal Road Home monies imparted no special incentive to do otherwise, and no federal compensation fund awaited those home owners and businesses that would have been affected by a hypothetical decision to shrink the city's footprint.

The entire city *could* come back, but how that city would look and function still remained an open question. Additional planning efforts—by the City Council–sponsored, Miami-based Lambert/Danzey consultants and by the foundation-supported Unified New Orleans Plan (UNOP)—provoked more civic engagement from meeting-weary New Orleanians during late 2006. The UNOP's "Citywide Strategic Recovery and Rebuilding Plan" plus numerous district plans hit the streets in draft form in early 2007, about the same time that Mayor Nagin appointed renowned disaster-recovery expert Dr. Edward Blakely as chief of the city's Office of Recovery Management. In March 2007, "Recovery Czar" Blakely unveiled yet another plan—of 17 "re-build," "re-develop," and "re-new" nodes throughout the city, marking spots for intensive infrastructure investment. Strikingly more modest and focused than the grandiose and sometimes radical visions of earlier plans, Blakely's plan aimed

> to encourage commercial investment—and with it stabilize neighborhoods—rather than defining areas that are off-limits to rebuilding. One such previous plan, advanced in early 2006 by Mayor Ray Nagin's Bring New Orleans Back Commission and backed by the widely respected Urban Land Institute, drew howls from residents who found their neighborhoods represented on maps by green dots that denoted redevelopment as perpetual green space.[17]

New Orleans ■ "Plandemonium"

Once again, citizens convened to discuss and debate this latest proposal and how it may or may not relate to the earlier plans of UNOP, Lambert/Danzey, the numerous neighborhood associations, the BNOB Commission, WRT, and the ULI. Some wags described the parallel, overlapping, and sometimes competing planning efforts as "plandemonium." Citizens grew cynical, not because of lack of commitment, but because too many soft promises and uncoordinated efforts chased too few of the hard resources and inspirational leadership needed for genuine problem solving.

Despite the heroic civic engagement demonstrated by thoughtful and intelligent New Orleanians during a very busy and stressful era, the plandemonium of postdiluvian New Orleans faces daunting odds of ever bearing fruit. History indicates that in the wake of urban disasters, the most ambitious and revolutionary rebuilding plans usually suffer the greatest likelihood of failure. Victims of trauma seek normalcy and a return to pretraumatic conditions; the last thing they want is more change. Attempts to instigate radical change after a disaster are viewed by victims as, at best, a misallocation of resources that ought to be going to them—or, at worst, as opportunistic scheming by sinister forces at their expense. Footprint renegotiation represented the most radical plan of all, and despite its compelling logic it suffered resounding defeat.

The defeat stemmed from the fact that Katrina's flood did not by any means wipe the slate clean. The antecedent urban layers in the flooded zones—including land title, property value, commercial investments, social networks, and personal attachments—were in fact inscribed deeply and survived easily. In the absence of generous and immediate compensation for the loss of all those prior investments, most flooded home owners—who understandably worried about *tomorrow*, not the distant and theoretical future—naturally gravitated to the default option of simply rebuilding in place. Local politicians, unable to guarantee an alternative and fearful of retribution at the polls if they proposed one, heard the "keep the footprint" consensus loud and clear and acted accordingly. Anti-shrinkage advocates cinched their victory by pointedly reminding critics that federal levee failure, not Hurricane Katrina per se, caused—or more accurately, failed to prevent—the flooding. What they ignored was the inconvenient geological truths beyond, and beneath, those breached levees.

The Katrina catastrophe inspired high levels of civic engagement in urban planning. Here citizens contribute to the Unified New Orleans Plan (UNOP) in late 2006. One lesson learned from the postdiluvian "plandemonium": The grander and more radical the plan, the more likely it is to fail. *Photograph by Richard Campanella, 2006.*

In most cases, momentum from the past is good for landscapes and cityscapes. It creates value, generates wealth, and makes places distinctive and interesting: Witness New Orleans's colorful street names, pedestrian-scale neighborhoods, and vast inventory of historical structures. But occasionally that momentum leads a community down a troubled path, in this case toward geological and environmental unsustainability.

The footprint controversy represented a genuine dilemma, with sound arguments and unpleasant consequences on either side. Dilemmas demand decisions—difficult choices—or else they persist and usually worsen. New Orleans's great footprint debate concluded when officials and society at large decided not to make the difficult choice of urban shrinkage. By 2009, four years after the flood, a population of at most 350,000 occupied a cityscape designed for well over 600,000.

The aftermath of this catastrophe, as often happens, may become the prelude to the next.

TIME LINE, 2006–2007

Fall 2006

Cityscape of flooded region is sprinkled with FEMA trailers, which reach their peak numbers a year after storm. Nearly 19,000 white tin boxes dot Orleans Parish, plus more than 20,000 in adjacent areas, offering flood victims convenient but cramped places to dwell as they repair their homes. Progress in rebuilding and concerns over formaldehyde cut trailer usage in half by early 2008.

2006–07

Army Corps of Engineers erects temporary closable gates at mouths of outfall canals to prevent repeat of surge-induced levee breaches during Katrina. Long recommended by Corps but resisted locally for fear of inhibiting canals' ability to remove runoff, gates represent significant improvement in flood protection for lakeside areas. Special bypass pumps are installed to allow for rainwater runoff removal if gates are closed for impending storm.

**Late 2006–
Early 2007**

With returning citizens comes a small but extremely violent number of criminals, who renegotiate flood-affected drug-distribution networks and gangster turf. While the city's returned population doubles between last quarters of 2005 and 2006, murders and overall violent crimes increase nearly six-fold. Murders of two particularly noteworthy citizens—a black male music teacher and a white female filmmaker—incite a massive March Against Crime on January 11, 2007.

2006–07

Canal Street is refurbished with granite sidewalks, palm trees, and other improvements, with aim of restoring artery's commerce and grandeur.

2006–07

Storm-related bankruptcies, lack of affordable housing, and influx of migrant workers contribute to burgeoning homeless population. Closure of downtown shelters shifts geography of homelessness to beleaguered Ozanam Inn on Camp Street, "the Wall" at foot of Elysian Fields, and a makeshift encampment under Duncan Plaza gazebo. Squatter colony of over 150 homeless people camped immediately outside City Hall forms striking statement on social problems of postdiluvian city.

163

New Orleans ▪ "Plandemonium"

Outfall canals draining runoff into Lake Pontchartrain remained ungated and open to gulf storm surges because local authorities worried that closing them in the face of oncoming storms would diminish their ability to pump rainwater out of the city. That policy was reversed after Hurricane Katrina's surge ruptured multiple floodwalls along those canals in August 2005. The Army Corps has since erected temporary floodgates at the mouth of each canal, with bypass pumps to eject runoff if and when the gates close. *Photograph by Richard Campanella, 2007.*

2007

Louisiana Road Home Program distributes billions of federal dollars to Katrina flood victims: maximum $150,000 per eligible home owner (based on home value), minus insurance settlements and FEMA grants. Home owners suffering greater than 50 percent damage opt to repair or rebuild in place; sell to state and purchase another home in Louisiana; or sell to state and not remain a home owner in Louisiana. Lengthy and slow-moving paperwork process enrages citizenry, delays rebuilding decisions, and dooms Gov. Kathleen Blanco's reelection efforts. Basing grants on home value rather than rebuilding costs hurts home owners in poor neighborhoods, a situation not remedied until late 2009.

2007–Present

Plan for gigantic medical complex involving new Louisiana State University (LSU) and Veterans Affairs (VA) hospitals promises economic development and health care for city but threatens demolition of nearly 30 blocks of historic Third Ward near intersection of Canal and South Galvez streets. Movement to reopen Charity Hospital and cluster new facilities within existing medical district footprint grows during 2008–09 but faces increasingly long odds.

Summer 2007

Three key entities—Army Corps of Engineers, New Orleans Sewerage and Water Board, and Jefferson Parish—agree to relocate pumping stations for the 17th Street, Orleans, and London Avenue outfall canals from their historical inland locations, which marked the city's edge when they were installed a century before, to new, higher lakefront locations. This would keep them out of flood-prone lowlands, allow outfall canals to flow below grade without floodwalls, and enable pumps to continue operating even when new storm gates are closed during high water. Plan, however, is extremely costly and disruptive.

Late 2007

Localism enjoys rare victory over national and global forces as Thibodaux-based Rouses grocery chain, known for its Louisiana foods and regional suppliers, takes over Sav-a-Center supermarket outlets. Change shifts city's food retail industry back into local hands, a position once enjoyed by locally owned Schwegmann's until Winn-Dixie and Wal-Mart moved into market in late 1990s and early 2000s.

2007–Present

Army Corps of Engineers embarks on $15 billion overhaul of region's flood protection—renamed risk reduction—system by 2011, engineered for storms with 1 percent chance of occurring in any given year. "Hundred-year protection plan" entails gating of outfall canals, rock barrier closing MR-GO, 1.8-mile-long barrier of "soldier pilings" across GIWW and MR-GO funnel, raising of existing levees to account for rising seas and subsidence, construction of new levees, installation of pumping stations to remove runoff while gates are closed, and reinforcement of weak spots in existing floodwalls and levees. Environmental assessment process is streamlined and contracts are arranged on a design-build basis, to enable completion by 2011. Project sends Army Corps of Engineers on regionwide search for 100 million cubic yards of clay.

165

New Orleans ■ "Plandemonium"

Cultural geographies of New Orleans. *Montage and most photographs by Richard Campanella, 2000–09.*

2007–Present New housing technologies in flood-affected zones alter city's inventory of building methods. Advances in stick-built (wooden frame) houses make timber more resistant to termites, mold, and wind; new poured-on-site concrete walls provide additional strength and insulation; *green building* becomes trendy buzz phrase. Modular homes, built off-site in factories and assembled rapidly on location, reduce costs but also design options, while circumventing local craftsmen. Stylistically, debate rages between Modernists and traditionalists on whether postdiluvian city should exhibit latest international architectural trends or respect traditional local aesthetics. Lakeview in particular experiments with wide range of building styles, types, sizes, and heights.

November 8, 2007 Louisiana enjoys productive day in Washington. Passage of Water Resources Development Act over presidential veto deauthorizes MR-GO Canal while authorizing (but not yet appropriating) about $7 billion for Louisiana coastal restoration, levee construction, and related projects. Same-day passage of defense-spending bill allocates $3 billion toward shortfall in Road Home monies, ensuring home owners will be reimbursed for federal government–caused flood damages.

Late 2007 Records from 2003 and 2007 gubernatorial elections reveal that black voters in Orleans Parish declined by more than 54 percent (84,584 to 38,738), while white voters declined by 27 percent (46,669 to 33,937). Studies show that New Orleans will remain majority African American but by slimmer margin than before storm.

167

December 20, 2007 Amid loud protests and national media attention, City Council and mayor unanimously approve razing and rebuilding of C. J. Peete, St. Bernard, B. W. Cooper, and Lafitte housing projects. Subsequent demolitions during 2008–09 put to rest city's most controversial issue since footprint debate of 2005–06.

New Orleans ▪ "Plandemonium"

CHAPTER 21   REPOPULATING THE DELTAIC CITY

The repopulation of postdiluvian New Orleans defies easy measure.[1] Residents living between places—repairing their homes during the day, for example, and returning nightly to apartments or relatives' houses in neighboring areas—plus temporarily broken-up families, transient workers, homeless people, and incoming rebuilding professionals all conspire to make the city's post-Katrina population and demographics hotly contested numbers. Most observers generally agree that the summer 2005 Orleans Parish population of between 450,000 and 455,000 dropped to nearly zero immediately after the flood, then rose to roughly 100,000 by year's end, to 200,000 on the first anniversary of the storm, 300,000 on the second anniversary, 320,000 on the third anniversary, and around 340,000 by summer 2009. When graphed, these figures depict a population recovery curve with a steep upward slope in the first year, which proceeds to level out and stabilize in subsequent years, though at levels different from before the trauma. This same flattening-curve pattern—not quite normal but "new normal"—may be seen in most other rebuilding metrics, from business reopenings to building permits to public school enrollments. Depending on individual circumstances, "new normal" became the prevailing narrative of New Orleanians around two to three years after the catastrophe—even as tens of thousands of homes remained blighted, and heavily damaged neighborhoods fought to regain half their antediluvian populations.

Indeed, the laissez-faire rebuilding decision inevitably drove what the ULI had dubbed a "jack-o'-lantern" pattern of erratic, piecemeal repopulation. The expression likened a cityscape of empty lots next to renovated houses next to blighted houses to the gap-toothed grin carved into a Halloween pumpkin. The "teeth" were irregularly interspersed not only horizontally among gaps but vertically as well because new homes were raised on piers to varying heights depending on when residents secured rebuilding permits and what FEMA regulations were in place at the time. New homes differed stylistically as well: Some owners opted for historicity, others for functionality, still others for opulence, economy, Modernism, or environmental sustainability.

The level of flood damage and pre-Katrina socioeconomics generally drove the geography of recovery. Affluent, unflooded areas saw nearly all their residents return by early 2006, while at the opposite end of the spectrum, poor, severely flooded areas remained only 10 to 20 percent repopulated into 2009. Most other areas, ranging from working-class lightly flooded areas to middle-class deeply flooded zones, by 2009 had returned to between half and two-thirds of their pre-Katrina population—though not necessarily with the same residents.

Occurring between decennial censuses, the Katrina catastrophe spawned a frustrating urban-planning challenge: lack of hard data on population, demographic composition, and spatial distribution. Estimates came from surveys, electricity usage, and postal service data, particularly on households receiving mail. Households, of course, do not correspond neatly to population, because a single-person apartment counts the same as a large family's home. Nevertheless, because these data are aggregated at the block level, they allow mapping and measuring of detailed residential settlement patterns.

As of June 2009, a total of 154,579 households were receiving mail in Orleans Parish. That was 24 percent fewer than in June 2005 but nearly 6 percent more than in June 2008—a slight uptick in the otherwise stabilizing population recovery curve.

How have those households shifted their occupancy of the cityscape? One way to answer this question is by determining the population centroid—the theoretical center of balance around which people are evenly distributed. For example, the population centroid of the United States in 1790 was in Maryland; two centuries of westward migration moved it to southern Missouri. Throughout the 1800s, New Orleans's population centroid edged slightly upriver from its original location in the central French Quarter, as the city spread predominantly uptown. In the 1900s, it shifted lakeward, as drainage allowed urbanization to spread into the lakeside swamps. Later in the 1900s, the centroid edged eastward, as people moved across the Industrial Canal into eastern Orleans Parish. By 2005, the centroid of households receiving mail throughout the east bank of Orleans Parish was located around the intersection of North Miro and Kerlerec streets, just off Esplanade Avenue in the Seventh Ward.

Four years after Katrina, that lakeward, eastward trend had reversed for the first time in the city's history. The 2009 centroid moved six blocks closer to the river and three blocks westward, to the intersection of North Miro and Dumaine streets in Tremé. That does not represent a huge shift, considering the post-storm visions of a smaller urban footprint. But the reversed direction is nevertheless notable. The reason behind it: Lower-lying areas to the north and east, which were closer to surge-prone canals and the storm path, flooded deeply during Katrina and have struggled to regain population, while in higher neighborhoods toward the river people returned more quickly and in higher numbers. The fact that the eastern half of the city has consistently been less affluent than the western half further beleaguers recovery in that zone.

These same factors explain why New Orleanians straddle the Industrial Canal differently today. In June 2005, 24 percent of east-bank Orleans Parish households lay east of the Industrial Canal. That figure dropped to 16 percent by June 2008 but rose to 18 percent during 2009, as more housing units in eastern New Orleans became available.

The parish population has also slightly shifted with respect to the Mississippi River. In June 2005, 11 percent of Orleans Parish households lay on the West Bank. That rose to 15 percent by June 2008 but dropped to 14 percent during the following year as more flooded east-bank homes came back on the market. Despite its lack of flood damage, the West Bank of Orleans Parish still lost nearly 1,200 households between 2005 and 2009, due in part to military transfers.

How has human geography shifted with regard to sea level? In 1900, nearly all New Orleanians lived above sea level because most homes were located on the higher ground close to the river and because the backswamp had not yet subsided below sea level. After two generations of drainage, subsidence, and urban expansion, 48 percent of the population lived above sea level in 1960. By 2000, that figure had dropped to 38 percent.

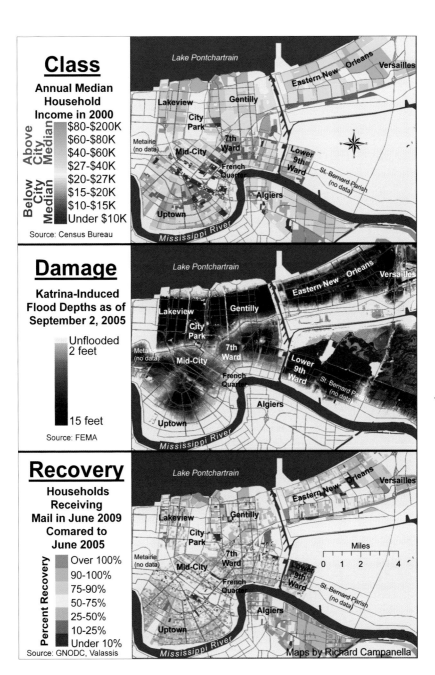

Class

Annual Median
Household
Income in 2000

Above City Median
$80-$200K
$60-$80K
$40-$60K
$27-$40K

Below City Median
$20-$27K
$15-$20K
$10-$15K
Under $10K

Source: Census Bureau

Damage

Katrina-Induced
Flood Depths as of
September 2, 2005

Unflooded
2 feet

15 feet

Source: FEMA

Recovery

Households
Receiving
Mail in June 2009
Comared to
June 2005

Percent Recovery
Over 100%
90-100%
75-90%
50-75%
25-50%
10-25%
Under 10%

Source: GNODC, Valassis

Maps by Richard Campanella

171

The geography of recovery has been strongly informed by neighborhoods' predisaster socioeconomic status and the level of damage inflicted by the disaster. *Maps by Richard Campanella based on data from U.S. Census, FEMA, and Greater New Orleans Community Data Center / Valassis, Inc.*

New Orleans ▪ Repopulating the Deltaic City

The flood reversed the century-long migration into lower areas. Lacking census data until 2010, we must switch metrics from population to households receiving mail to measure the shift. By March 2008, 54 percent of households receiving mail were located above sea level compared to 43 percent just before the storm. As flooded neighborhoods recovered, however, that percentage dropped by June 2009 to 51 percent living above sea level. Like the city itself, New Orleanians now roughly straddle the level of the sea—half above, half below.

How have demographics changed? This will be answered by the 2010 census. Recent surveys indicate that New Orleans remains majority African American, but the percentage dropped from 68–70 percent before the storm to around 61 percent in 2009. The electorate is closer to fifty-fifty, probably slightly majority black. The Latino population has increased markedly, although this population is particularly difficult to estimate. A small but high-profile group of young professionals has also arrived. Combine these trends with the departure of many native-born citizens, and we can expect a decline in New Orleans's nativity rate, which was the highest in the nation in 2000 (77.4 percent according to the Census).

Surveys also indicate that the poor, seniors, and other vulnerable groups returned in disproportionately lower numbers. The same may be said of renters, particularly those in the subsidized public-housing projects now undergoing reconstruction. The displacements have made post-Katrina New Orleans, statistically speaking, a wealthier city, with higher income levels and lower poverty rates. But it is wealthier for the wrong reasons.

New Orleans's population ranking among American cities suffered its most precipitous drop ever after Katrina. The third-largest city in America in 1840, New Orleans ranked around 10th largest in the late 1800s and stabilized at around the 15th largest between 1910 and 1960. Suburban exodus lowered it to the 31st position in 2000; now it is roughly the 60th-largest city in the nation.

A glance at a 2009 recovery map reveals a number of spots of extremely low repopulation rates. They include the high-velocity flood zone in the rear of the Lower Ninth Ward, where home owners sold out their properties to the state in the highest concentration, as well as some Section 8 multifamily housing complexes in New Orleans East. The lowest repopulation

rates—zero, in many cases—occur in the footprints of the public housing projects. These subsidized apartments were the subject of some of the most controversial urban-planning decisions at both the federal and local levels over the past two decades. The decisions stemmed from an initiative by the Department of Housing and Urban Development (HUD): Project HOPE (Homeownership and Opportunity for People Everywhere), which entailed replacing the complexes built circa 1940s–1950s with lower-density mixed income neighborhoods designed according to the sensibilities of new urbanism. Working with the Housing Authority of New Orleans (HANO), HUD razed the St. Thomas Projects in the Irish Channel during 2000–01 and erected scores of new homes and apartments reflecting traditional New Orleans styles. Some saw the HOPE idea as a long-overdue acknowledgment of a failed policy that only isolated the poor, fostered intergenerational dependency, and exacerbated social pathologies. Others viewed HOPE as an attack on underprivileged people, their sense of place in the urban fabric, and on public housing in general.

Katrina's floodwaters rendered the HOPE initiative even more controversial, in light of the postdiluvian housing shortage of 2006–07. When HUD and HANO proceeded with pre-storm plans to demolish and rebuild the C. J. Peete, St. Bernard, B. W. Cooper, and Lafitte projects, a small number of passionate activists challenged the effort as designed to deny poor, displaced African Americans their right to return to the

Restored house, raised house, razed house, ruined house: Seventh Ward streetscape four years after Hurricane Katrina. *Photograph by Richard Campanella, 2009.*

173

New Orleans ■ Repopulating the Deltaic City

city. Given the housing shortage and high homeless population at the time, their case rested upon the "bird in the hand is worth two in the bush" argument: Why destroy existing high-quality housing stock when the promise to redevelop it may not be kept and when basic financing had not yet been secured?

Those favoring the demolition pointed to 40 years of deteriorating structural and social conditions as sufficient reason to proceed with HOPE. They also noted that many refurbished HANO apartments had failed to attract tenants, indicating that displaced residents were not being denied their wish to return. While the public-housing residents in question were overwhelmingly black, both sides in the controversy claimed diversity among their supporters; the dispute explicitly did not break down along race and class lines.

The agencies agreed to stagger the demolition and reconstruction so that some residents could return as work progressed, but otherwise they did not waver in their intention to proceed with the HOPE plan. All that kept the bulldozers from rolling was the approval of the City Council and mayor. The controversy climaxed on December 20, 2007, when the council, amid violent scuffles inside and outside City Hall, unanimously voted to approve the demolitions. Mayor Nagin concurred and in early 2008 signed off on the demolition permits. By 2009, the C. J. Peete, St. Bernard, B. W. Cooper, and Lafitte projects lay mostly in rubble. Plans entail replacing the "Big Four" complexes' 4,500 units with 3,343 subsidized apartments, 900 market-rate apartments, and another 900 homes for sale.[2]

We do not yet know if the HOPE concept will improve life in the housing projects. Nor do we know if displaced denizens will return to their home city once the replacement structures are completed, nearly a half decade after Katrina. The future of New Orleans's public-housing population invokes an even greater unknown: how a sprawling cityscape originally designed for over 600,000 people will function efficiently and economically with a population and tax base of 350,000.

TIME LINE, 2007–PRESENT

2007–08

Army Corps of Engineers releases flood-risk maps showing how hundred-year protection plan, promised by 2011, will affect greater New Orleans. Basin-by-basin maps depict likely flood depths produced by medium to extreme storms under various scenarios: before Katrina, in the present day, and after 2011, with pumping capacities of 0, 50, and 100 percent. Best-case scenario indicates light flooding in some low-lying suburban subdivisions; worst-case scenario shows severe deluges in most areas that lie below sea level. Most likely scenario shows marked improvements since 2005. Maps are aimed at helping residents understand that risk is not evenly distributed spatially, nor can it be eliminated entirely. Revealingly, Army Corps of Engineers changes name of hurricane *protection* system to Greater New Orleans Hurricane and Storm Damage *Risk Reduction* System (emphasis added).

175

The Industrial Canal, which joins the Mississippi River (extreme upper left) with gulf-access navigation canals and Lake Pontchartrain, benefited New Orleans by creating ample deep-draft, private-sector dock space in the heart of the Ninth Ward. That same access, however, allowed hurricane-induced storm surges into the inner core of the bowl-shaped metropolis. The two most severe levee failures during Hurricane Katrina (2005) occurred along the Industrial Canal's floodwalls at lower right. This 2009 aerial photograph shows the piecemeal recovery of the Lower Ninth Ward (foreground) during the ensuing four years. *Photograph by Jaap van der Salm / David Waggonner,* Dutch Dialogues, *2009.*

New Orleans ▪ Repopulating the Deltaic City

2008 Thousands of flooded properties bought out from home owners through Road Home program face uncertain future. Properties are initially transferred to Louisiana Land Trust, which then gradually turns them over to New Orleans Redevelopment Authority. The authority opts to repair or rebuild for market-rate or affordable housing, to convert to green space, or to enroll in Lot Next Door program, in which home owners may purchase adjacent parcels. It must decide similar fate for 10,000 blighted houses and possibly 15,000 additional substandard houses, putting city agency in charge of momentous decisions influencing future urban geography of New Orleans.

2008 Make It Right Foundation, sponsored by actor Brad Pitt, commences building affordable green residences in Lower Ninth Ward, adjacent to now-repaired levee breach. Effort aims to reconstitute local neighborhood—with pre-storm residents whenever possible—while introducing bold new architectural designs with a prioritization for environmental sustainability and a wink to historicity. Styles are seen as inspired by some, bizarre by others. Project comes to symbolize post-storm urban sustainability movement and makes Pitt local hero.

2008–09 Plans to raze nearly 30 blocks of historic Third Ward for LSU and VA medical complex (in lieu of reopening Charity Hospital and concentrating new facilities in extant medical district) replace demolition of housing projects (2006–07) and footprint shrinkage (2005–06) as most controversial urban-planning issue in postdiluvian city.

2008–09 "Pump to the River" concept gains momentum for Hoey's Basin (between Metairie Ridge and Mississippi River) in Jefferson Parish, in which runoff would be pumped southward into river rather than northward through Orleans Parish's drainage apparatus connecting with Lake Pontchartrain. Engineers and citizens in Orleans Parish, with support from visiting Dutch flood-control experts, also advocate relocating century-old pumps to lakefront at mouths of canals, so that water is pulled and lifted into Lake Pontchartrain at the last moment, thus allowing outfall canals to flow below grade without breachable floodwalls. Proposal is widely viewed as optimal solution for draining east bank of New Orleans west of Industrial Canal but comes with highest price tag.

Winter–Spring 2008 B. W. Cooper, C. J. Peete, St. Bernard, and Lafitte housing projects are demolished and prepared for mixed income redevelopment.

New Orleans ▪ Repopulating the Deltaic City

Lessons learned from the Great Mississippi River Flood of 1927 inspired the construction of the Bonnet Carré Spillway in the 1930s. Instead of restraining the river during high water with "levees only" (as the old policy was called), the spillway accommodates the will of the river by diverting excess water into Lake Pontchartrain. Shown here is the April 2008 opening, the spillway's ninth since 1937. *Photograph by Richard Campanella, 2008.*

April 2008

As Mississippi River nears flood stage (17 feet above sea level at Carrollton Gauge), Army Corps of Engineers opens Bonnet Carré Spillway for ninth time since its installation in 1930s and first time since 1997.

**August 31–
September 1, 2008**

As citizens mark third anniversary of Katrina, Hurricane Gustav approaches Gulf Coast at angle potentially threatening entire Louisiana coastal region. Largest evacuation in American history proceeds relatively smoothly compared to 2004–05 experiences. Federal, state, and local authorities work well together; newly elected governor Bobby Jindal gains national attention for no-nonsense crisis management and fact-filled press conferences. Gustav's surge enters GIWW and MR-GO funnel, fills Industrial Canal, and overtops floodwalls, as apprehensive evacuees watch on live television. But floodwalls and levees hold, and city suffers mostly wind damage. Central Louisiana takes harder hit. Hurricane Ike threatens region again 10 days later and eventually devastates Galveston, Texas, on September 13. Delayed and confusing reentry directions for New Orleans evacuees, coupled with weeks-long disruption of commerce and education, make some residents vow never again to evacuate. Gustav demonstrates substantial improvements in city's ability to withstand storms but broaches question of whether metropolis can survive repeated full-scale mobilizations even *without* flooding.

177

New Orleans ■ Repopulating the Deltaic City

In 2007, the Army Corps of Engineers embarked on a $15 billion overhaul of New Orleans's flood protection system, designed to resist storms with a 1 percent chance of occurring in any given year. Promised by 2011, the so-called "hundred-year protection plan" entails repairing damaged levees and floodwalls, raising and constructing other levees, gating outfall canals and installing bypass pumps to remove runoff if and when gates are closed, blockading the MR-GO Canal, and erecting a barrier of 1,271 "soldier pilings" (see here in October 2009) across the funnel-shaped junction of the Gulf Intracoastal Waterway / MR-GO Canal. The Corps fast-tracked the complex projects, which ordinarily would have taken decades to plan and construct, by streamlining the environmental assessment process and arranging contracts on a design-build basis. *Photographs by Richard Campanella, 2009.*

178

2008–09

Weary of toothless urban plans and obsolete zoning ordinances, voters in November 2008 grant upcoming New Orleans Master Plan and Comprehensive Zoning Ordinance the force of law, even before it is written. Throughout 2009, City Planning Commission and Boston-based consultants Goody Clancy assemble new plan with input from experts, community groups, and previous post-Katrina plans. Unlike planning efforts elsewhere, which generally write master plan first and devise zoning and land-use ordinances afterward over a period of years, New Orleans fast-tracks both components simultaneously in a single year. Draft plan raises eyebrows for proposal to study removing Claiborne Avenue I-10 overpass; garners support from preservationists, opposition from commuters, and mixed feelings in Tremé. Final passage of master plan will follow public hearings, amendments, and approval by City Planning Commission and City Council.

2008–09

Hundreds of new apartments, including in the renovated Falstaff Brewery, open in vicinity of Tulane Avenue and Jeff Davis Parkway. Spurred by tax credits, aimed at residents of various income levels, and positioned to benefit from controversial LSU and VA hospital expansion plans, new affordable housing opportunities may increase Mid-City's population from pre-Katrina levels.

179

2009

Rock barrier at Bayou La Loutre, rising seven feet above sea level, closes MR-GO Canal to shipping and reduces damaging effects of intruding saltwater. Closer to metro area, 144-foot-long soldier pilings are hammered across 1.8-mile-wide GIWW and MR-GO funnel, to protect city from gulf storm surges. Vital components of the 2011 commitment for protection against "1 percent storms," barriers represent attempt to reverse environmental mistakes 80 years in the making.

2009

Courthouses are demolished at Duncan Plaza, ending progressive Modernist "Civic Center" vision dating to Mayor Morrison's administration of late 1950s. Mayor Nagin nearly succeeds in relocating City Hall away from Duncan Plaza as well, but City Council rejects plan. Future seat of city government remains in question.

New Orleans ■ Repopulating the Deltaic City

Summer 2009

Nature Geoscience article reports that, even if sediment loads are restored, Mississippi River will lack sufficient sediment supply to counter predicted one-meter rise in sea level during 21st century. Authors conclude that "significant drowning" of the Mississippi Delta is inevitable "because sea level is now rising at least three times faster than during delta-plain construction." Every decade of delaying massive coastal restoration "will increase the mass balance deficiency by more than a billion tons of sediment." They warn that we must "restore the delta region to a desired level of sustainability, or plan an inevitable retreat."[3]

February 2010

Within span of one remarkable weekend, New Orleanians elect new city government on Saturday and witness beloved, beleaguered Saints football team win first-ever Super Bowl on Sunday. Historic election of Mitch Landrieu as mayor, with landslide support across racial and geographical lines, is overwhelmed by citywide jubilation over Saints' exciting underdog victory. Coming in midst of Carnival season, events garner worldwide attention for city and set optimistic tone for new decade.

CHAPTER 22   DELTA URBANISM: LESSONS FROM NEW ORLEANS

What can we learn from 300 years of urbanizing the Mississippi Delta?

Delta cities are great places. The strategic natural advantages that encourage delta urbanization render culturally rich and diverse places, manifested in everything from architecture to linguistics, food, music, traditions, atmosphere, and civic spirit. Deltaic cities also usually claim tumultuous political and military histories, making them among the most fascinating places on Earth. Deltaic cities are treasure troves of the human experience, worth sustaining for their past but even more so for their current and future functions.

Deltas need freshwater and sediment. Deltas are floodplains. They are existentially tied to occasional inundations. Riverine injections of freshwater and sediment counteract the soil compaction and wave action that naturally reduce alluvial deposits. Building deltaic cities in a manner that accommodates seasonal flooding—by primarily urbanizing higher natural levees, leaving low-lying swamps and marshes undeveloped to store water, and strategically perforating riverfront levees—balances urban requirements with deltaic processes. Perforating riverfront levees means diverting the river's water and sediment (suspended load as well as bedload) out of the channel and onto adjacent wetlands, via controlled diversions, sediment siphons, and uncontrolled crevasses. Sediment dredged from navigation-impeding shoals, which develop wherever the river is diverted, should be siphoned into wetlands, not merely mobilized in the water column and dumped uselessly into the sea. Sediment may also be excavated from the bottom of nearby bays and pumped onto wetlands—dedicated dredging—to speed the land-creation process.

Strengthen existing levees, but avoid building new ones. Deltas are products of fluidity and dynamism. Humans resist such geological volatility and seek to tame it by imposing rigidity, constraint, and order upon it. Levees are the premier tool of anthropogenic control of unruly alluvial environments, and when built sturdily they succeed in reducing the nuisance of springtime floods. But they inevitably trigger sinkage of the soils behind them, particularly when accompanied by municipal drainage. They also eliminate freshwater and sediment inputs to the backswamp and marshes, compromising their ecological and geological health. *Existing* levees that protect populated areas must of course be maintained, strengthened, heightened, and regularly inspected, but *new* levees across open marsh are usually ill-advised, as they will further strangle coastal processes and continue to lure people into harm's way.

Soft edges can protect better than hard edges. New Orleans's 19th-century floods inundated only about one-tenth the population, damaged a small percentage of homes, destroyed even fewer, and hardly killed anyone. What made New Orleans resilient to those historical floods was the fact that the city's rear flank petered out softly into the backswamp; most floodwaters accumulated harmlessly in vacant lowlands while higher urbanized areas generally remained dry. It was not until humans built levees and drained and populated those lowlands that flooding became problematic there. Deltaic urbanism is safer when the "soft" protections of natural topography and marshy buffers are exploited to the maximum and the "hard" protection of levees, floodwalls, gates, and barriers are deployed only when necessary.

Where hard edges are necessary... Breaches during Hurricane Katrina revealed certain truisms about levee construction. The best levees are built of pure, cohesive clays with a minimum of organic matter and a minimum of coarse soil particles such as sand. Levee elevations must be periodically raised to account for local subsidence and sea-level rise. If floodwalls are built atop or in lieu of earthen levees, their steel sheet piling should penetrate the earth in the form of a stable T-wall, rather than the unstable I-walls lacking lateral support that Katrina's surges pushed over. Sheet piling should penetrate deeply, beyond the porous layers of peat and sand that allow seepage to pass. Floodwalls should also have con-

crete aprons on their dry sides, to prevent undermining if and when overtopping occurs. Short sheet pilings, excessive organic matter, inconsistent soil texture, insufficient height, inadequate lateral support, and unprotected shoulders were the immediate causes of most Katrina levee failures. Centuries of environmental manipulation and deltaic deterioration were the ultimate cause.

Healthy deltas need healthy valleys. Water quality, volume, sediment load, biota, and other inputs arrive at a delta from across hundreds of thousands of square miles, regardless of jurisdictional lines. Integrated management among the various basins, agencies, states, and nations that a watershed comprises is necessary to maintain the health of a delta. The New Orleans region bears a disproportionate share of the burden of basin wide environmental impacts, including dam and lock construction on sediment-bearing tributaries, diminishing sediment supply in the river; fertilizer and urban runoff, causing the hypoxic dead zone in the Gulf of Mexico; pollutants in the river, affecting drinking water supplies; and invasive species such as the zebra mussel and Asian carp.

Raised houses individualize flood protection. All structures, particularly residences, should be raised

Hard lines in soft environments: Much of the Mississippi Delta's land loss can be attributed to the excavation of oil, gas, navigation, and other man-made canals, which cause saltwater intrusion, swamp die-off, erosion, and surge funneling. Photograph by Peter Hermans/David Waggonner, Dutch Dialogues, 2009.

183

New Orleans ▪ Delta Urbanism: Lessons

on pilings or piers. This tradition prevailed in New Orleans for over 200 years, only to be abandoned after World War II in favor of cheap concrete slabs poured at grade level. Living at grade level places too much faith in flood-control and drainage infrastructure. Building above the grade empowers the individual to play a role in minimizing personal flood damage should other systems fail.

Municipal drainage comes at a cost. Draining the swamps around New Orleans helped solve the problem of insufficient living space. It also created a new problem. Water being a major component of deltaic soils, drainage caused the soil body to shrink and collapse, sending half the metropolis below sea level. Finding an aesthetic way to integrate runoff into the cityscape—through canals, as the Dutch do—or to store it in specially designed areas that double as parks when dry, restores the hydric component to the soil body and reduces subsidence rates. Storing water on the cityscape also reduces pump capacity requirements and minimizes the need to activate the pumps after every rainfall.

Pumping stations should be optimally sited. Pumping stations, which remove runoff via outfall canals into adjacent water bodies, should be located at the mouths of those canals, not at their headwaters. In this manner, runoff is pulled from throughout the city via low, below-grade outfall canals and raised at the very last moment. Such pumps can also double as canal gates, preventing outside water from intruding inland. This design eliminates the need for levees and floodwalls intruding into neighborhoods. New Orleans in the 1890s located its pumps in the middle of the area being drained, at the headwaters of the outfall canals, where they pushed runoff into Lake Pontchartrain. Decades of subsidence forced the pumps to push that runoff uphill by increasingly steeper inclines. This meant that the outfall canals had to flow above houses, requiring levees and floodwalls to contain them. It also meant that incoming storm surges penetrated the (ungated) outfall canals and dangerously raised water levels—until, finally, the point of floodwall collapse during Katrina. Most planners now agree that pumping stations should be relocated to the lakefront, as they are in Jefferson Parish and New Orleans East, which learned from New Orleans's mistake. Such a relocation would allow canals to be redesigned to flow below grade and beautified into urban amenities, as they are in Amsterdam. Financial constraints, however, currently prevent this costly correction from being enacted. There is also a concern that below-grade canals would increase subsidence rates.

Canals usually bear more costs than benefits. Deltaic cities often begin as transshipping nodes and develop into ports of national or international importance. Competition forces ports to make docking at their wharves as fast, cheap, and efficient as possible, a pressure that often justifies the excavation of navigation canals. Throughout coastal Louisiana, oil and gas companies joined the shipping industry in scoring and scouring the deltaic plain with innumerable man-made waterways. Most seemed to make sense at the time, but their long-term costs may ultimately kill this place. Canals that have proven to be more detrimental than beneficial should be barricaded with rock barriers, pilings, gates, or other devices to prevent further saltwater intrusion—and, if feasible, filled in with sediment.

Diversions alone may not be sufficient to rebuild coastal marshes. Diverting the Mississippi River out of its man-made straitjacket and allowing it to deposit its sediment-laden waters into adjacent coastal wetlands is widely viewed as fundamental to saving the Mississippi Delta. Crevasses—that is, uncontrolled diversions—are even better. But locks and dams on the western distributaries of the Mississippi River system have so radically reduced the quantity and quality of sediment reaching the delta that diversions and crevasses are no longer sufficient to restore coasts. Sediment must be actively mined from the bottom of the river and bays and siphoned into the marshes. Gravity alone will not solve this problem.

Legal issues complicate restoration efforts. Over three-quarters of the Louisiana coastal region is in private hands. Leases of adjacent water bodies for fisheries and other resources further complicate the cadastral landscape. A single coastal restoration proposal thus affects numerous parties, livelihoods, and ways of life. Coping with this complexity requires legal mechanisms, compensation funds, mitigation plans, and other creative solutions.

Expect the paradoxical in the wake of urban disasters. Planners might reasonably view the aftermath of an urban disaster as an opportunity to correct entrenched problems with ambitious and revolutionary rebuilding

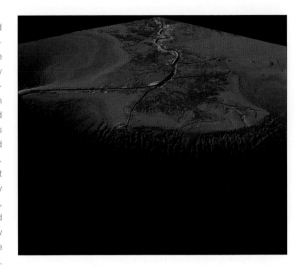

This computer-generated perspective of the active "birdfoot" delta of the Mississippi River, vertically exaggerated fortyfold for visibility purposes, derives from multibeam SONAR-based water depth measurements combined with LIDAR-based terrestrial elevation data. Riverborne sediment that once dispersed laterally throughout the deltaic plain, building up its soils and nourishing its biota, now spills out uselessly on the continental shelf (foreground). *GIS processing by Richard Campanella based on data from C&C, Louisiana Department of Natural Resources, and University of Louisiana at Lafayette.*

plans. Post-Katrina New Orleans certainly saw its share of bold urban planning visions, offered by some of the best minds in the profession. All failed, in large part because flood victims primarily sought to return to normalcy, not further tumult. Planners should expect particularly fierce resistance if their plan entails moving people out of harm's way by closing down unsustainable neighborhoods— *footprint shrinkage*, in post-Katrina parlance. In the absence of immediate and generous compensation, home owners affected by disaster will defend the one major life investment they still possess—their property—and advocate for the default plan of simply rebuilding in place, regardless of future risk.

Deltaic sustainability entails grappling with dilemmas. Whereas a problem typically ends with a solution, a dilemma usually ends with a choice—a difficult value judgment, which yields unpleasant consequences and unhappy stakeholders. Saving deteriorating deltas will mean that some human communities, despite their historical, cultural, and economic significance, will have to relocate to minimize future loss and allow aggressive coastal restoration to commence. Resistance will be passionate and often imbued with social tensions and historical distrusts. But the geophysical realities of sea-level rise demand that we make mature decisions about where and how humans inhabit deltas—or else they will be made for us.

ENDNOTES

INTRODUCTION

1. Statistics vary on the urbanization and population of the world's deltas because both deltas and cities have "soft" edges and thus a wide range of measurements depending on definitions and methodologies. These figures come from James P. M. Syvitski et al., "Sinking Deltas Due to Human Activities," *Nature Geoscience*, published online September 20, 2009, 10.1038/NGEO629, 1 (www.nature.com/ngeo/journal/v2/n10/abs/ngeo629.html); and Organization for Economic Co-operation and Development, "Ranking Port Cities with High Exposure and Vulnerability to Climate Extremes," November 2007, 12, available through www.oecd.org.

CHAPTER 1: DELTA FORMATION

1. This chapter is an updated adaptation drawn from the author's previous books, including *Bienville's Dilemma: A Historical Geography of New Orleans* (Lafayette, La.: University of Louisiana Press, 2008); *Geographies of New Orleans: Urban Fabrics Before the Storm* (Lafayette, La.: University of Louisiana Press, 2006); and *Time and Place in New Orleans: Past Geographies in the Present Day* (Gretna, La.: Pelican Publishing, 2002).

2. Samuel L. Clemens, *Life on the Mississippi* (New York: Harper & Row, 1883; repr., 1958), 4.

3. Basil Hall, *Travels in North America in the Years 1827 and 1828*, 3rd ed. (Edinburgh: Robert Cadell, and Simpkin and Marshall, 1830), 3:317–18 (emphasis added).

4. Elisée Réclus, *A Voyage to New Orleans*, ed. John Clark and Camille Martin (1855; trans., Thetford, Vt.: Glad Day Books, 2004), 42.

5. John McPhee, *The Control of Nature* (New York: Farrar, Straus and Giroux, 1989), 5.

6. D. A. Ross, *Introduction to Oceanography* (New York: Harper Collins College, 1988), 318.

7. Roger T. Saucier, *Geomorphology and Quaternary Geologic History of the Lower Mississippi Valley* (Vicksburg, Miss.: U.S. Army Engineer Waterways Experiment Station, 1994), 1:276.

CHAPTER 2: DELTA TOPOGRAPHY

1. This chapter is an updated adaptation drawn from the author's previous books, including *Bienville's Dilemma*, *Geographies of New Orleans*, and *Time and Place in New Orleans*.

2. "Letter from Father Vivier to the Society of Jesus, to a Father of the same Society," in *The Jesuit Relations and Allied Documents: Travels and Explorations of the Jesuit Missionaries in New France 1610–1791*, vol. 26, *All Missions, 1710–1756*, ed. Reuben Gold Thwaites (New York: Pagent Book Company, 1959), 213.

3. Elisée Réclus, *A Voyage to New Orleans*, ed. John Clark and Camille Martin (1855; trans., Thetford, Vt.: Glad Day Books, 2004), 50.

CHAPTER 3: SETTLING THE DELTA

1. This chapter is an updated adaptation drawn from the author's previous books, including *Bienville's Dilemma, Geographies of New Orleans*, and *Time and Place in New Orleans*.

2. Father Zenobius Membré, "Narrative of La Salle's Voyage Down the Mississippi, By Father Zenobius Membré," in *The Journeys of René-Robert Cavelier Sieur de La Salle*, ed. Isaac Joslin Cox (1905; repr., Austin, Tex.: Pemberton Press, 1968), 1:145.

3. M. Cavelier de La Salle, "Memoir of M. Cavelier de La Salle," in *On the Discovery of the Mississippi*, ed. Thomas Falconer (1680s; trans., London: Samuel Clarke, 1844), Appendix 3–4, 24–27.

4. Incredibly, La Salle's shipwreck and encampment were discovered in 1995.

5. As quoted by Tennant S. McWilliams in Pierre Le Moyne, Sieur d'Iberville, *Iberville's Gulf Journals*, ed. and trans. Richebourg Gaillard McWilliams (1700; trans., University, Ala.: University of Alabama Press, 1991), 4.

6. Le Moyne, Sieur d'Iberville, *Iberville's Gulf Journals*, 53.

7. As quoted by Marc de Villiers du Terrage, "A History of the Foundation of New Orleans (1717–1722)," *The Louisiana Historical Quarterly* 3, no. 2 (April 1920): 174 (emphasis in original).

8. Ibid.

CHAPTER 4: URBANIZING THE DELTA

1. This chapter is an updated adaptation drawn from the author's previous books, including *Bienville's Dilemma, Geographies of New Orleans*, and *Time and Place in New Orleans*.

2. Thomas Jefferys, *The Natural and Civil History of the French Dominions in North and South America* (London: T. Jefferys, 1760), 148–49.

3. A footnote in the colonist Dumont's journal, as well as a number of tertiary sources, date this hurricane to September 11, 1721, but 1722 is the more likely date.

4. Adrien de Pauger, as quoted by Samuel Wilson, Jr., *The Vieux Carre, New Orleans: Its Plan, Its Growth, Its Architecture* (New Orleans: Bureau of Government Research, 1968), 13.

5. Ibid.

6. Diron d'Artaguiette, as quoted in ibid.

7. Malcolm Heard, *French Quarter Manual: An Architectural Guide to New Orleans' Vieux Carré* (New Orleans: School of Architecture, Tulane University, 1997), 1.

8. Heloise H. Cruzat, trans., "Allotment of Building Sites in New Orleans (1722)," *The Louisiana Historical Quarterly* 7, no. 4 (October 1924): 564–65.

9. M. Dumont, "History of Louisiana, Translated from the Historical Memoirs of M. Dumont," in *Historical Memoirs of Louisiana, From the First Settlement of the Colony to the Departure of Governor O'Reilly in 1770*, ed. B. F. French (New York: Lamport, Blakeman & Law, 1853), 41.

CHAPTER 5: WHY THERE?

1. This chapter is an updated adaptation drawn from the author's previous books, including *Bienville's Dilemma, Geographies of New Orleans*, and *Time and Place in New Orleans*.
2. Readers are directed to Peirce F. Lewis's discourse on site versus situation in his classic monograph *New Orleans: The Making of an Urban Landscape* (Cambridge, Mass.: Ballinger Publishing, 1976), 17–30.
3. Francois Marie Perrin Du Lac, *Travels Through the Two Louisianas . . . in 1801, 1802, & 1803* (London: Richard Phillips, 1807), 87–88, including asterisked footnote. Despite his appreciation for New Orleans's challenges, Du Lac was not particularly impressed with the city. "New Orleans," he wrote, "does not merit a favourable description."
4. Friedrich Ratzel, *Sketches of Urban and Cultural Life in North America*, trans. and ed. Stewart A. Stehlin (1876; trans., New Brunswick, N.J.: Rutgers University Press, 1988), 196 (emphasis added).

CHAPTER 6: COLONIAL-ERA FLOOD CONTROL

1. This chapter is an updated adaptation drawn from the author's previous books, including *Bienville's Dilemma, Geographies of New Orleans*, and *Time and Place in New Orleans*.
2. Jeffrey Alan Owens, "Holding Back the Waters: Land Development and the Origins of Levees on the Mississippi, 1720–1845" (Ph.D. diss., Louisiana State University, 1999), quoted from abstract.
3. E. W. Gould, *Fifty Years on the Mississippi; Or, Gould's History of River Navigation* (St. Louis: Nixon-Jones Printing, 1889), 224–25.
4. Le Page du Pratz, *The History of Louisiana*, ed. Joseph G. Tregle, Jr. (1758; repr. of 1774 ed., Baton Rouge, La.: Louisiana State University Press, 1976), 54.
5. Capt. Philip Pittman, *The Present State of the European Settlements on the Missisippi* (1770; facsimile, Gainesville, Fla.: University of Florida Press, 1973), 10.
6. Laura L. Porteous, trans., "Governor Carondelet's Levee Ordinance of 1792," *The Louisiana Historical Quarterly* 10, no. 4 (October 1927): 513–14.
7. Stanford E. Chaillé, "Inundations of New Orleans and Their Influence on Its Health," *New Orleans Medical and Surgical Journal* (July 1882), excerpt in Tulane University Special Collections Vertical File, Flooding folder, 3.

CHAPTER 7: A RADICAL CHANGE OF DESTINY

1. This chapter is an updated adaptation drawn from the author's previous books, including *Bienville's Dilemma, Geographies of New Orleans*, and *Time and Place in New Orleans*.
2. Zadok Cramer, *The Navigator, or the Traders' Useful Guide in Navigating the Monongahela, Allegheny, Ohio, and Mississippi Rivers* (Pittsburgh: Zadok Cramer, 1806), 128.

3. Ibid.
4. Hugh Murray, *Historical Account of Discoveries and Travels in North America* (London: Longman, Rees, Orme, Brown, & Green, 1829), 426.
5. Daniel Blowe, *A Geographical, Historical, Commercial, and Agricultural View of the United States of America* (London: Edwards & Knibb, 1820), 64–65.

CHAPTER 8: UNWRITTEN RULES OF URBAN EXPANSION

1. This chapter is an updated adaptation drawn from the author's previous books, including *Bienville's Dilemma, Geographies of New Orleans*, and *Time and Place in New Orleans*.
2. The present-day Orleans–Jefferson parish line at Monticello Street also dates back to 1805 but had been changed to Felicity Street in 1812 and thence relocated throughout present-day uptown over the next six decades. Former upper boundaries of New Orleans include an old plantation line near St. Joseph Street (1797), Monticello Street (1805), Felicity Street (1812), an old plantation line between Foucher and Antonine streets (1818), Felicity Street again (1833), Toledano Street (1852), Lowerline Street (1870), and finally Monticello Street again (1874), where it remains today. Sam R. Carter, "Growth in Area: New Orleans, Louisiana," foldout map, in *A Report on Survey of Metropolitan New Orleans Land Use, Real Property, and Low Income Housing Area* (New Orleans: Works Projects Administration, Louisiana State Department of Public Welfare, and Housing Authority of New Orleans, 1941).
3. City Planning and Zoning Commission–Advisory Commission, *The Handbook to Comprehensive Zone Law for New Orleans, Louisiana* (New Orleans, 1929–33), Chap. 3, 1, Rare Book Room, Louisiana Supreme Court Law Library, New Orleans.
4. Ibid., Chap. 1, 1–2, and Chap. 3, 1.

CHAPTER 9: THE UNPLANNED STREET PLAN

1. This chapter is an updated adaptation drawn from the author's previous books, including *Bienville's Dilemma, Geographies of New Orleans*, and *Time and Place in New Orleans*.
2. Henry P. Dart, trans., "The First Law Regulating Land Grants in French Colonial Louisiana" in "The Edict of Louis XV of October 12, 1716," *The Louisiana Historical Quarterly* 14, no. 3 (July 1931): 347.
3. Toponyms such as 40-Arpent Canal and Eighty Arpent Road survive today throughout the region.
4. I borrow the term *antecedent cadaster* from the late geographer Milton Newton, Jr., *Louisiana: A Geographical Portrait* (Baton Rouge, La.: Geoforensics, 1987), 211.
5. See, for example, the City Planning and Zoning Commission's *Major Street Report* (New Orleans: City Planning and Zoning Commission, 1927).
6. Frank Haigh Dixon, *A Traffic History of the Mississippi River System, National Waterways Commission, document no. 11* (Washington, D.C.: Government Printing Office, 1909), 15.

CHAPTER 10: ANTEBELLUM FLOOD CONTROL

1. This chapter is an updated adaptation drawn from the author's previous books, including *Bienville's Dilemma, Geographies of New Orleans*, and *Time and Place in New Orleans*.
2. George E. Waring Jr., *Report on the Social Statistics of Cities, Part II: The Southern and the Western States* (Washington, D.C.: Government Printing Office, 1887), 261.
3. Wilton P. Ledet, "The History of the City of Carrollton," *The Louisiana Historical Quarterly* 21, no. 1 (January 1938): 228.
4. Stanford E. Chaillé, "Inundations of New Orleans and Their Influence on Its Health," *New Orleans Medical and Surgical Journal* (July 1882), excerpt in Tulane University Special Collections Vertical File, Flooding folder, 5.
5. Fred B. Kniffen, "The Lower Mississippi Valley: European Settlement, Utilization and Modification," *Geoscience & Man 27* (1990): 6–7.
6. Adam Hodgson, *Remarks During a Journey Through North America in the Years 1819, 1820, and 1821* (New York: Samuel Whiting, 1823), 163.
7. Joseph Holt Ingraham, *The South-West by a Yankee* (New York: Harper and Brothers, 1835), 1:78–79.
8. Hurricane Katrina's maximum flood line was also at the Bourbon-Canal intersection.
9. "The Inundation," *Daily Picayune*, June 4, 1849, evening edition, 2.
10. Stanford E. Chaillé, "Inundations of New Orleans and Their Influence on Its Health," *New Orleans Medical and Surgical Journal* (July 1882), excerpt in Tulane University Special Collections Vertical File, Flooding folder, 5, 9–12.
11. John M. Barry, *Rising Tide: The Great Mississippi River Flood of 1927 and How It Changed America* (New York: Simon & Schuster, 1997), 32–45.
12. Albert E. Cowdrey, *Land's End: A History of the New Orleans District, U.S. Army Corps of Engineers* (New Orleans: U.S. Army Corps of Engineers, 1977), 9.

CHAPTER 11: POPULATING THE ANTEBELLUM CITY

1. William Darby, *A Geographical Description of the State of Louisiana* (Philadelphia: John Melish, 1816), 186; Joseph Holt Ingraham, *The South-West by a Yankee* (New York: Harper and Brothers, 1835), 1:99; H. Didimus, *New Orleans As I Found It* (New York: Harper & Brothers, 1845), 29–30. Material in this chapter is drawn from Richard Campanella's previous books, including *Bienville's Dilemma, Geographies of New Orleans, and Time* and *Place in New Orleans*.
2. Joseph G. Tregle Jr., "Creoles and Americans," *Creole New Orleans: Race and Americanization*, ed. Arnold R. Hirsch and Joseph Logsdon (Baton Rouge, La.: Louisiana State University Press, 1992), 154–57, 164.
3. Numerical evidence of this and other ethnic geographical patterns described here briefly are presented in detail in the author's 2006 book, *Geographies of New Orleans: Urban Fabrics Before the Storm* (Lafayette, La.: University of Louisiana Press/Center for Louisiana Studies).

4. David C. Rankin, "The Forgotten People: Free People of Color in New Orleans, 1850–1870" (Ph.D. diss., Johns Hopkins University, 1976), 81; Larry Ford and Ernst Griffin, "The Ghettoization of Paradise," *Geographical Review* 69, no. 2 (April 1979): 156–57.
5. "A Kaleidoscopic View of New Orleans," *Daily Picayune*, September 23, 1843, 2.
6. Treasury Department, Bureau of Statistics, *Tables Showing Arrivals of Alien Passengers and Immigrants in the United States from 1820 to 1888* (Washington, D.C.: Government Printing Office, 1889), 108–9.
7. Ronald Van Kempen and A. Sule Özüekren, "Ethnic Segregation in Cities: New Forms and Explanations in a Dynamic World," *Urban Studies* 35, no. 10 (1998): 1631.

CHAPTER 12: POPULATING THE POSTBELLUM CITY

1. This chapter is an updated adaptation drawn from the author's previous books, including *Bienville's Dilemma, Geographies of New Orleans*, and *Time and Place in New Orleans*.
2. Dale A. Somers, "Black and White in New Orleans: A Study in Urban Race Relations, 1865–1900," *Journal of Southern History* 40, no. 1 (February 1974): 21; John W. Blassingame, *Black New Orleans, 1860–1880* (Chicago: University of Chicago Press, 1973), 60–61.
3. Peirce F. Lewis, *New Orleans: The Making of an Urban Landscape* (Cambridge, Mass.: Ballinger Publishing, 1976), 44–46; Sam R. Carter, *A Report on Survey of Metropolitan New Orleans Land Use, Real Property, and Low Income Housing Area* (New Orleans: Work Projects Administration, 1941), foldout map following p. 136.
4. Ernest W. Burgess, "The Growth of the City: An Introduction to a Research Project," in *The City*, ed. Robert E. Park, Ernest W. Burgess, and Roderick D. McKenzie (Chicago: University of Chicago Press, 1925), 47–62.
5. Paul Knox, *Urban Social Geography: An Introduction* (Essex, England: Longman Scientific & Technical and John Wiley & Sons, 1987), 256.
6. David Ward, *Cities and Immigrants: A Geography of Change in Nineteenth Century America* (New York: Oxford University Press, 1971), 106.
7. Burgess, "Growth of the City," 47–62.
8. Ernst von Hesse-Wartegg, *Travels on the Lower Mississippi, 1879–1880: A Memoir by Ernst von Hesse-Wartegg*, ed. and trans. Frederic Trautmann (Columbia, Mo.: University of Missouri Press, 1990), 161.

CHAPTER 13: DRAINING THE DELTAIC CITY

1. This chapter is an updated adaptation drawn from the author's previous books, including *Bienville's Dilemma, Geographies of New Orleans*, and *Time and Place in New Orleans*.
2. Ari Kelman, "A River and Its City: Critical Episodes in the Environmental History of New Orleans" (Ph.D. diss., Brown University, 1998), 251–53, 267.
3. "Report on the Drainage of the City of New Orleans by the Advisory Board, Appointed by Ordinance No. 8327, Adopted by the City Council, November 24, 1893," as summarized in ibid., 269.

4. George Washington Cable, "New Orleans Revisited," *The Book News Monthly* (April 1909): 564, 560, as quoted in ibid., 281.

5. City Planning and Zoning Commission, *Major Street Report* (New Orleans: City Planning and Zoning Commission, 1927), 75.

6. Sewerage and Water Board of New Orleans, *The Sewerage and Water Board of New Orleans: How It Began, the Problems It Faces, the Way It Works, the Job It Does* (New Orleans: Sewerage and Water Board of New Orleans, 1998), 9–11.

7. "New Orleans Is Getting Hotter—Increases in Temperature in Summer Attributed to the Drainage System," *Columbus Ledger-Enquirer*, Columbus, Ga., June 13, 1918, 1.

8. Gilbert Fowler White, "Human Adjustment to Floods" (Ph.D. diss., Chicago: University of Chicago Department of Geography, 1945), 2.

CHAPTER 14: TURN-OF-THE-CENTURY FLOOD CONTROL

1. This chapter is an updated adaptation drawn from the author's previous books, including *Bienville's Dilemma, Geographies of New Orleans*, and *Time and Place in New Orleans*.

2. Stanford E. Chaillé, "Inundations of New Orleans and Their Influence on Its Health," *New Orleans Medical and Surgical Journal* (July 1882), excerpt in Tulane University Special Collections Vertical File, Flooding folder, 3; E. W. Gould, *Fifty Years on the Mississippi; Or, Gould's History of River Navigation* (St. Louis: Nixon-Jones Printing, 1889), 225; John Smith Kendall, *History of New Orleans* (Chicago: Lewis Publishing, 1922), 1:167–69; Army Corps of Engineers, New Orleans District, "Bonnet Carré Spillway" (agency booklet, circa 2000), 3.

3. As cited by Richard Joel Russell, "Physiography of Lower Mississippi River Delta" in "Lower Mississippi River Delta: Reports on the Geology of Plaquemines and St. Bernard Parishes," *Geological Bulletin 8* (1936): 19.

4. Regional Planning Commission, Jefferson, Orleans, St. Bernard Parishes, *History of Regional Growth of Jefferson, Orleans, and St. Bernard Parishes, Louisiana* (New Orleans: Regional Planning Commission, 1969), 6.

5. Ari Kelman, "A River and Its City: Critical Episodes in the Environmental History of New Orleans" (Ph.D. diss., Brown University, 1998), 311.

6. Act 93 of the 1890 General Assembly of the State of Louisiana (July 7, 1890), as quoted in *Orleans Levee District, The Orleans Levee District—A History* (New Orleans: Orleans Levee District, 1999); and *The Mississippi River Levee* (New Orleans: Orleans Levee District, 1999).

7. Kelman, "A River and Its City," 311–13.

8. "Louisiana, in Favor of Nationalizing the Levees of the Mississippi River," U.S. House of Representatives, Mis. Doc. no. 41, January 13, 1873, in reference to H.R. 3419, 10.

CHAPTER 15: BUFFERING THE DELTAIC CITY

1. This chapter is an updated adaptation drawn from the author's previous books, including *Bienville's Dilemma, Geographies of New Orleans,* and *Time and Place in New Orleans*.

193

2. Judy A. Filipich and Lee Taylor, *Lakefront New Orleans: Planning and Development, 1926–1971* (New Orleans: Urban Studies Institute, Louisiana State University in New Orleans, 1971), 7–13; Association of Levee Boards of Louisiana, *The System That Works to Serve Our State* (New Orleans: Association of Levee Boards of Louisiana, 1990), 43–44.

3. Peirce F. Lewis, *New Orleans: The Making of an Urban Landscape* (Cambridge, Mass.: Ballinger Publishing, 1976), 65–66.

4. Orleans Levee Board, "Building a Great City," New Orleans, 1954, pamphlet.

5. City Planning and Zoning Commission, *Major Street Report* (New Orleans: Planning and Zoning Commission, 1927), 9.

CHAPTER 16: TWENTIETH-CENTURY DELTA URBANISM

1. City Planning and Zoning Commission, *Major Street Report* (New Orleans: Planning and Zoning Commission, 1927), 26–28.

2. John Magill, "A Conspiracy of Complicity," *Louisiana Cultural Vistas* 17, no. 3 (Fall 2006): 43.

3. H. W. Gilmore, *Some Basic Census Tract Maps of New Orleans*, map book, 1937, C5-D10-F6, Tulane University Special Collections, New Orleans.

4. Daphne Spain, "Race Relations and Residential Segregation in New Orleans: Two Centuries of Paradox," *The Annals of the American Academy of Political and Social Science* 441 (January 1979): 82.

CHAPTER 17: PERCEIVING THE DELTAIC CITY

1. This chapter is an updated adaptation drawn from the author's previous book *Bienville's Dilemma*.

2. For an analysis of uptown and downtown, see Richard Campanella, *Geographies of New Orleans: Urban Fabrics Before the Storm* (Lafayette, La.: University of Louisiana Press/Center for Louisiana Studies, 2006), 157–67.

3. John Pope, "Evoking King, Nagin Calls N.O. 'Chocolate' City," *The Times-Picayune*, January 17, 2006, 1.

4. Michel Faulkner, as quoted by George Will, "Charter Schools Fight an Old Bigotry," *The Times-Picayune*, December 6, 2007, B-9.

5. City Planning and Zoning Commission-Advisory Commission, *The Handbook to Comprehensive Zone Law for New Orleans*, Louisiana (map insert), Rare Book Room, Louisiana Supreme Court Law Library, New Orleans.

CHAPTER 18: ENVIRONMENTAL CONSEQUENCES OF DELTA URBANISM

1. This chapter is an updated adaptation drawn from the author's previous books, including *Bienville's Dilemma, Geographies of New Orleans,* and *Time and Place in New Orleans*.

2. As cited by Stanley C. Arthur, *A History of the U.S. Custom House at New Orleans* (Baton Rouge, La.: Work Projects Administration of Louisiana, 1940), 45.

3. "How Much of City Is Below Sea Level?" *New Orleans Item*, April 13, 1948, 12.

CHAPTER 19: DEVASTATING THE DELTAIC CITY

1. Chronologies in this section are drawn in part from the author's previous writings and personal experiences, and based on the research of M. Kok et al., "Polder Flood Simulations for Greater New Orleans: Hurricane Katrina August 2005" (Technical University at Delft and Svasek Hydraulics, July 2007).

CHAPTER 20: "PLANDEMONIUM"

1. This chapter is an updated adaptation drawn from the author's previous book *Bienville's Dilemma*.
2. Timothy M. Kusky, "Time to Move to Higher Ground," *Boston Globe*, September 25, 2005, D12.
3. Gary Rivlin, "New Orleans Forms a Panel on Renewal," *New York Times*, October 1, 2005, A11.
4. Martha Carr, "Citizens Pack Rebirth Forum," *The Times-Picayune*, November 15, 2005, Metro section, 1.
5. Urban Land Institute, map in "New Orleans, Louisiana: A Strategy for Rebuilding—an Advisory Services Program Report" (Power-Point file, November 12–18, 2005), 45.
6. Frank Donze, "Don't Write Us Off, Residents Warn," *The Times-Picayune*, November 29, 2005, 1.
7. Ibid.
8. Ibid.
9. Bring New Orleans Back Commission, "Parks and Open Space Plan," map in "Action Plan for New Orleans: the New American City" (PowerPoint file, January 11, 2006), 31.
10. Gordon Russell and Frank Donze, "Rebuilding Proposal Gets Mixed Reception," *The Times-Picayune*, January 12, 2006, 1.
11. Frank Donze and Gordon Russell, "Four Months to Decide," *The Times-Picayune*, January 11, 2006, 1.
12. "Meetings," *The Times-Picayune*, September 30, 2006, Metro section, 4.
13. Neighborhood Partnership Network, www.npnnola.com/associations. Many of these associations predate Katrina but renewed their efforts after the storm.
14. Analysis by Richard Campanella using Lexis-Nexis to search for occurrence of "civic association" and "neighborhood association" in the full text of *The Times-Picayune* from February 2004 through April 2007.
15. Analysis by Richard Campanella.
16. Stephanie Grace, "Will Plan Lift the Curse of the Green Dot?" *The Times-Picayune*, April 1, 2007, Metro section, 7 (emphasis added).
17. Michelle Krupa and Gordon Russell, "N.O. Post-K Blueprint Unveiled," *The Times-Picayune*, March 29, 2007, 1.

CHAPTER 21: REPOPULATING THE DELTAIC CITY

1. Analyses in this chapter are by the author. Components are drawn from the author's previous book *Bienville's Dilemma* and other writings.
2. Coleman Warner and Gwen Filosa, "Unanimous: Council Votes to Raze 4,500 Units," *The Times-Picayune*, December 21, 2007, 1.

3. Michael D. Blum and Harry H. Roberts, "Drowning of the Mississippi Delta Due to Insufficient Sediment Supply and Global Sea-Level Rise," *Nature Geoscience*, letters, published online June 28, 2009 (www.nature.com/ngeo/journal/v2/n7/abs/ngeo553.html), 1–3.

196

BIBLIOGRAPHY

"A Kaleidoscopic View of New Orleans." *Daily Picayune,* September 23, 1843, 2.

Arthur, Stanley C. *A History of the U.S. Custom House at New Orleans.* Baton Rouge, La.: Work Projects Administration of Louisiana, 1940.

Association of Levee Boards of Louisiana. *The System That Works to Serve Our State.* New Orleans: Association of Levee Boards of Louisiana, 1990.

Barry, John M. *Rising Tide: The Great Mississippi River Flood of 1927 and How It Changed America.* New York: Simon & Schuster, 1997.

Blassingame, John W. *Black New Orleans, 1860–1880.* Chicago: University of Chicago Press, 1973.

Blowe, Daniel. *A Geographical, Historical, Commercial, and Agricultural View of the United States of America.* London: Edwards & Knibb, 1820.

Blum, Michael D., and Harry H. Roberts. "Drowning of the Mississippi Delta Due to Insufficient Sediment Supply and Global Sea-Level Rise." Letters. *Nature Geoscience*, published online June 28, 2009. Available at www.nature.com/ngeo/journal/v2/n7/abs/ngeo553.html.

Brasseaux, Carl A., trans. and ed. *A Comparative View of French Louisiana, 1699 and 1762: The Journals of Pierre Le Moyne d'Iberville and Jean-Jacques-Blaise d'Abbadie.* 2nd ed. Lafayette, La.: Center for Louisiana Studies, 1981.

Bring New Orleans Back Commission. "Action Plan for New Orleans: the New American City." PowerPoint file, New Orleans, January 11, 2006.

Brooks, Jane S. *On the Avenue: A Plan to Revitalize the Lower St. Charles Corridor.* New Orleans: St. Charles Avenue Merchants Association and College of Urban and Public Affairs, University of New Orleans, 1996.

Bureau of Governmental Research. *Plan and Program for the Preservation of the Vieux Carré: Historic District Demonstration Study.* New Orleans: City of New Orleans, 1968.

———. *Wards of New Orleans.* New Orleans: City of New Orleans, 1961.

Burgess, Ernest W. "The Growth of the City: An Introduction to a Research Project." In *The City*, ed. Robert E. Park, Ernest W. Burgess, and Roderick D. McKenzie, 47–62. Chicago: University of Chicago Press, 1925.

Burkett, Virginia R., David B. Zilkoski, and David A. Hart. "Sea-Level Rise and Subsidence: Implications for Flooding in New Orleans, Louisiana." *Measuring and Predicting Elevation Change in the Mississippi River Deltaic System.* Louisiana Governor's Office of Coastal Activities Conference, New Orleans, December 8–9, 2003.

Cable, George Washington. "New Orleans Revisited." *The Book News Monthly* (April 1909): 564, 560. Quoted by Ari Kelman, "A River and Its City: Critical Episodes in the Environmental History of New Orleans." Ph.D. diss., Brown University, 1998.

Campanella, Richard. *Bienville's Dilemma: A Historical Geography of New Orleans.* Lafayette, La.: University of Louisiana Press/Center for Louisiana Studies, 2008.

———. "An Ethnic Geography of New Orleans." *Journal of American History* 94, no. 3 (December 2007): 704–16.

———. *Geographies of New Orleans: Urban Fabrics Before the Storm.* Lafayette, La.: University of Louisiana Press/Center for Louisiana Studies, 2006.

———. "Geography, Philosophy, and the Build/No-Build Line." *Technology in Society: An International Journal* 29 (2007): 169–72.

———. "A Proposed Reconstruction Methodology for New Orleans." *Journal of Architectural Education* 60, no. 1 (September 2006): 12–13.

———. "Street Survey of Business Reopenings in Post-Katrina New Orleans." CBR Whitepaper/National Science Foundation Award 0554937, New Orleans, May 2006 and January 2007. Available at www.kerrn.org/pdf/campanella2.pdf.

———. *Time and Place in New Orleans: Past Geographies in the Present Day.* Gretna, La.: Pelican Publishing, 2002.

Carr, Martha. "Citizens Pack Rebirth Forum." *The Times-Picayune*, November 15, 2005, Metro section, 1.

Carter, Sam R. *A Report on Survey of Metropolitan New Orleans Land Use, Real Property, and Low Income Housing Area.* New Orleans: Works Projects Administration, Louisiana State Department of Public Welfare, and Housing Authority of New Orleans, 1941.

Chaillé, Stanford E. "Inundations of New Orleans and Their Influence on Its Health." *New Orleans Medical and Surgical Journal*, July 1882. Flooding folder, Special Collections Vertical File, Howard-Tilton Library, Tulane University, New Orleans.

City Planning and Zoning Commission. *Major Street Report.* New Orleans: City Planning and Zoning Commission, 1927.

City Planning and Zoning Commission–Advisory Commission. *The Handbook to Comprehensive Zone Law for New Orleans, Louisiana.* New Orleans, 1929–33. Rare Book Room, Louisiana Supreme Court Law Library, New Orleans.

Clemens, Samuel L. *Life on the Mississippi.* 1883. Republished, New York: Harper & Row, 1958.

Conway, Alan A. "New Orleans as a Port of Immigration, 1820–1860." *Louisiana Studies* 1 (Fall 1962): 1–22.

Cowdrey, Albert E. *The Delta Engineers: A History of the United States Army Corps of Engineers in the New Orleans District.* New Orleans: U.S. Army Corps of Engineers, 1971.

———. *Land's End: A History of the New Orleans District, U.S. Army Corps of Engineers.* New Orleans: U.S. Army Corps of Engineers, 1977.

Cramer, Zadok. *Navigator, or the Traders' Useful Guide in Navigating the Monongahela, Allegheny, Ohio, and Mississippi Rivers*. Pittsburgh: Zadok Cramer, 1806.

Cruzat, Heloise H., trans. "Allotment of Building Sites in New Orleans (1722)." *The Louisiana Historical Quarterly* 7, no. 4 (October 1924): 564–66.

Curtis and Davis. *New Orleans Housing and Neighborhood Preservation Study*. New Orleans: Curtis and Davis, 1974.

D'Iberville, Pierre Le Moyne, Sieur. *Iberville's Gulf Journals,* ed. and trans. Richebourg Gaillard McWilliams. University, Ala.: University of Alabama Press, 1991.

Darby, William. *A Geographical Description of the State of Louisiana*. Philadelphia: John Melish, 1816.

Dart, Henry P., trans. "The First Law Regulating Land Grants in French Colonial Louisiana." *The Louisiana Historical Quarterly* 14, no. 3 (July 1931): 347.

Day, John W., Jr., et al. "Pattern and Process of Land Loss in the Mississippi Delta: A Spatial and Temporal Analysis of Wetland Habitat Change." *Estuaries* 23 (August 2000): 425–38.

Didimus, Henry. *New Orleans As I Found It*. New York: Harper & Brothers, 1845.

Dixon, Frank Haigh. *A Traffic History of the Mississippi River System*. National Waterways Commission, Document no. 11. Washington, D.C.: Government Printing Office, 1909.

Donze, Frank. "Don't Write Us Off, Residents Warn." *The Times-Picayune*, November 29, 2005, 1.

Donze, Frank, and Gordon Russell. "Four Months to Decide." *The Times-Picayune*, January 11, 2006, 1.

Drainage Advisory Board. *Report on the Drainage of the City of New Orleans*. New Orleans: T. Fitzwilliam & Co., 1895.

Dumont, M. "History of Louisiana, Translated from the Historical Memoirs of M. Dumont." In *Historical Memoirs of Louisiana, From the First Settlement of the Colony to the Departure of Governor O'Reilly in 1770*, ed. B. F. French. New York: Lamport, Blakeman & Law, 1853.

Filipich, Judy A., and Lee Taylor. *Lakefront New Orleans: Planning and Development, 1926–1971*. New Orleans: Urban Studies Institute, Louisiana State University in New Orleans, 1971.

Fisk, H. N. *Geological Investigations of the Alluvial Valley of the Lower Mississippi River*. Vicksburg, Miss.: U.S. Army Corps of Engineers and Mississippi River Commission, 1944.

Ford, Larry R., and Ernst Griffin. "The Ghettoization of Paradise." *Geographical Review* 69 (April 1979): 140–58.

Friends of the Cabildo. *New Orleans Architecture*. 8 vols. New Orleans: Friends of the Cabildo and Pelican Publishing, 1971–97.

Gagliano, Sherwood M. "Mississippi River Sediment as a Resource." In *Modern Mississippi Delta—Depositional Environments and Processes*, ed. Ram S. Saxena, 103–25. New Orleans: New Orleans Geological Society, 1976.

———, and Johannes L. Van Beek. "Geologic and Geomorphic Aspects of Delta Processes, Mississippi Delta System: Hydrologic and Geologic Studies of Coastal Louisiana." Report 1. Baton Rouge, La.: Louisiana State University, Center for Wetland Resources, 1970.

Gilmore, H. W. "The Old New Orleans and the New: The Case for Ecology." *American Sociological Review* 9, no. 4 (August 1944): 385–94.

———. *Some Basic Census Tract Maps of New Orleans*. New Orleans: Tulane University, 1937. C5-D10-F6, Tulane University Special Collections, New Orleans.

Gould, E. W. *Fifty Years on the Mississippi; Or, Gould's History of River Navigation*. St. Louis, Mo.: Nixon-Jones, 1889.

Grace, Stephanie. "Will Plan Lift the Curse of the Green Dot?" *The Times-Picayune*, April 1, 2007, Metro section, editorial, 7.

Hall, Basil. *Travels in North America in the Years 1827 and 1828*. 3rd ed. Vol. 3. Edinburgh: Robert Cadell, and Simpkin and Marshall, 1830.

Heard, Malcolm. *French Quarter Manual: An Architectural Guide to New Orleans' Vieux Carré*. New Orleans: School of Architecture, Tulane University, 1997.

Hesse-Wartegg, Ernst von. *Travels on the Lower Mississippi, 1879–1880: A Memoir by Ernst von Hesse-Wartegg*. Ed. and trans. Frederic Trautmann. Columbia, Mo.: University of Missouri Press, 1990.

Hodgson, Adam. *Remarks During a Journey Through North America in the Years 1819, 1820, and 1821*. New York: Samuel Whiting, 1823.

Houck, Oliver. "Can We Save New Orleans?" *Tulane Environmental Law Journal* 19, no. 1 (Spring 2006): 2–67.

"How Much of City Is Below Sea Level?" *New Orleans Item*, April 13, 1948, 12.

Ingraham, Joseph Holt. *The South-West by a Yankee*. 2 vols. New York: Harper and Brothers, 1835.

"The Inundation." *Daily Picayune,* June 4, 1849, evening edition, 2.

Jefferys, Thomas. *The Natural and Civil History of the French Dominions in North and South America*. London: T. Jefferys, 1760.

Kelman, Ari. "A River and Its City: Critical Episodes in the Environmental History of New Orleans." Ph.D. diss., Brown University, 1998.

Kendall, John Smith. *History of New Orleans*. 2 vols. Chicago: Lewis Publishing, 1922.

Kniffen, Fred B. "The Lower Mississippi Valley: European Settlement, Utilization and Modification." *Geoscience & Man* 27 (1990): 6–7.

Knox, Paul. *Urban Social Geography: An Introduction*. Essex, U.K.: Longman Scientific & Technical and John Wiley & Sons, 1987.

Kok, M., et al., "Polder Flood Simulations for Greater New Orleans: Hurricane Katrina August 2005." Technical University at Delft, The Netherlands, and Svasek Hydraulics, July 2007.

Krupa, Michelle. "City Hall Begins a Building Boom." *The Times-Picayune*, February 23, 2008, B1–B3.

———, and Gordon Russell. "N.O. Post-K Blueprint Unveiled." *The Times-Picayune*, March 29, 2007, A1.

Kusky, Timothy M. "Time to Move to Higher Ground." *Boston Globe,* September 25, 2005, D12.

Le Page Du Pratz, Antoine. *The History of Louisiana*. 1758. Reprint of 1774 edition. Ed. Joseph G. Tregle Jr. Baton Rouge, La.: Louisiana State University Press, 1976.

Ledet, Wilton P. "The History of the City of Carrollton." *Louisiana Historical Quarterly* 21, no. 1 (January 1938): 220–81.

Lemann, Bernard. *The Vieux Carré—A General Statement*. New Orleans: School of Architecture, Tulane University, 1966.

Lewis, Peirce F. *New Orleans: The Making of an Urban Landscape*. Cambridge, Mass.: Ballinger Publishing, 1976.

Magill, John. "A Conspiracy of Complicity." *Louisiana Cultural Vistas* 17, no. 3 (Fall 2006): 43–53.

McPhee, John. *The Control of Nature*. New York: Farrar, Straus and Giroux, 1989.

McQuaid, John, and Mark Schleifstein. *Path of Destruction: The Devastation of New Orleans and the Coming Age of Superstorms*. Boston: Little, Brown, 2006.

"Meetings," *The Times-Picayune*, September 30, 2006, Metro section, 4.

Membré, Zenobius. "Narrative of La Salle's Voyage Down the Mississippi, By Father Zenobius Membré." In *The Journeys of René-Robert Cavelier Sieur de La Salle*, ed. Isaac Joslin Cox. Vol. 1. 1905. Reprint, Austin, Tex.: Pemberton Press, 1968.

Murray, Hugh. *Historical Account of Discoveries and Travels in North America*. London: Longman, Rees, Orme, Brown, & Green, 1829.

"New Orleans Is Getting Hotter—Increases in Temperature in Summer Attributed to the Drainage System." *Columbus Ledger-Enquirer*, Columbus, Ga., June 13, 1918, 1.

Newton, Milton B., Jr. *Louisiana: A Geographical Portrait*. Baton Rouge, La.: Geoforensics, 1987.

Organization for Economic Co-operation and Development, "Ranking Port Cities with High Exposure and Vulnerability to Climate Extremes." November 2007. Available through www.oecd.org.

Orleans Levee Board. *Building a Great City*. New Orleans: Orleans Levee Board Reports, 1954.

Orleans Levee District. *The Orleans Levee District—A History*. New Orleans: Orleans Levee District, 1999.

———. *The Orleans Levee District—The Hurricane Levee System*. New Orleans: Orleans Levee District, 1999.

Owens, Jeffrey Alan. "Holding Back the Waters: Land Development and the Origins of Levees on the Mississippi, 1720–1845." Ph.D. diss., Louisiana State University, 1999.

Penland, S., et al. "Geomorphic Classification of Coastal Land Loss Between 1932 and 1990 in the Mississippi River Delta Plain, Southeastern Louisiana." Study sponsored by U.S. Geological Survey, University of New Orleans, and Army Corps of Engineers–New Orleans District, 1998.

———, and R. Boyd. *Transgressive Depositional Environments of the Mississippi River Delta: A Guide to the Barrier Islands, Beaches, and Shoals in Louisiana*. Baton Rouge, La.: Louisiana Geological Society, 1983.

Perrin Du Lac, M. *Travels Through the Two Louisianas . . . in 1801, 1802, & 1803*. London: Richard Phillips, 1807.

Pittman, Captain Philip. *The Present State of the European Settlements on the Mississippi*. 1770. Facsimile. Gainesville, Fla.: University of Florida Press, 1973.

Pope, John. "Evoking King, Nagin Calls N.O. 'Chocolate' City." *The Times-Picayune*, January 17, 2006, 1.

Porteous, Laura L., trans. "Governor Carondelet's Levee Ordinance of 1792." *The Louisiana Historical Quarterly* 10, no. 4 (October 1927): 513–14.

Powell, Lawrence N. "What Does American History Tell Us About Katrina and Vice Versa?" *The Journal of American History* 94, no. 3 (December 2007): 863–76.

Rankin, David C. "The Forgotten People: Free People of Color in New Orleans, 1850–1870." Ph.D. diss., Johns Hopkins University, 1977.

Ratzel, Friedrich. *Sketches of Urban and Cultural Life in North America*. 1876. Trans. and ed. Stewart A. Stehlin. New Brunswick, N.J.: Rutgers University Press, 1988.

Réclus, Elisée. *A Voyage to New Orleans*. 1855. Ed. John Clark and Camille Martin. Thetford, Vt.: Glad Day Books, 2004.

Regional Planning Commission, Jefferson, Orleans, St. Bernard Parishes. *History of Regional Growth of Jefferson, Orleans, and St. Bernard Parishes, Louisiana*. New Orleans: Regional Planning Commission, 1969.

"Report on the Drainage of the City of New Orleans by the Advisory Board, Appointed by Ordinance No. 8327, Adopted by the City Council, November 24, 1893." Summarized by Ari Kelman, "A River and Its City: Critical Episodes in the Environmental History of New Orleans." Ph.D. diss., Brown University, 1998.

Rivlin, Gary. "New Orleans Forms a Panel on Renewal." *New York Times*, October 1, 2005, A11.

Ross, D. A. *Introduction to Oceanography*. New York: Harper Collins College, 1988.

Russell, Gordon, and Frank Donze. "Rebuilding Proposal Gets Mixed Reception." *The Times-Picayune,* January 12, 2006, 1.

Russell, Richard Joel. "Physiography of Lower Mississippi River Delta." In *Lower Mississippi River Delta: Reports on the Geology of Plaquemines and St. Bernard Parishes*. Geological Bulletin no. 8. New Orleans: Department of Conservation and Louisiana Geological Society, 1936.

Saucier, Roger T. *Geomorphology and Quaternary Geologic History of the Lower Mississippi Valley*. 2 vols. Vicksburg, Miss.: U.S. Army Engineer Waterways Experiment Station, 1994.

———. *Recent Geomorphic History of the Pontchartrain Basin*. Coastal Studies Series 9. Baton Rouge, La.: Louisiana State University Studies, 1963.

Schleifstein, Mark. "Corps Moves to Close MR-GO." *The Times-Picayune*, November 17, 2007, 1.

Sewerage and Water Board of New Orleans. *Report on Hurricane "Betsy," September 9–10, 1965*. New Orleans: Sewerage and Water Board, October 8, 1965.

———. *The Sewerage and Water Board of New Orleans: How It Began, the Problems It Faces, the Way It Works, the Job It Does*. New Orleans: Sewerage and Water Board of New Orleans, 1998.

Snowden, J. O., W. C. Ward, and J. R. J. Studlick. *Geology of Greater New Orleans: Its Relationship to Land Subsidence and Flooding*. New Orleans: New Orleans Geological Society, 1980.

Somers, Dale A. "Black and White in New Orleans: A Study in Urban Race Relations, 1865–1900." *Journal of Southern History* 40, no. 1 (February 1974): 19–42.

Soniat, Meloncy C. "The Faubourgs Forming the Upper Section of the City of New Orleans." *The Louisiana Historical Quarterly* 20 (January 1937): 192–211.

Spain, Daphne. "Race Relations and Residential Segregation in New Orleans: Two Centuries of Paradox." *The Annals of the American Academy of Political and Social Science* 441 (January 1979): 82–96.

Syvitski, James P. M., et al. "Sinking Deltas Due to Human Activities." *Nature Geoscience*, published online September 20, 2009, 10.1038/NGEO629. Available at www.nature.com/ngeo/journal/v2/n10/abs/ngeo629.html.

Thwaites, Reuben Gold, ed. *The Jesuit Relations and Allied Documents: Travels and Explorations of the Jesuit Missionaries in New France, 1610–1791.* Vol. 69, *All Missions, 1710–1756.* New York: Pagent Book Company, 1959.

Treasury Department, Bureau of Statistics. *Tables Showing Arrivals of Alien Passengers and Immigrants in the United States from 1820 to 1888.* Washington, D.C.: Government Printing Office, 1889.

Tregle, Joseph G., Jr. "Creoles and Americans." In *Creole New Orleans: Race and Americanization*, ed. Arnold R. Hirsch and Joseph Logsdon. Baton Rouge, La.: Louisiana State University Press, 1992.

University of Michigan. "CensusScope: Social Science Data Analysis Network." Available at www.CensusScope.org.

Urban Land Institute. "New Orleans, Louisiana: A Strategy for Rebuilding—an Advisory Services Program Report." PowerPoint file, New Orleans, November 12–18, 2005.

U.S. Army Corps of Engineers, New Orleans District. "Bonnet Carré Spillway." Agency booklet, circa 2000.

———. "Freshwater Diversion." Agency brochure, circa 2001.

———. "Old River Control." Agency booklet, 1999.

U.S. Army Corps of Engineers, New Orleans District and State of Louisiana. "Louisiana Coastal Area: Most Efficient Comprehensive Coastwide Ecosystem Restoration Plans." Agency document, 2003.

U.S. Census Bureau. "Aggregate Amount of Persons Within the United States in the Year 1810: Aggregate Amount of Each Description of Persons Within the Territory of Orleans, 1810." Government Documents, Howard-Tilton Memorial Library, Tulane University, New Orleans.

———. *Census of 1820.* Washington, D.C.: Gales & Seaton, 1821.

———. *Census of 1980.* Washington, D.C.: Bureau of the Census, 1981.

———. "Census Tract Statistics—New Orleans, Louisiana." Ch. 36 of Vol. 3, *1950 Population Census Report.* Washington, D.C.: Government Printing Office, 1952.

———. "Census 2000 Full-Count Characteristics (SF1)." Compiled by Greater New Orleans Community Data Center.

———. *Fourteenth Census of the United States Taken in the Year 1920.* Vol. 3, *Population 1920*, especially Enumeration Districts 31, 34, and 35. Washington, D.C.: Government Printing Office, 1922.

———. *Louisiana 1910 Census: Orleans Parish (Part).* Digital database of 1910 Census population schedules. North Salt Lake City, Utah: HeritageQuest, 2003.

———. *Population and Housing, 1960: Census Tracts—New Orleans, La.* Washington, D.C.: Government Printing Office, 1961.

———. *Population and Housing Statistics for Census Tracts—New Orleans, La.* Washington, D.C.: Government Printing Office, 1942.

———. *Population 1910: Reports by States, with Statistics for Counties, Cities, and Other Civil Divisions, Alabama–Montana.* Washington, D.C.: Government Printing Office, 1913.

———. "Profile of Selected Social Characteristics, 2000, Census 2000 Summary File 3 (SF 3) Sample Data." http://factfinder.census.gov.

———. *Statistics of the Population of the United States at the Tenth Census.* Washington, D.C.: Government Printing Office, 1883.

203

———, Population Division. "Region and Country or Area of Birth of the Foreign-Born Population, With Geographic Detail Shown in Decennial Census Publications of 1930 or Earlier: 1850 to 1930." Table 4, Tech Paper 29.

U.S. House of Representatives, "Mississippi Levees: Memorial of Citizens of the State of Louisiana, in Favor of Nationalizing the levees of the Mississippi River," Mis. Doc. No. 41, January 13, 1873, in reference to H.R. 3419.

Vale, Lawrence J., and Thomas J. Campanella, eds. *The Resilient City: How Modern Cities Recover from Disaster*. New York: Oxford University Press, 2005.

Van Kempen, Ronald, and A. Sule Özüekren. "Ethnic Segregation in Cities: New Forms and Explanations in a Dynamic World." *Urban Studies* 35 (1998): 1631–56.

Villiers du Terrage, Marc de. "A History of the Foundation of New Orleans (1717–1722)." *The Louisiana Historical Quarterly* 3, no. 2 (April 1920): 157–251.

Viosca, Percy, Jr. "Flood Control in the Mississippi Valley in Its Relation to Louisiana Fisheries." Technical Paper No. 4, State of Louisiana Department of Conservation–Division of Fisheries, New Orleans, 1927.

Ward, David. *Cities and Immigrants: A Geography of Change in Nineteenth Century America*. New York: Oxford University Press, 1971.

Waring, George E., Jr. *Report on the Social Statistics of Cities, Part II: The Southern and the Western States*. Washington, D.C.: Government Printing Office, 1887.

Warner, Coleman, and Gwen Filosa. "Unanimous: Council Votes to Raze 4,500 Units." *The Times-Picayune*, December 21, 2007, 1.

White, Gilbert Fowler. *Human Adjustment to Floods*. Research Paper no. 29, 1942. Chicago: University of Chicago Department of Geography, 1945.

Will, George. "Charter Schools Fight an Old Bigotry." *The Times-Picayune*, December 6, 2007, B-9.

Wilson, Samuel, Jr. *The Vieux Carre, New Orleans: Its Plan, Its Growth, Its Architecture*. New Orleans: Bureau of Government Research, 1968.

Winkler-Schmit, David. "The Long Road Ahead." *Gambit Weekly*, December 18, 2007, 9–11.

Zimpel, Charles F. *Topographical Map of New Orleans and Its Vicinity*. 1834. Original copy stored at Southeastern Architectural Archive, Tulane University Special Collections, New Orleans.

INDEX

205

New Orleans ■ Index

213

ABOUT THE AUTHOR

Tulane University geographer Richard Campanella maps and analyzes the physical and human geography of the New Orleans region. Among his four previous books are *Bienville's Dilemma* and *Geographies of New Orleans*, both winners of the Louisiana Endowment for the Humanities Book of the Year Award. His research has also been published in *Journal of American History*, *Technology in Society*, *Journal of Architectural Education*, *Photogrammetric Engineering and Remote Sensing*, *Environmental Geochemistry and Health*, and elsewhere. Campanella and his wife, Marina, live in downtown New Orleans.